Parent Child Journey

Parent Child Journey

AN INDIVIDUALIZED APPROACH TO RAISING YOUR CHALLENGING CHILD

• • •

Dan Shapiro M.D.
Illustrations by John Watkins-Chow

CreateSpace Independent Publishing Platform, North Charleston, SC

ISBN: 1536914320
ISBN 13: 9781536914320
Library of Congress Control Number: 2016912942
CreateSpace Independent Publishing Platform
North Charleston, South Carolina

To Mom and Dad for showing me how to paddle
Ben, Sarah, AJ, Aaron, and Barry for traveling along
Ella and Charlie for flying ahead
Dr. Jeff Bernstein for the life jacket
And Robin for the nest, boat, navigational support, and love

Birches

By Robert Frost (1969)

• • •

When I see birches bend to left and right
Across the lines of straighter darker trees,
I like to think some boy's been swinging them.
But swinging doesn't bend them down to stay
As ice-storms do. Often you must have seen them
Loaded with ice a sunny winter morning
After a rain. They click upon themselves
As the breeze rises, and turn many-colored
As the stir cracks and crazes their enamel.
Soon the sun's warmth makes them shed crystal shells
Shattering and avalanching on the snow-crust—
Such heaps of broken glass to sweep away
You'd think the inner dome of heaven had fallen.
They are dragged to the withered bracken by the load,
And they seem not to break; though once they are bowed
So low for long, they never right themselves:
You may see their trunks arching in the woods
Years afterwards, trailing their leaves on the ground
Like girls on hands and knees that throw their hair
Before them over their heads to dry in the sun.
But I was going to say when Truth broke in
With all her matter-of-fact about the ice-storm

I should prefer to have some boy bend them
As he went out and in to fetch the cows—
Some boy too far from town to learn baseball,
Whose only play was what he found himself,
Summer or winter, and could play alone.
One by one he subdued his father's trees
By riding them down over and over again
Until he took the stiffness out of them,
And not one but hung limp, not one was left
For him to conquer. He learned all there was
To learn about not launching out too soon
And so not carrying the tree away
Clear to the ground. He always kept his poise
To the top branches, climbing carefully
With the same pains you use to fill a cup
Up to the brim, and even above the brim.
Then he flung outward, feet first, with a swish,
Kicking his way down through the air to the ground.
So was I once myself a swinger of birches.
And so I dream of going back to be.
It's when I'm weary of considerations,
And life is too much like a pathless wood
Where your face burns and tickles with the cobwebs
Broken across it, and one eye is weeping
From a twig's having lashed across it open.
I'd like to get away from earth awhile
And then come back to it and begin over.
May no fate willfully misunderstand me
And half grant what I wish and snatch me away
Not to return. Earth's the right place for love:
I don't know where it's likely to go better.
I'd like to go by climbing a birch tree,
And climb black branches up a snow-white trunk

Toward heaven, till the tree could bear no more,
But dipped its top and set me down again.
That would be good both going and coming back.
One could do worse than be a swinger of birches.

Contents

You never step in the same river twice, for it's not the same river, and you're not the same you.

—Heraclitus

Acknowledgments

• • •

Over the past thirty years, in spurts and sputters, I have developed the Parent Child Journey program and written this book. It is impossible to thank everyone who helped, but I'll try.

In the early days, Dr. Jeff Bernstein, partner and mensch, supported the first incarnations of this program in our primary care pediatric practice. Without him, I would have certainly gone the way of the dodo.

More recently, Dr. Sarah Wayland has joined me in offering this program. She has made many important contributions in its development by broadening its availability in our community and improving its overall quality. She made helpful additions and suggestions regarding the Gander (formerly known as the Quick Scan). Because of her, the journey has been better for parents and for me.

Throughout the writing process, over these many years, dear friends and colleagues read drafts and offered many useful suggestions. With gratitude, I especially want to acknowledge help from Polly Panitz, Tom Holman, Bill Stixrud, Joel Swerdlow, Rhona Gordon, Bonnie Curl, Chelsea Kaplan, Jack Naglieri, Sarah Wayland, and Bertha Green. I deeply appreciate their time, expertise, and honesty.

I especially want to thank John Watkins-Chow, my incredibly talented illustrator. Working with John has been a true joy. Every step of the way, he has been enthusiastic, unselfish, and creative. He has believed in this project and believed in me. On scraps of paper at Starbucks, I had a front-row seat to his imagination and artistry. What an honor and a pleasure.

My dear friend Jonathan Band has been extraordinarily generous with his expertise, time, and support.

My dear friend Bruce Louryk provided invaluable editorial support.

Throughout the text, I gratefully acknowledge the work of many experts, past and present, on whom this program has been built.

Unfortunately, it is not possible to name the thousands of parents and children to whom I owe the largest debt. Still, I thank you all for sharing your lives with me.

And, of course, thanks to Robin, Ben, Sarah, AJ, Aaron, and Barry, for teaching me more than I could ever write, supporting me more than I will ever deserve, and giving me more joy than I could ever say.

Overview: Different Children, Different Parents, Different Journey

• • •

There are many parenting books and programs out there. In several important ways, this *Parent Child Journey* is as different as the children and parents it serves.

"I Would If I Could"

Whether inborn or conditioned, children have brain-based differences over which they have little control. These differences underlie your child's challenging behaviors. Noncompliant or oppositional behaviors are not the result of willful disobedience. Even if you feel like it some days, your child does not wake up each morning plotting how to make your life miserable. Just as important, parents also "would if you could." After all, parents have their own behavioral styles, skill deficits, and environmental stresses too. Some parents have had less-than-optimal childhood experiences or adult role models. In any case, difficult children can make the most wonderful parents feel incompetent. But what good does it do to dwell on unmet expectations? Let's move beyond blame, guilt, and shame toward practical solutions.

Integrated Approach: The Parent Child Journey builds on a long tradition of parent training programs (McMahon & Forehand, 2005; Patterson, 1977). I am most obviously indebted to the work of Skinner (1976), Ginott

(2003), Barkley (2013a), Greene (2014a), Levine (2003), Carey (2004), and Seligman (2006), plus too many others to name. Mostly, I am indebted to the thousands of parents and children who have shared their experiences over the years. *Parent Child Journey* resolves old conflicts between different schools of thought. I believe that children are best served if we stir together important ingredients from a wide range of programs, combine "wisdoms" from different schools of thought, and throw in a large pinch of clinical experience. For years, battles have been fought between behaviorists and psychotherapists, Lovaas and Greenspan, Barkley and Greene, tough love and soft love, neurodiversity advocates and disability interventionists, and so on (Maurice & O'Hanlon, 2010). The same professionals who warn parents to avoid power struggles with their children seem to engage in gratuitous battles with one another! This is unfortunate, unnecessary, and counterproductive. I hope to show that many of these approaches have something to offer, but none is generally better than another. Different pieces of different approaches work better for some children, in some families, some of the time. By combining tools from a range of workshops, *Parent Child Journey* helps you build a larger and more versatile tool kit. Then you will have everything you need for effective—and individualized—assessment and management.

Comprehensive Assessment

For each child and each job, how do you know which tool to use? It all starts with good assessment. "Defiant children," "noncompliant children," "explosive children," "autistic children," "ADHD children," "anxious children," and so on, are far more different from one another than they are alike; that is, of course, if you move beyond these diagnostic categories and take the time to really get to know them as individuals! In the First Mile (session one) of our journey together, I will guide you through a comprehensive assessment of your child, using what I call "the Gander," as in, "take a gander"; a quick but meaningful look. This functional assessment tool will allow you to see the true sources of your child's behavior and thus individualize your management strategy.

Behaviors as Secondary Symptoms, Not Primary Diagnoses

The so-called diagnosis of ODD (oppositional-defiant disorder) should be thrown away. This label is too broad, too pejorative, too negative, too confusing, and too permanent sounding. Many children do have oppositional and defiant *behaviors*—but for many different and ever-changing reasons. The question should not be: "Does your child have ODD?" Or, "What do we do with children who have ODD?" Rather, it should be: "For this child, at this phase in his or her life, in this situation, where do the oppositional-defiant behaviors come from?" Just like fever is a common symptom of many possible microscopic diseases, oppositional-defiant behaviors are always secondary to developmental differences. Also, most children with challenging behaviors do not have just one underlying problem. Usually, they have a constellation of developmental differences, all existing in dynamic interplay. Furthermore, let's keep in mind that oppositional-defiant behaviors do not always represent disorder in the child. Rather, challenging behaviors can signify appropriate reactions of a child to disorder in his or her environment, such as, inappropriate expectations or demands. Lastly, some childhood oppositional-defiant behaviors can represent the normal and healthy development of autonomy.

Understanding the Whole Child

When thinking about diagnosis, too many parents and professionals fall into an "either/or" trap. They confine themselves to considering whether a child has "this *or* that," for example, ADHD *or* learning disability. Most children don't have just one thing *or* another. Rather, they have complicated profiles: "this *and* that *and* that *and* that." For example, ADHD *and* learning disabilities *and* anxiety *and* environmental stresses. As Levine (1992) would say, most children have, "Dysfunction at the junction of the functions." Meaning that if you look at just one aspect of a child's profile, you might say, "No big deal." And then if you look at another one of your child's developmental differences, again, you would be right to conclude, "This kid should not be having trouble *just because of that.*" It's like the parable of the many blind men who try to identify an elephant by each touching just one isolated body part. If you view each aspect of your child's complicated profile separately and out of natural context, you will often be misled. Oversimplification leads to confusion. It's more accurate and useful to examine all the different aspects of your child's profile. How do all the pieces overlap and affect one another? This interplay of developmental differences is not hidden. You just need to know how to look. And look you should because the "junction of the functions" can be a very big deal.

Understanding the Child's Whole World

Children do not exist in a vacuum. Their developmental differences are embedded within contexts and relationships, and across family members, peers, school, and community. These complicated systems and cultures are just as relevant as neurobiology in understanding the source of your child's behavior. Your family has an impact on your child's behavior and your child's behavior has an impact on your family. Understanding your child must include an understanding of these larger systems.

The Gander

So, how are we going to capture all of this complexity? Well, just because children are complicated, does not mean they are incomprehensible. In the First Mile session, you will be introduced to the Gander, a developmental-behavioral assessment instrument designed to help you move beyond simplistic diagnostic categories to a more detailed, comprehensive, and useful understanding of your child. The Gander is just a screening instrument. It does not take the place of standardized neuropsychological or multidisciplinary assessment. However, it is broad, quick, and inexpensive. Find it in this book and for free at ParentChildJouney.com. The Gander can lead you to a practical understanding of your child's behavior. You know your children best. If asked the right questions, you can describe your child's developmental profile in rich and accurate detail. But what about your child's world? Especially, what about your child's relationship with you? Are all parents alike? You have developmental differences of your own. What about the junction between parent and child functions? To answer these questions, you will be taking a gander at yourself too. The Gander will not just explain the source of your child's challenging behavior. It will also shed light on issues related to "goodness of fit"—between you, your child, and others—across different situations. Beyond assessment, the Gander will also serve as a guide to individualizing behavior management for your unique child.

The Tool Kit

We should not treat children as if they are all alike. Some approaches work better for some children than others. Nor should we treat all families as if they are alike. What works for one parent-child dyad may not work for another. When adult differences have the potential to create disagreement about what's best for the child, it's better to understand the source of those differences and resolve them up front. As I will repeat throughout this book, raising a challenging child can stress the best of parents and the best of families. You deserve some support too. Not only that, research—and common sense—suggests that effective support for parents leads to better outcomes for kids. And let's not forget siblings, grandparents, friends, and other significant adults. By understanding how parent-child-sib-peer-other adult profiles are intertwined, you can choose the right tools for you and your child across many different tasks, people, and settings. Moving beyond a limited focus on one child "with problems," *Parent Child Journey* is designed to support the entire family system. So yup, you will need a pretty large tool kit with a really good instruction manual.

Multimodal Presentation

It seemed to me that a book about developmental differences and individualized management should practice what it preaches. What if parents learn differently? Shouldn't this book offer a variety of learning modalities for you? So instead of the usual restriction to text and print, I have deliberately "gone multimodal." Throughout the *Parent Child Journey*, parents *and* children can opt to learn through fable, illustrations, and maps. Most importantly, each "mile" in the Journey ends with homework for experiential learning. For those of you who are especially creative, I have included suggestions on how to draw your own picture, write your own song, and map your own journey; each of you according to your own preferences and needs.

The book is divided into two parts: Your Gander Instruction Manual in the back and the Journey in the front.

The Gander assessment tool helps you describe your child's individual differences using whatever approach works for you. The Gander is presented in five different ways:

1. In the First Mile as a standard rating scale
2. In Your Gander Instruction Manual, Part A: The Gander Explained as an expanded discussion
3. In Your Gander Instruction Manual, Part B: Know Your Boat as a picture

4. In Your Gander Instruction Manual, Part C: Know Your Song through music
5. In the First Mile and included in Your Gander Instruction Manual Part D: Know Your Map as a graph

The *Journey: An Individualized Approach to Raising Your Challenging Child* is presented as ten miles; that is, ten chapters or sessions. Each mile covers a different set of strategies and is presented in four different ways:

1. **Standard text** is used to present a variety of behavioral strategies.
2. A **fable** with illustrations, *The Tale of Hawk and Raph*, is used to present the relationship between parent and child as they journey together.
3. **Homework**, learning by doing, is crucial to progress. After each mile, you will have behavioral strategies to practice at home. I strongly recommend that you read this book no faster than one to two chapters per week. This will give you time to do your homework.
4. As originally conceived, *Parent Child Journey* is a ten-week **parent group training** program. Some of you will be using this book as a supplement to a group experience, including learning from others, discussion, role-play, and mutual support. (For more information about parent groups, go to www.parentchildjourney.com.)

Don't worry about being overwhelmed. The bulk of the book is old-fashioned text. You can choose to supplement with these extra modalities—or not. By the end of this book, you might have written your own script, drawn your own picture, composed your own song, drafted your own map, and practiced your own homework. Or you might decide to just read and do. You might just do the Gander as presented in the First Mile and not even look at Your Gander Instruction

Manual in the back. Or you might choose to spend a lot of time with the instruction manual for more in-depth discussion and varied representations. Whatever your approach to this book, I hope that you choose a combination of learning options that makes helping your challenging child more effective and enjoyable.

By integrating schools of thought, emphasizing the importance of comprehensive assessment, and presenting all of this in a variety of ways, this ten-mile course offers an individualized approach for helping parents help their challenging children.

Time for introductions. Throughout this different kind of book, we will be joined by two birds of a different feather, Hawk and Raph. Their story will weave in and out of ours. I hope that you enjoy their company. After all, we are all in the same boat.

The Tale of Hawk and Raph

• • •

There is grandeur in this view of life.

—Charles Darwin, *On the Origin of Species*

Hawk soared high over the river. Down below, he saw a little boat with a funny-looking bird. It was drifting downstream, toward Great Falls. Hawk flew down and perched on the boat. Hawk screeched, "You're going to kill yourself staying in that tiny tub! Fly away, you stupid bird!"

But the strange bird just stood there in its boat and said, "I would if I could."

Hawk couldn't believe it. Incredulously, he asked, "What kind of bird doesn't even know how to fly?"

The odd bird answered, "*Raphus cucullatus*, of course. You can call me Raph." Then Raph added, "I want tambalacoque."

Well, Hawk had never heard of a *Raphus cucullatus* bird-or tambalacoque! All Hawk knew was that Raph was soon to be a goner. The sound of Great Falls was getting louder and louder. Hawk grabbed Raph in his talons and flapped his wings-hard. Hawk didn't get twenty feet before realizing that Raph was just too heavy, so Hawk dropped Raph back on the boat and thought, *Not much more I can do here.*

Hawk started to fly away, but Raph called out, "I want tambalacoque."

Hawk muttered, "What am I getting myself into?" Hawk sighed, swooped back down, and perched on the back of the boat. Hawk's talons dug deep into the stern. Hawk's wings flapped hard. The little boat moved up the river, far away from the falls. Raph was safe, but Hawk was exhausted. No way could Hawk push Raph's boat all the way up the river. What to do?

Just then, for no good reason, Raph said, "I want to go back down the river."

Hawk said, "Remember Great Falls. Raph, you need to go up the river!"

Raph said, "No, I don't. I don't care about Great Falls!"

Hawk yelled, "You have to do as I say!"

Again, Raph yelled back, "No, I don't!"

Back and forth they fought. The little boat rocked from side to side. Before they knew it, they'd thrown each other overboard. Underwater, they struggled to breathe-but they kept on fighting.

Finally, the fight ended. Maybe Hawk won the fight. Or maybe Hawk just gave up. Who can remember, and what did it matter? Raph and Hawk drifted backward in the cold water. The boat drifted beside them. The sound of Great Falls again grew louder. Somehow, Hawk and Raph dragged themselves back onto the boat. Hawk flapped and pushed the boat ashore, safe once more. Staying at different ends of the boat, not saying a word, they caught their breath. Just then, a round fruit fell out of a tree and into the boat.

Raph cried, "Tambalacoque!" and ate it with one joyful gulp.

Hawk smiled and thought, *So that's what tambalacoque is.* At that moment, Hawk knew they were in this boat together.

• • •

Outline of the Parent Child Journey

Some children are more challenging than others. When home life is difficult, parents might blame the child. More often they blame themselves. But a challenging child is nobody's fault. The ten-session *Parent Child Journey* is designed to help parents understand where challenging behavior comes from and what to do about it.

Let's start by taking a look at what happens when you and your child end up "knocking each other overboard." Contemporary experts in child behavior have provided some very useful descriptions of all-too-familiar parent-child power struggles, meltdowns, and rage cycles.

Power Struggles and Irrational Brains

Barkley (2013a) describes a vicious cycle of parent-child interaction. The parent has an expectation, gives a command, or assigns a task. The child resists. The parent repeats. Again, the child defies. The parent increases the intensity of the command and usually adds a threat: "If you don't (*command*), then I'll have to (*threat*)!" The child digs in. Back and forth they go with escalating volleys of intensity and counterintensity. The child may fight, flee, or freeze. So might the parent. Often the volume goes up. There can be disruption, screaming, property damage, or aggression. Some power struggles can be heard by neighbors down the street. Some children end up running down the street! Other power struggles are quieter, more internal affairs. The child might just withdraw from the room or into him- or herself. Similarly, parents might retreat, feeling defeated, not sure what to do. Once power struggles begin, they're hard to stop.

Greene (2014a) outlines phases to meltdown. When parents and children are locked in a power struggle, emotional brains turn on and rational brains turn off. "Vaporlock," "brainlock," or "short circuiting" can represent a crossroads on the way to possible meltdown. The child has to shift gears but has trouble. He or she gets frustrated. Rational thinking starts clouding up. The parent and child are able to maintain good communication and avoid a crisis—or not. Either the rational brain gets back on top, or it further caves to emotion. If things get worse, the rational brain can become totally flooded and hijacked by emotion. Things fall apart. Here, if parents try to intervene, "inflexibility plus inflexibility leads to further meltdown."

Myles and Southwick (2005) present parent-child conflict as a "rage cycle." Once children start to "rumble," whatever capacity they might have had for rational discussion can go right out the window. If "rage" ensues, teaching and mutual problem-solving become impossible. Some children "recover" from these episodes fairly quickly—within minutes. Others take a much longer time—hours or even days. However long the rage cycle lasts, parents should not expect emotional children to act as if they are calm, cool, and rational. During the rage cycle, they are not available for learning. As children rumble, rage, and recover, their all-too-human parents react in parallel. When children are emotional, so are parents. Children are more rational and teachable well before the rumble-rage-recovery cycle begins and well after it ends—but not while it's happening. Likewise, parents are better teachers when their emotional brains are quiet and their rational brains are in control.

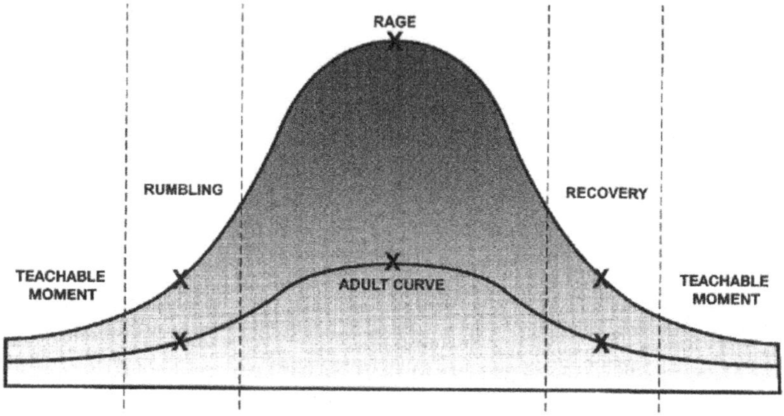

Used with permission from Dr. Brenda Smith-Myles

Power Struggles Never End Well

Barkley emphasizes that power struggles can only end in one of two ways…and neither is desirable. Parents can *overpower* the child verbally, emotionally, or physically. This increases mutual animosity and leaves everyone feeling bad—certainly not the kind of relationship parents and children would like to have with one another. Moreover, the child learns that "might makes right." On the other hand, and just as undesirable, parents might feel that overpowering is not worth it and simply *give up*. The parent drops the command, and peace is restored, but at a cost. The parent had reasonable expectations, but they are now lowered. Parent and child lose faith in their ability to work through challenging situations. Whether the parent overpowers or gives up, the child learns nothing worthwhile.

Understanding the Source of Power Struggles

Sometimes these power struggles might make parents feel as if their child is being willfully disobedient. But there is always a reason. In *Parent Child Journey*, we will spend considerable time looking for **potential breakdown points** that lie at the root of all noncompliant behaviors:

1. ***Readiness***
   a. *Engagement:* Your child might not have been sufficiently engaged or attentive.
   b. *Understanding:* Your child might not have understood exactly what to do.
2. ***Willingness:*** Your child might have had too little motivation; that is, there was not enough in it for him or her. Or maybe the task was not immediately gratifying.
3. ***Ability:*** For your child, the task might have been too difficult.

Most often it's not just one of these factors, but a combination that leads to noncompliance or disappointing performance. In any case, if your child is not sufficiently engaged, understanding, willing, or able, how can you reasonably expect anything but noncompliance? Whatever caused the initial noncompliance does not magically disappear. Parents who do not fix these underlying problems simply end up repeating the same ineffective command.

Understanding the Source of Your Child's Behavior

Children learn to repeat problem behavior only if it gets them something. They give up behavior that doesn't get them anything. Behaviors only continue if they serve one of four broad functions (Cooper, Heron, & Heward, 2007):

1. ***The behavior gets a reaction (attention) from someone else.*** Think about your child's behavior when you have to take a phone call, do some work, or otherwise withdraw your attention. Often these are the times when children "act out" to regain some attention. If your child learns that a certain behavior captures your attention, he or she is more likely to do that behavior again. Sometimes it may feel like your child is misbehaving to get your reaction. However, just because a behavior is attention-*getting* does not mean that it was attention-*seeking*. Your reaction can certainly reinforce the behavior. However—at least initially—your child might have wanted something besides your attention.
2. ***The behavior gets the child what he or she wants.*** Most often children misbehave to get something: a toy, food, or other objects of desire. Or they might want do a certain activity: play or use electronics. If your child learns that a certain behavior gets him or her what he or she wants, the child is more likely to do that behavior again.
3. ***The behavior gets the child out of uncomfortable or undesirable situations.*** Often children misbehave to avoid unpleasant situations, demands, or tasks, such as homework and chores. If your child learns that a certain behavior gets him or her out of these uncomfortable or difficult situations, then he or she is more likely to use that behavior again to successfully escape.
4. ***The behavior results in a desirable sensation.*** For some children, what they want is a certain type of self-stimulation, such

as thumb-sucking, fingernail biting, masturbation, or autistic repetition. It might seem illogical, but some painful sensations are desirable. Specific types of self-injury may produce a certain kind of pleasure. This can stem from a sense of self-control, fascination, or differences in sensory processing. Examples include cutting, biting, and head-banging.

Sometimes children use words to tell us exactly what they want. Other times their behavior is their only mode of communication. As Martin Luther King Jr. once wrote: "A riot is at bottom the language of the unheard." When a child "riots," it is our responsibility to try to understand where the behavior is coming from and what to do about it.

Proactive and Reactive Strategies

Proactive strategies are key to effective behavior management. Far too many behavior-management programs focus on what to do when a child misbehaves instead of how to avoid misbehavior by setting up a child for success. Through understanding your child's developmental profile, you can recognize the source of his or her challenging behavior. For each of your child's problem behaviors and problem situations, we will analyze what it is about your child that interferes with engagement, understanding, willingness, and/or ability. From the Second Mile through the Seventh Mile in the *Parent Child Journey*, you will learn how to foster compliance by modifying expectations and commands. Then you will be able to follow with positive reinforcement for success. This does not mean lowering expectations. In fact, effective proactive strategies will decrease power struggles, increase the chance of success, and allow both parents and children to "raise the bar."

Although effective proactive strategies will lessen the need for reactive strategies, nothing ever works perfectly. Effective *reactive strategies* will also be necessary. Instead of repeating requests and getting sucked into power struggles, parents have three better alternatives. As explained in the eighth and ninth miles, there are three types of preferred reactive strategies, symbolized as follows:

1. ***"Logs" for ignoring:*** You can float right over a log. Ignoring can be used when there is no significant threat to safety and the misbehavior is of no serious consequence.
2. **"Lightning" for time-out:** You better get to safety. Time-out should be used when a significant threat to person or property makes intervention necessary.
3. ***"Rocks" for pausing for empathy and self-reflection:*** You can't ignore a rock, but it's easy to get around if you just stop and consider a change of direction. Pausing for empathy and self-reflection is always preferred but not always practical.

Ignoring is very different from *giving up*, *time-out* is very different from *overpowering*, and *pausing* is very different from *power struggles*. Time-out and ignoring are immediate, nonverbal, and nonemotional; both create physical and emotional distance. The parent is in control. There is no power struggle. Giving up and overpowering occur only after a power struggle; both lead to more prolonged, negative, and intense interactions. The parent is out of control. Pausing for empathy and self-reflection brings parents and children together, but in positive ways that represent the very antithesis of the power struggle.

These *reactive strategies* work well to keep parents and children out of power struggles, but only if parents use excellent technique. We will cover effective technique for reactive strategies in detail, but not until miles eight and nine. Parents who need some reactive strategy help *now* can skip ahead to those discussions. By design, the first seven sessions in this program will focus on proactive strategies. After all, an ounce of prevention is worth a pound of cure. *Parent Child Journey* is an integrated program. Each session builds on the last so that the whole is greater than the sum of the parts. For different situations, you will need to choose different combinations of tools from your kit.

First Mile: Know Your Child/Know Yourself (Birds of a Different Feather)

• • •

All real living is meeting.

—Martin Buber, *I and Thou* (2010)

As they fell asleep, exhausted, Hawk wondered, *What kind of bird is this anyhow?*

• • •

The Behavioral Topography Survey and the Gander

What is it about your child's developmental profile that explains his or her problem behaviors? What makes certain situations difficult for you and your child? What are your child's relative strengths and interests? What makes some situations relatively easy?

Behavioral Topography

Before starting any river journey, it's important to know what lies ahead. If you know a river well, you can anticipate hazards. If you're unfamiliar with it, you need to rely more on maps. For example, the International Scale of River Difficulty is used to rate the challenges of navigating any stretch of flowing water: Class I for the easiest ripples through Class VI for the most dangerous rapids. Knowing the river topography, you can anticipate trouble and plan accordingly.

Likewise, navigating the *Parent Child Journey* is much easier if you know what to expect. What is a typical day with your child? A typical week? When does there tend to be trouble? What happens? How bad is it? Fortunately, your child's problem situations and behaviors are mostly predictable. After all, you know your child's patterns very well. When you think about it, how often does your child really throw you anything new? Not very. This is good news. After all, if history tends to repeat itself, you have the opportunity to analyze and strategize.

Let me introduce the Behavioral Topography Survey, a checklist that helps you anticipate problems and strategize proactively. The Behavioral Topography Survey includes challenging situations and behaviors and is adapted from the most widely accepted diagnostic manual (American Psychiatric Association, 2013). Feel free to add to this list. For each item, consider frequency, severity, duration, disruption, and distress. In other words, "how big a deal" is this? For each problem situation or behavior, how hard is it for you to "keep from capsizing and stay out of treacherous water"? Rate the challenges of navigating each behavioral "bend" according to the following scale:

- 0, no problem
- 1, little problem
- 2, medium problem
- 3, big problem

The Behavioral Topography Survey, a map of your child's problem situations and problem behaviors, not only identifies targets for behavior management, but also serves as a baseline against which to measure the success of the *Parent Child Journey* program. At the end of this ten-session program, I will remind you to redo the Behavioral Topography Survey and see how much progress you have made.

Behavioral Topography Survey

Name: ______________________________ Date: ____________ Rater: ____________

Circle best answer: *0, no problem; 1, little problem; 2, medium problem; 3, big problem*

Problem Situations

HOME

0	*1*	*2*	*3*	Getting ready to go in the morning
0	*1*	*2*	*3*	Transitioning into the car
0	*1*	*2*	*3*	Riding in the car
0	*1*	*2*	*3*	Arriving home
0	*1*	*2*	*3*	Transitioning out of the car
0	*1*	*2*	*3*	Mealtime (circle: before, during, after)
0	*1*	*2*	*3*	Playing with other children
0	*1*	*2*	*3*	While using electronic devices (which ones? ____________)
0	*1*	*2*	*3*	When asked to stop using electronic devices
0	*1*	*2*	*3*	During unstructured free time
0	*1*	*2*	*3*	When visitors come over
0	*1*	*2*	*3*	When visiting others
0	*1*	*2*	*3*	In public places (which one[s]? ____________________)
0	*1*	*2*	*3*	With adult(s) (which one[s]? ____________________)
0	*1*	*2*	*3*	With sibling(s) (which one[s]? ____________________)
0	*1*	*2*	*3*	With babysitter(s) (which one[s]? ______________)
0	*1*	*2*	*3*	Homework (circle: starting, during, finishing)
0	*1*	*2*	*3*	Doing chores (which one[s]? ________________)
0	*1*	*2*	*3*	Getting ready for bed (washing, bathing, teeth-brushing, etc.)
0	*1*	*2*	*3*	Getting into bed
0	*1*	*2*	*3*	Falling asleep
0	*1*	*2*	*3*	Staying asleep
0	*1*	*2*	*3*	*Other:* ____
0	*1*	*2*	*3*	*Other:* ____

SCHOOL

0	*1*	*2*	*3*	Arriving at school
0	*1*	*2*	*3*	During class (Which one? __________________________)
0	*1*	*2*	*3*	In school hallways/bathrooms
0	*1*	*2*	*3*	Recess at school
0	*1*	*2*	*3*	Lunch at school
0	*1*	*2*	*3*	School field trips
0	*1*	*2*	*3*	With adult (name: ____________________________)
0	*1*	*2*	*3*	Pickup at school
0	*1*	*2*	*3*	School bus
0	*1*	*2*	*3*	*Other:* ____
0	*1*	*2*	*3*	*Other:* ____

COMMUNITY				
0	*1*	*2*	*3*	Grocery store
0	*1*	*2*	*3*	Eating out
0	*1*	*2*	*3*	House of worship
0	*1*	*2*	*3*	Shopping
0	*1*	*2*	*3*	Neighborhood playground
0	*1*	*2*	*3*	Festivals
0	*1*	*2*	*3*	Outdoor events
0	*1*	*2*	*3*	Indoor events (concerts, movies, etc.)
0	*1*	*2*	*3*	*Other:* ____________________
0	*1*	*2*	*3*	*Other:* ____________________

Problem Behaviors				
0	*1*	*2*	*3*	Actively defies/refuses to comply
0	*1*	*2*	*3*	Loses temper
0	*1*	*2*	*3*	Argues with adults
0	*1*	*2*	*3*	Deliberately annoys people
0	*1*	*2*	*3*	Blames others for his or her mistakes or misbehaviors
0	*1*	*2*	*3*	Is touchy or easily annoyed by others
0	*1*	*2*	*3*	Is angry or resentful
0	*1*	*2*	*3*	Is spiteful or vindictive
0	*1*	*2*	*3*	Bullies, threatens, or intimidates others
0	*1*	*2*	*3*	Initiates physical fights
0	*1*	*2*	*3*	Lies/"cons"
0	*1*	*2*	*3*	Skips school
0	*1*	*2*	*3*	Is physically cruel to people or animals
0	*1*	*2*	*3*	Has stolen items of nontrivial value
0	*1*	*2*	*3*	Deliberately destroys other's property

Other problem behaviors and situations:				
0	*1*	*2*	*3*	____________________
0	*1*	*2*	*3*	____________________

The Gander

Now that you have a baseline problem list, it's time to figure out where these problems came from. The questionnaire that follows—the Gander—guides parents through an analysis of their child's unique profile. The Gander allows you to summarize how your child is "built." It provides a "here and now" description of your child's development and behavioral style. Understanding your child's profile will serve two important functions.

1. *Explain the source of his or her behavioral challenges.* In other words, what is it about your child that interferes with engagement, understanding, motivation, and/or ability and naturally leads to the problem situations and behaviors listed on the Behavioral Topography Survey?
2. Allow you *to customize your behavioral approach;* that is, modify your expectations, commands, and tasks—in a truly individualized way—to ensure success.

So we will be referring to this Gander throughout the *Parent Child Journey* to guide assessment and custom-design effective management strategies.

The Gander is designed to be functional. This practical approach deliberately steers away from fuzzy debates about "normal versus abnormal," "diversity versus disorder," and "difference versus disability." After all, where is the line between eccentricity and autism? Moodiness and bipolar illness? Blues and depression? High energy and ADHD? Learning difference and learning disability? These distinctions may be important in research and some types of treatment, but they are really just artificial categories that often get in the way of individualized and effective behavior management. Children who share a diagnostic label are usually more different from one another than they are alike. Plus, most children have more than one important difference or diagnosis anyway! *Parent*

Child Journey will help you move beyond simplistic diagnostic categories to a full description of your child's functional profile.

With this here-and-now approach, we will try not to worry too much about the future. If we can make things better day by day and week by week, then the future will take care of itself. For the purposes of behavior management, I prefer to keep things results oriented. Together, we will stick to practical questions:

- Is there a problem?
- Where did it come from?
- What should we do about it?
- How did that work?

Introducing the Gander and Your Gander Instruction Manual

The Gander guides you through a detailed description of your child's profile within the following broad domains:

- Behavioral Style/temperament
- Sensory
- Skills
- Environmental

Your Gander Instruction Manual: As you go through the Gander, if you're not sure what something means, you can find more detailed explanation in Your Gander Instruction Manual in the back half of the book. Each part of Your Gander Instruction Manual presents the Gander in different ways: in words, pictures, music, and graphs. I hope that you find this more thorough discussion and creative presentation helpful, interesting, and fun. Whatever works best for you. Children have different ways of processing, learning, understanding, and remembering. So do parents.

And So Our Journey Begins

While working through the Gander, you should begin to see your child in a new way. The Gander is designed to be both comprehensive and practical. Start by focusing on just one child. Once you get a feel for it, you can have a Gander at other children. You should take a Gander at yourself too. Greene says, "Children do well when they can." Likewise, I believe, "Parents do well when they can." Just as it is important to understand the source of your child's behavior problems, it is also crucial for you to consider the source of your own difficulties. After completing the Gander and beginning to analyze problems in these terms, parents often feel liberated; no more blame or guilt. According to this view, childhood behavior challenges are not the result of willful disobedience or poor parenting; rather, they are the natural outgrowth of developmental differences stemming predictably from a problematic fit between the child and environmental demands. By understanding the reasons for problem behaviors, parents lay an important foundation for building effective behavioral strategies. This understanding puts parents and children well on their way to positive growth and change.

So let's have a Gander!

The Gander

Child's name: ______________________________ Age: ____________

Rater's name: ______________________________ Date: ____________

Please circle the most appropriate number.

Behavioral Style/Temperament

Motor Activity Level:

3	2	1	0	1	2	3
High activity			Average			Low activity

Impulsivity

3	2	1	0	1	2	3
Acts before thinking			Average			Thinks before acting

Attention Span

3	2	1	0	1	2	3
Short			Average			Long

Initial Reaction

3	2	1	0	1	2	3
Slow to warm up			Average			Quick to warm up

Adaptability

3	2	1	0	1	2	3
Very inflexible			Average			Very flexible

Intensity of Reaction

3	2	1	0	1	2	3
Dramatic			Average			Reserved

Usual Mood

3	2	1	0	1	2	3
Unpleasant, serious, tense			Neutral		Pleasant, joyful, relaxed	

Regularity/Predictability

3	2	1	0	1	2	3
Low regularity, unpredictable		Average	High regularity, predictable			

Sensory Profile

Hearing Speech

3 2 1 0 1 2 3

Tunes in people talking — Average — Tunes out people talking

Hearing Noise

3 2 1 0 1 2 3

Oversensitive — *Sounds and noises* — Undersensitive

Vision

3 2 1 0 1 2 3

Quick to notice — *Visual stimuli* — Slow to notice

Taste

3 2 1 0 1 2 3

Oversensitive — *Changes in foods, hidden tastes* — Undersensitive

Smell

3 2 1 0 1 2 3

Oversensitive — *Odors* — Undersensitive

Light Touch

3 2 1 0 1 2 3

Oversensitive — *Sensitive to light touch, tickling, clothing texture* — Undersensitive

Deep Touch

3 2 1 0 1 2 3

Avoids, dislikes — *Physically close contact* — Seeks, likes

Movement/Body Position in Space

3 2 1 0 1 2 3

Avoids — *Moving, spinning through space (swing, seesaw, rides, heights)* — Likes

Internal Body Awareness/Physical Symptoms

3 2 1 0 1 2 3

Overreports — *Symptoms of illness, not feeling well* — Underreports

Skills Profile

Fine Motor

3 2 1 0 1 2 3

Difficulty, avoids — *Manipulating small objects* — Ease, enjoys

Handwriting

3 2 1 0 1 2 3

Difficulty, avoids — *Writing with crayons, pencils, markers* — Ease, enjoys

Gross Motor

3 2 1 0 1 2 3

Difficulty, avoids — *Running, jumping, climbing, playing sports/athletics, dancing* — Ease, enjoys

Speaking

3 2 1 0 1 2 3

Difficulty — *Putting thoughts into words* — Ease

Listening

3 2 1 0 1 2 3

Difficulty — *Understanding spoken communication* — Ease

Writing

3 2 1 0 1 2 3

Difficulty — *Putting thoughts onto paper* — Ease

Reading

3 2 1 0 1 2 3

Delayed — *Reading skills* — Advanced

Understanding Spatial Relations

3 2 1 0 1 2 3

Poor — *Understanding puzzles, shapes, block design, maps* — Excellent

Visual Arts

3 2 1 0 1 2 3

Poor — *Drawing, crafts, painting* — Excellent

Music

3 2 1 0 1 2 3

Poor — *Musical ability* — Excellent

Math

3 2 1 0 1 2 3

Delayed — *Math ability* — Advanced

Time Awareness

3	2	1	0	1	2	3
Difficulty, inaccuracy			*Estimating, pacing*			Ease, accuracy

Planning, Organization, and Implementation

3	2	1	0	1	2	3
Difficulty			*Planning ahead/ strategizing/ sequencing/ preparing*			Ease

Social Skills

3	2	1	0	1	2	3
With difficulty, rejected			*Makes friends*			Easily, popular

Physical Health, Family, Environmental, and other Life Stresses

Problems with Physical Health

3	2	1	0	1	2	3
Severe			Average			None

Family, Environmental or Life Stresses

3	2	1	0	1	2	3
Severe			Average			None

Other Family, Environmental, or Life Stresses (experienced by child)

Circle best answer according to* current *impact:
0 = no problem; 1 = little; 2 = medium; 3 = big problem

FAMILY STRESSES				
0	*1*	*2*	*3*	Death of parent
0	*1*	*2*	*3*	Death of other family member
0	*1*	*2*	*3*	Death of pet
0	*1*	*2*	*3*	Substance abusing parent(s)
0	*1*	*2*	*3*	Physical or sexual abuse of family member
0	*1*	*2*	*3*	Mental or behavioral disorder of parent or sibling
0	*1*	*2*	*3*	Disability of parent or sibling
0	*1*	*2*	*3*	Physical illness of parent or sibling
0	*1*	*2*	*3*	Addition of a sibling
0	*1*	*2*	*3*	Physical separation from primary caregiver
0	*1*	*2*	*3*	Change in primary caregiver
0	*1*	*2*	*3*	Caregiver does not speak language of community
0	*1*	*2*	*3*	Marital discord
0	*1*	*2*	*3*	Separation/divorce
0	*1*	*2*	*3*	Parent dating
0	*1*	*2*	*3*	Remarriage
0	*1*	*2*	*3*	Blended family
0	*1*	*2*	*3*	Domestic violence
0	*1*	*2*	*3*	Parent or family member with crime problem
0	*1*	*2*	*3*	Parent underemployed
0	*1*	*2*	*3*	Parent working long hours outside the home
0	*1*	*2*	*3*	Lack of support from extended family

CHILD'S PERSONAL STRESSES				
0	*1*	*2*	*3*	Physical changes (e.g., weight, acne, puberty, etc.)
0	*1*	*2*	*3*	Sexual/gender identity issues
0	*1*	*2*	*3*	Physical or sexual abuse
0	*1*	*2*	*3*	Neglect
0	*1*	*2*	*3*	Foster care/institutional care
0	*1*	*2*	*3*	Adoption
0	*1*	*2*	*3*	Witness to violence
0	*1*	*2*	*3*	Chronic, long-term, or undiagnosed illness
0	*1*	*2*	*3*	Disability (diagnosed or undiagnosed): ____________
0	*1*	*2*	*3*	Not enough free time

PEER RELATIONSHIP STRESSES				
0	*1*	*2*	*3*	Discord with peers (e.g., bullying, exclusion, etc.)
0	*1*	*2*	*3*	Not enough peers with shared interests
0	*1*	*2*	*3*	Loss of a good friend
0	*1*	*2*	*3*	Friends who are struggling
0	*1*	*2*	*3*	Social media stress
COMMUNITY STRESSES				
0	*1*	*2*	*3*	Adjustment to a new and different culture
0	*1*	*2*	*3*	Social discrimination or isolation of family
0	*1*	*2*	*3*	Religious or spiritual problem
EDUCATIONAL STRESSES				
0	*1*	*2*	*3*	Inadequate school facilities
0	*1*	*2*	*3*	New school and/or new teacher (circle)
0	*1*	*2*	*3*	Unexpected change of teacher or classroom (circle)
0	*1*	*2*	*3*	Does not get along with teacher(s)
0	*1*	*2*	*3*	Does not get along with classmates
0	*1*	*2*	*3*	Poor academic performance
0	*1*	*2*	*3*	Homework problems
0	*1*	*2*	*3*	Undiagnosed/unrecognized/unsupported disability
INADEQUATE RESOURCES				
0	*1*	*2*	*3*	Food insecurity/lack of adequate nutrition
0	*1*	*2*	*3*	Homelessness or uncertain housing
0	*1*	*2*	*3*	Financial instability
0	*1*	*2*	*3*	Lack of adequate health care
ENVIRONMENTAL STRESSES				
0	*1*	*2*	*3*	Unsafe neighborhood
0	*1*	*2*	*3*	Dealing with relatives
0	*1*	*2*	*3*	Exposure to upsetting news stories
0	*1*	*2*	*3*	Natural disaster
OTHER STRESSES				
0	*1*	*2*	*3*	______________________________
0	*1*	*2*	*3*	______________________________
0	*1*	*2*	*3*	______________________________
0	*1*	*2*	*3*	______________________________

Know Your Map

It might be easier for some of you to sum up your child's Gander profile on a graph. And it's kind of cool to see how a Gander graph maps out over a river, for both your child and for you. For ease of use, I repeat the following presentation of the river map in both the First Mile of the Journey and as Part D of Your Gander Instruction Manual.

Behavioral Style and Sensory Profile

Near shore, midriver, or far shore

For behavioral style and sensory profile, go ahead and plot points on the river map that correspond to each facet of your child's Gander profile. Then connect the dots and see your child's natural path through the water. Does your child tend to travel along the near shore, up the middle of the river, or along the far shore? Maybe your child's profile is all over the river?

With great hesitation, let me make some very imperfect generalizations about temperament and this river map. In the context of our cultural expectations, the "near shore" tends to be easier; the "far shore" more difficult; the "middle of the river" not a big deal either way. This is consistent with the work of Chess and Thomas (1989) and Carey (2004), who made generalizations about certain temperament constellations or groupings being relatively "easy" and others more "difficult." Although often helpful, labeling these personality types or river paths in such a way will not be accurate for all children in all situations. As emphasized throughout part A of Your Gander Instruction Manual, there is no such thing as a "good" or "bad" temperament, just "goodness or badness of fit," depending on the task or situation at hand. Sometimes the "near shore" is harder, and the "far shore" is easier. Even so, I offer these labels and generalizations because they tend to apply more often than not. Whatever your child's differences in temperament, it's up to you to decide when that behavioral style represents an advantage (near shore) or a disadvantage (far shore).

Staying mindful of this warning against generalizations, go ahead and see how your child's Gander behavioral style and sensory profile maps onto the river. Then, if you like, use a different color to map your own natural path onto the same graph. This makes it easier to see when you and your child tend to travel together or apart.

MAPPING BEHAVIORAL STYLE AND SENSORY PROFILE

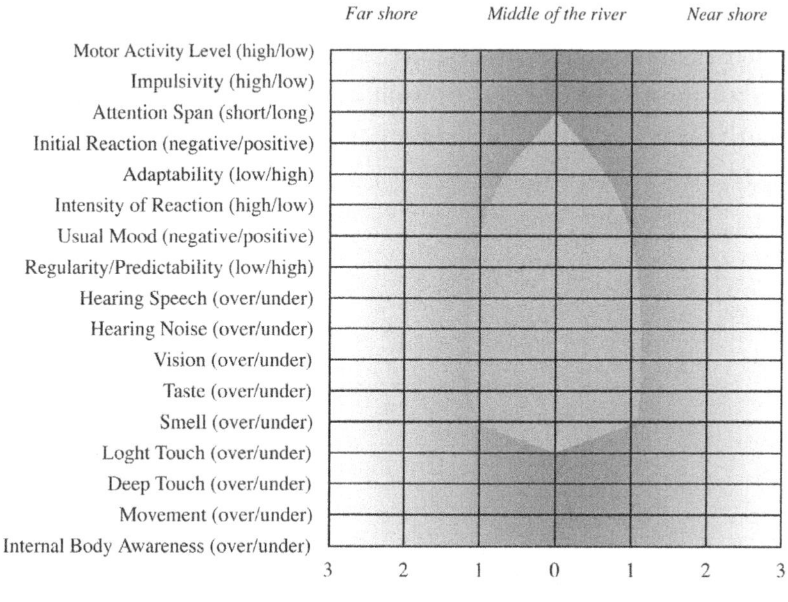

SKILLS (STRENGTHS AND WEAKNESSES)
Fly above water level (sails) or sink below (holes)

Now do the same thing for your child's skills profile. Plot your child's Gander strengths and weaknesses, then connect those dots. For which developmental domains does your child's boat tend to "fly" above the water, travel along at water level, or "sink" below? (See Tenth Mile for more detailed discussion of strengths and weaknesses.) Most children have uneven profiles, with some skills in the average range, others above, and others below. Most children will have some weaknesses—"holes in their boats"—that require bailing (accommodations) or patching (interventions), but they also have strengths—"sails"—for catching favorable winds (enrichment). As before, using a different color, plot your own skills profile on the same graph with your child's. Which of your strengths and weaknesses map along with your child's? Which of your skills are different from theirs?

MAPPING SKILLS PROFILE

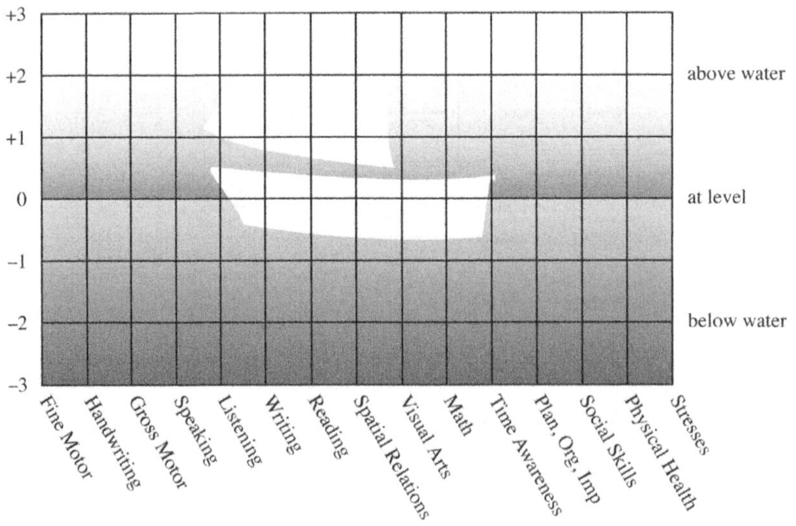

How the Gander Explains the Behavioral Topography

To see how the Gander explains the behavioral topography, let's consider the example of Timmy, a six-year-old boy.

> *Each morning, Timmy refuses to get ready for school. His "noncompliance" with the morning routine has been getting worse. His mother says, "Time to get up," "Time to get dressed," "Time to eat breakfast," "Time to brush teeth," "Time to get your backpack," and then "Time to go." Each step of the way, he knows what to do, but he simply doesn't do it. Timmy acts like he doesn't hear his mother. Or he might start doing what he's supposed to do but then get sidetracked. His mother gets frustrated. She raises her voice. She tries to physically guide him. He has a tantrum. She gets more upset. The whole process is prolonged and very unpleasant. He's late for school. She's late for work. They're both demoralized.*

Where does Timmy's morning problem come from, and what can his mother do about it? The Gander explains the source of the problem. Your Gander Instruction Manual in the back of this book suggests some individualized accommodations.

- Gander: Timmy has short attention span and high impulsivity. This makes it hard for him to stay on track through the multistep morning routine. *Accommodations: Timmy's mom can be more proactive breaking down the multistep routine into single subtasks. She can communicate her expectations more effectively by using visuals, such as schedules, checklists, or picture guides. And she can be sure to give plenty of immediate positive reinforcement.*
- Gander: Timmy is inflexible and has a high intensity of reaction. This causes difficulty making transitions and keeping cool. *Accommodations: Timmy's mom can give warnings, extra time, and plenty of empathy.*

- Gander: Timmy is hypersensitive to touch. This contributes to his overreaction. *Accommodations: His mom can use* non*physical means to engage and direct him, especially when Timmy is not expecting to be touched or when he is very emotional.*
- Gander: Timmy has relatively weak fine motor skills. This makes it a bit cumbersome to tie shoes and brush teeth. *Accommodations: Timmy can wear Velcro shoes and use an electric toothbrush.*
- Gander: The school program is heavy on worksheets. This causes Timmy to anticipate trouble keeping pace with his classmates. He is nervous about going to school. *Accommodations: The teacher can reduce Timmy's written workload and allow him to dictate his answers.*
- Gander: Timmy has difficulty with organization of language on demand. This makes it hard for him to "use his words" and calmly negotiate. So he defaults to having a tantrum. *Accommodations: Timmy's mom can help him put his feelings into words.*
- Gander: Timmy has very poor awareness of time passing. So when he thinks he's getting around to it, his mother thinks he's not making any progress at all. *Accommodations: Use a timer for each subtask.*
- Gander: Timmy's mother is stressed at work and very anxious about arriving late. Her own high intensity of reaction and inflexibility causes her trouble, both at home and at the office. Her angry reaction to Timmy's noncompliance prolongs the morning routine. This allows him to successfully delay arrival to school. *Accommodations: Timmy's mom might benefit from some counseling and better self-care.*

Homework for the First Mile

There will be homework after every "mile." For this First Mile, the homework is a "thought exercise." In all the miles to follow, you will be implementing very specific behavioral strategies; that is, not just "thinking about stuff" but "doing stuff." Just learning about these strategies is not the same as actually putting them into practice. More on that in the miles ahead. For the First Mile:

1. Finish listing and rating your child's problem situations and problem behaviors on the Behavioral Topography Survey.
2. Finish the Gander; first on your child and then on yourself. If you have more than one child, pick just one for now. You can Gander other children and adults later.
3. If you have questions about how to complete the Gander, go to Your Gander Instruction Manual, Part A: The Gander Explained.
4. Feel free to represent your child's Gander profile in whatever way appeals to you. See Your Gander Instruction Manual:
    a. Part B: Know Your Boat
    b. Part C: Know Your Song
    c. Part D: Know Your Map
5. Analyze:
    a. For now, choose just one problem situation from the Behavioral Topography Survey. You can analyze others later. What is it about your child's Gander profile that explains this problem situation? (Note: Do not choose a problem *behavior* to analyze. Problem behaviors are always secondary to problem *situations*.)
    b. How does your usual reaction to these problem behaviors either increase or decrease the frequency and severity of recurrence?
    c. What accommodations would make a difference? If you're not sure, check out Your Gander Instruction Manual at the end of the book.

Second Mile: Time-in and Self-Care *(Off the River)*

• • •

Alice: How long is forever?
White Rabbit: Sometimes, just one second.

—Lewis Carroll, *Alice's Adventures in Wonderland* (1898)

In the morning, Hawk and Raph started up the river. The current was strong. It wasn't long before they ran into trouble. There were logs. There was lightning. There were rocks. It wasn't easy traveling.

After a while, Hawk decided that they should take a break and just let the boat drift ashore. They pulled up on the bank. Raph was relieved to get back on land. Hawk was glad to perch up in a tree. First Raph pooped. Then Raph kicked a pebble into the water and watched it skip across the surface. Raph glanced up to see if Hawk was watching. Hawk smiled. Raph kicked another pebble. It skipped even farther. Raph looked up again. Hawk flew down and tried kicking a pebble like Raph did. They had fun kicking pebbles together.

Raph said, "I didn't know hawks kicked pebbles."

Hawk said, "I didn't know hawks kicked pebbles either."

They both laughed. Then Hawk flew off high into the sky. Hawk had been stuck on the boat with Raph awhile. It felt good to be airborne again. After a good fly, Hawk collected a few more tambalacoque fruit and came back to Raph.

• • •

In this session, we will be discussing two equally important kinds of time-in:

1. Time-in (for children)
2. Self-care (for parents)

Why Do Time-in with Your Child?

Time-in is a central component of all parent training programs. Time-in goes by different names: "special time," "positive pairing," "child-directed interaction," and others (Barkley & Benton, 2013; Cooper et al., 2007; McNeil, Hembree-Kigin, & Anhalt, 2010). But the principles are pretty much the same.

Parents sometimes focus too much on their children's problem behaviors and not enough on their good behavior. The consequences are significant. All children need some regular time-in.

- ***Getting off the negative:*** Children who feel that they are not getting regular positive attention and emotional nurturing may increase their undesirable behavior just to get any kind of reaction—even if it's negative. Regularly admonishing children about what they shouldn't do never works as well as praising them for what they should do. Children learn best through positive engagement. Moreover, parents find that doing time-in every day creates a whole new atmosphere in their home. By design, time-in is one of the first sessions in the *Parent Child Journey.* Over the years, many parents have reported that this simple practice was the most powerful component of the entire program. Until you start doing time-in regularly, you may not realize how much of your interaction with your children has revolved around their negative behaviors. Time-in is your opportunity to help your child "notice being noticed" and "feel felt." If done routinely, time-in becomes a wonderfully positive foundation for you and your child.
- ***"Push off with the left hand, pull near with the right":*** This ancient proverb sums up the importance of time-in as a counterweight to limit-setting. Sometimes parents may have to use "ignoring" or "time-out." These are important tools in the behavior management tool kit, which we will discuss in detail. In

a nutshell, time-out and ignoring work by creating physical and emotional distance when there would otherwise be physical and emotional intensity. By deliberately creating separation, parents avoid power struggles and teach children that certain behaviors will not be rewarded with attention. But unless parents give regular positive attention for desirable behaviors, these standard techniques for managing misbehavior will not work. Parents and teachers cannot *effectively* withdraw positive attention if it is not regularly provided. For example, if a child does not regularly receive encouraging reinforcement in a classroom, being sent to the principal's office for misbehavior might actually be a huge relief; that is, the acting-out behavior effectively allows the child to escape what for him or her was an unrewarding, stressful, or even toxic classroom environment. Furthermore, parents and teachers who routinely practice time-in should not feel guilty when they do have to use ignoring or time-out, or otherwise set limits. "Soft love" balances "tough love."

- ***Relationship repair and maintenance:*** The relationship between parent and child suffers if too many interactions center on misbehavior. Over time, children can become conditioned to dread the sound of their own name. Just hearing, "Tommy," might elicit a reflexive negative reaction: "What did I do wrong? What difficult thing are they going to ask me to do now?" Similarly, parents can become conditioned to dread the sound of their child's voice. "Mommy" or "Daddy" might elicit reflexive withdrawal or resentment. "What is he going to demand now? How much more incompetent is he going to make me feel as a parent?" Regular time-in is an opportunity for children and parents to hit the reset button on their relationship, unlearn these automatic thoughts, and turn to the sound of their names with positive—even joyful—expectation. In these ways, time-in helps parents and children get off the negative and rebuild their relationship. Parents and children both deserve a chance to share regular oases in time when they can truly relax and enjoy one another's company. At first, time-in may not come easily. But time-in is time and effort very well spent. Try to make time-in a priority in your lives.

- ***Stress reduction:*** Imagine you and your child looking forward to spending time together just for the simple pleasure of it. The crazier your lives, the more you need time-in. The less time you think you have for time-in, the more you need it. When your child has had a rough day at school, when you've had a rough day at work, time-in can be a shared safe harbor. Instead of time together feeling like just one more stress on top of everything else, time-in can promise a chance to decompress; get off the treadmill; and take a slow, deep breath. You and your child, together. Wouldn't it be nice to have some measure of unconditional acceptance and undivided attention - with our children, with our friends, with our spouse? Couldn't we all use just a little time-in each day?

Time-in is not a way of life. Outside of time-in, good parents should command, teach, and question. These jobs go much more smoothly if the parent-child relationship is first built on a positive foundation. For all these reasons, as much as possible, time-in should be an essential part of the day.

How to Do Time-in with Your Child

Time-in is all about giving your child unconditional, positive attention. The goal is simple: pleasant time together. If there are no expectations, then there will be no behavior problems.

- To make time-in work for you and your child, you need to ***plan*** ahead.
- As with all strategies discussed in the *Parent Child Journey*, it is crucial to ***individualize*** your approach.

- ***Relax.***
- And just follow your ***child's lead.***

To do time-in well, just **PIRCh**:

- **P**lan: For some parents, the hardest thing about doing time-in is finding the time off from life's craziness. With planning and commitment, you can build time-in into your lives. Make time-in a regular priority. Try for fifteen to thirty minutes each day. Consider: what is going to work best for you and your child?
  - ***Select an appropriate physical space:*** Where to do time-in? The space should be safe. There should be an adequate supply of child-friendly toys and materials. This can be a playroom, backyard, or fenced neighborhood playground. Choose a time-in environment where there's stuff your child will enjoy and you can allow free choice without having to worry about safety, property damage, or very problematic behavior. Time-in settings should not be where parents will have to say no or redirect. Try to create an electronics-free zone. We will discuss setting limits on screen time in the miles ahead. Here, suffice it to say that you do not want to compete with electronics. Your child will be much more interested in active time-in play if electronics are unavailable.
  - ***Get one-on-one:*** It is very important to do time-in without any distractions or interruptions. If at all possible, other children and adults should be out of sight, out of hearing, and out of mind. Turn phone ringers off. Or if the phone rings, don't answer. Instead, send your child a powerful message about the importance and priority you've attached to this sacred time together: "I'm not going to get that. This is my special time with you."
  - ***Each child, each parent:*** Parents should take turns doing time-in with each of their children. At a minimum, parents

can alternate days. Single parents can take turns with each child. Parents often begin time-in because one child has behavior problems or developmental challenges. However, siblings of challenging children have special needs too. If you feel that the "squeaky wheel" in your family gets a disproportionate amount of your attention, time-in for siblings can be a wonderful counterbalance. If one parent logs more direct child time than another, then time-in is a positive way for the other parent to give his or her partner a break. Sometimes time-in comes more naturally to one parent than another—all the more reason for both parents to practice time-in and discover their own best way. By rotating time-in pairings, each parent can solidify and enrich his or her own relationship with each child. For larger families and single parents, this can be logistically challenging. But each parent and each child should have some special time-in together. Do the best you can.

- ***Dividing and peeling:*** Of course, time-in is easier when there is only one child. The more children, the more planning. Some kids don't want to spend time-in separate from their siblings. Or they might be too easily distracted when others are around. So without being too obvious, look for opportunities to "peel" away the other kids. For the "time-in child," siblings should be out of sight and out of mind. "Non–time-in siblings" can be occupied by activities with another parent or adult. Look for chances to spend time-in with one child while the others are in school or attending scheduled extracurricular programs. The first child up in the morning or the last one to bed at night could get some early or late time-in while others are snoozing. Some siblings might be sufficiently engaged doing independent activities, such as building, crafts, reading, computer, or TV. In some households, it helps to let everyone know when his or her turn is due. If you think this kind of transparency and explicit structure would backfire, then you can at least have a time-in rotation worked out in your own mind.

- ***Starting and stopping:*** With some children, it works best if the time-in schedule is set. You can use visual schedules, clocks, and timers to ensure clear communication and sufficient warning. Other children do better with a more free-flowing, stealthy, and indirect approach. During unstructured time, you can pause and observe and then, very gradually, "mosey on over" and join your child's chosen activity. Just as casually, time-in can end with a subtle shift to other activities. If your child does not want to stop time-in (a nice problem to have), you can spend the last minutes gradually dialing back your attentiveness. You might have to strategically avoid transitioning from time-in to a nonpreferred activity, such as homework, chores or bed. Better to have a relatively preferred activity next, such as snack, play, or—if necessary—electronics.
- ***Time-in is not just for parents:*** Other adults in your child's life—teachers, tutors, coaches, doctors—should make time to connect in ways that send a clear message of unconditional acceptance. Obviously, such engagement must be modified to fit the setting. But the chart, curriculum, agenda, and schedule should sometimes be put aside to allow for some special moments of shared engagement. Adults should not underestimate the importance of noticing and talking about a child's interests. A gentle touch, a hug, or a smile can make a big difference. These little shows of positive attention may be subtle and easy, but they are powerful. Some of these other adults in your child's life might need to be reminded, respectfully and diplomatically, about the importance of these precious moments. Help them plan how to deliver mini-time-ins on a regular basis.

- Individualize: During time-in, make sure to customize how you give positive attention. Different children like to be noticed in different ways. Take a Gander. What works for one child or feels most natural to one parent might backfire for others. Think about the best way to show your child that you enjoy what he or she is doing. Depending on your child's profile, do whatever works.
    - ***Verbal attention:*** Some children do best with very explicit verbal feedback. If your child likes hearing your words, describe out loud what he or she is doing. While giving this kind of verbal positive attention, think of yourself as a narrator or broadcaster. Be specific about what you see your child doing. Focus on the activity, not the child. For example: "Hey, look at the way you..." or, "I like how you..." Keep up a running commentary. Many children love this kind of overt praise.
    - ***Nonverbal attention:*** Other children feel that verbal feedback is phony and irritating. They may look at you disdainfully, as if you've just read or participated in some birdbrained parent training program! For others, words just don't seem to register. For these children, try nonverbal positive attention. Refer to the Gander and think about your child's preferred sensory channels and relative strengths. Consider using any of the following—alone or in combination—depending on your child's profile and preferences:
        - *Facial expressions:* Appreciative smiles, winks, simple eye contact.
        - *Gestures*: Thumbs-up, "OK" signs (index finger and thumb forming a circle), applause.
        - *Touch:* Gentle strokes, big hugs, high fives.
        - *Music:* Singing, humming, or whistling a song that fits the activity, like providing a movie sound track.

    - *Just being present:* Simply let your child feel your attentive, unwavering, and appreciative presence. For some very sensitive children, just "being there" is more than enough.
  - ***Volume adjustment:*** Whether using verbal or nonverbal attention, think about your child's individual preferences regarding "volume." During time-in, some children like their parents to be loud, amped up, and animated. For "low-intensity" parents, this might not come naturally. But if this is what your child needs, you can modify your usual style. With other children, parents might have to take an approach that is more indirect, subtle, stealthy, quiet, and muted. If you are a naturally "high-octane" parent, you might have to tone it down. Pause to notice your child's intensity level. If necessary, adjust accordingly.
- **R**elax: Time-in should not be done when you are in a hurry or preoccupied. Your child should have your undivided attention. That's the whole idea. This is the Zen of Parenting. Take a cleansing breath. Shift gears. Forget about the past and don't worry about the future. During time-in, there is only the present moment. For this short time, you don't have to "parent." Leave the world behind. The more stressful your life, the more you need time-in. Not just for your child, but for yourself too. Learn to look forward to this time-in together. Couldn't we all use just a little time-in everyday? Your child deserves it. You deserve it too.
- **Ch**ild-led: Get into whatever your child wants to do.
  - ***Follow:*** Depending on their child, some parents announce, "It's time-in. I'm all yours!" Others have a regular activity that they look forward to doing together. But many parents find it's best not to be so direct and explicit. With a lot of children, it works best to just casually join whatever they are doing. First, pause. There's no rush. Just observe. See the

world through your child's eyes. Reflect on what he or she is doing. Right now, in this moment, what seems interesting to your child? Then mosey up slowly and gradually, and follow along. Different kids will want to spend time-in in very different ways. Some children will gravitate to quiet play, others more active. Legos, imaginary play, sports, games, dancing, drawing—whatever your child wants to do—that's what you focus on too.

- ***No questions, no commands, no teaching*** (Barkley, 2013a): For many parents, self-restraint is easier said than done. Good parents *should* question, command, and teach—but not during time-in. Whenever you ask a question, give a command, or suggest a better way, you are not following your child's lead. You are expecting him or her to respond. That could set up a power struggle and defeat the purpose of time-in. Life is too full of times when your child has to answer, comply, and learn. Time-in is a break from all that; a task-free zone not just for your child, but for you too.
- ***For the teenager:*** Some parents might be made to feel that their adolescent never wants to spend any kind of time together. Given their normal drive for independence, time-in with teenagers can be challenging. But try to spot natural opportunities. Teen time-in might be very late at night, just sitting on the bedroom floor and talking. Keeping with the spirit of time-in, don't comment. Just listen. Reflect. Empathize. In the morning, make breakfast for your teenager and relax just eating at the table—together. During the teen years, time-in can happen without warning or preparation: in the car, in front of the TV, or listening to music. Seize the moment when it presents itself. Catch some time-in when you can.

Some Common Questions about Time-in Activities

Q: What if I *don't enjoy* what my child wants to do during time-in?
A: If you don't like sports or dolls or bugs but your child does—tough. Get into it anyhow. Make sure to carve out time for yourself too, but *this* time-in is about your child's needs, not yours.

Q: What if my child wants to do some very *passive, self-absorbed,* or *isolating activities,* such as watching TV, listening to music, or playing video or computer games?
A: These activities do not work very well for time-in. When a child is just sitting there, parents do not have the same kind of opportunity to give meaningful positive attention. Some of these activities are such that the child may not even notice that the parent is in the room. This defeats the whole purpose. You might have to control the environment. Try to do time-in where access to these types of isolating activities is limited and there are other things to do. However, with some children, parents have to take what they can get. If your child truly gives you no alternative, you may have to default and sit along for TV shows, video games, or rap music. At least you have the chance to share enjoyment in parallel. It's not ideal, but desperate times call for desperate measures. Hopefully, this suboptimal time-in evolves into something more interactive. So for starters, settle: "If you can't beat 'em, join 'em." It's still way better than nothing.

Q: What if I *don't approve* of what my child wants to do during time-in?
A: This is not a time for teaching or commanding. There will be plenty of time for that later. During time-in, let it go. If there are violent themes in play, simply narrate: "That (action figure) sure is angry!" If there is cheating, simply play with your child's creative rewriting of the rules. If your child is focused on winning, enjoy letting yourself get beaten. If he or she wants to use a book or chess set in ways that defy custom, that's fine: "That book looks like a teepee!" or "That pawn has magic flying powers." During time-in, we simply abandon our preconceptions about how things are supposed to be done. If your child turns against you, don't admonish. Just go along. For example:

Angry child: "*You never do it the right way!*"
Calm parent: "*Oh no. Looks like I messed up again.*"

If parents are using good time-in technique, and the environment is suitable, children do not usually get aggressive or destructive. In fact, time-in behavior problems are rare. Children love time-in. After all, they are doing what they want to do and getting undivided attention for it. If your child's play has violent themes, try to roll with it: "I'm mortally wounded!" If absolutely necessary, try to distract, redirect, or briefly ignore. If that doesn't work, quietly end time-in, find something else to do, and think about what went wrong. Was there a problem with the environment or your technique? Tune it up and try again tomorrow. Give your child a clean slate. Time-in should never depend on good behavior. Over the many miles ahead in our Journey, we will be turning to behavior modification. But time-in should continue as an oasis of unconditional acceptance.

Self-Care (or Time-in) for Parents

Time-in is not just for children. It's hard to take care of your child if you don't take care of yourself. You need—and deserve—regular opportunities for unconditional acceptance and relaxation. Adult time-in or self-care can be with your coworkers, friends, or spouse. But so often adult time-in is something you can—or must—give yourself. Each and every day, couldn't you use just a little more time-in?

Self-Acceptance

You dreamed about becoming a parent. Having children was going to make your life more complete. You would enjoy love-filled times together. You would sing and dance. You would play catch in the backyard and bake cookies in the kitchen. You and your children would be good—perhaps best—friends. You would discuss art, nature, and politics. You would teach your children what you know. Your children would follow your good example. Your children would grow up to be moral, compassionate, talented, and successful. You would raise your children better than your parents raised you—or hope to do at least half as well.

But then, the dream of having the ideal child becomes tempered by reality. Your baby cries. You cannot provide comfort. Your toddler won't eat or sleep or toilet train. Even your ordinary expectations are met with resistance. Your young child might not talk, learn, move, or play like other children. Despite your best efforts, progress is slow. Simple things prove difficult: getting ready in the morning and evening, starting and stopping, doing as told. There are tears and tantrums, fears and withdrawal. Reality hits hard. Other people don't seem to be having these problems with their children, and you feel that they are making judgments about your ability to parent. You begin to make similar judgments about yourself. Your preconceptions of family life did not include developmental difference, challenging behavior, and stress. Yours is not such a perfect child. And, as it turns out, you do not feel like such a perfect parent.

When parents confront the daily realities of having a challenging child, they go through different emotional phases (Featherstone, 1981). Eichenstein (2015) describe five phases of adjustment. Similar to stages of grief, raising a child with developmental differences involves a kind of mourning (Kübler-Ross & Kessler, 2014).

1. *Denial:* Like most parents, you may have a hard time letting go of the ideal child you expected and accepting the child you have. "This must be just a phase. I was just like him when I was a kid, and I turned out OK. My ideal child will soon magically appear. This can't be happening. Tomorrow it will all be better. There's nothing really wrong. Nobody else really understands. My spouse, my parents, my friends, that teacher, that doctor—they

don't know what they're talking about. It's no big deal." Denial can protect you from feelings of powerlessness. But denial makes it harder to cope and move ahead.

2. *Anger and blame:* When denial fades and reality hits, many parents feel intense anger and overwhelming fear. You might take out your anger on those closest to you: your spouse, parents, or children. You might blame babysitters, teachers, and doctors. You might blame modern culture or environmental exposures. You might blame your child or yourself. This anger can be motivating but it can also become paralyzing and cause all sorts of additional trouble in your relationships.
3. *Bargaining and seeking solutions:* Sooner or later, motivated by your love for your child and the reality of the situation, you act. Sometimes this takes the form of striking a deal with another person, God, or the universe: "I promise to be the best parent in the world, if only_____." Hopefully, guided by research and experience, you will pursue effective supports and interventions. However, desperate for a miracle fix, you might be drawn to unproven "alternative" therapies.
4. *The depression trap:* Anxiety to find a fix can easily turn to despair and hopelessness. You wonder, when—even if—things will ever get better. Your mind runs from present concerns to future catastrophes. The dream of the ideal child is replaced by despair. You feel more isolated and helpless. The stress of parenting a challenging child becomes truly overwhelming.
5. *Active acceptance:* With time, you can adjust to these unanticipated challenges. You can learn to let go of old expectations and "play the cards you've been dealt." You get used to things as they are. You adapt a more realistic mind-set and accept that you and your child are doing the best you can. You grow not despite your child's challenges, but because of them. As a result, you feel compassion and offer help to others in similar circumstances. You might even become an advocate or activist. Although these

challenges do not disappear, you embrace your life as it is, joyfully and purposefully.

Parents do not go through all these phases in some orderly progression. You might move back and forth between phases, skipping some or staying put in others. You may be affected by watching other families experience certain milestones that you are not going through. Just as you have to let go of some preconceptions you had about your child, you should also acknowledge and simply accept whatever phase you're in as a parent.

Distorted versus Realistic Thinking

Making a healthy adjustment to raising your challenging child depends on recognizing distorted thoughts and substituting more accurate ones (Burns, 1999). When we face the stresses and strains of parenting, our minds can run wild. Irrational or overly pessimistic problem statements make it impossible to effectively solve problems and cope (Seligman, 2006). This does not mean sugarcoating. The principles of cognitive-behavioral therapy just guide us to be realistic.

Types of Distorted Thoughts

It's helpful to catch yourself before falling too far into some of these common cognitive traps.

- All or nothing: You might overgeneralize about your child's challenges in absolute terms, thinking in black-and-white, all-or-nothing terms. Problems that are temporary or situational might seem way too pervasive, permanent, and severe.
- Magnification or minimization: You might be guilty of either overstating or understating problems. This leads to unhelpful denial or catastrophizing. By inappropriately making either "mountains out of molehills" or "molehills out of mountains,"

your level of concern will be out of proportion to the severity of the problem at hand.

- Glass half-empty: You might dwell too much on the negative and ignore or discount the positive. Overly pessimistic problem statements become self-fulfilling prophecies. You feel stuck in the mud just when it's most important to take some kind of action or make some kind of change.
- Emotional reasoning: You might let your feelings cloud your thoughts. Depression and anxiety might interfere with level-headed analysis. You might say, "I don't feel like it," rather than ask, "What's really going to work best here?"
- Jumping to conclusions: You might make assumptions about what others are thinking or what the future holds. This kind of mind reading or fortune-telling can lead to misunderstandings and erroneous predictions.
- Perfectionism, personalization, and self-labeling: You might hold yourself to an impossible standard. You might blame yourself for things that were not entirely your fault. Instead of saying, "I made a mistake," you say, "I'm so stupid."
- Shifting blame: When you might have contributed to a problem, you blame others. You might dwell on how others should be rather than squarely facing how things are and what you need to do to make things better.

Examples of Distorted Thoughts

These types of distorted thoughts can be paralyzing. For example, you might—*falsely*—say to yourself:

- If I give up even a little bit of control, disaster is inevitable. I always need to be on top of every detail and stay totally rational.
- My child's developmental differences and challenging behavior mean that he or cannot have a good life.

- A few steps backward mean irreversible freefall.
- My child is so dependent and helpless. He or she never be an independent adult in the real world.
- If I disagree with my spouse or we have different parenting styles, our children will be totally messed up, and our marriage will be a disaster. If my friends are insensitive or do not understand, I will be alone.
- I don't deserve compassion. I should be able to do this parenting thing on my own. I'm a bad parent if I feel shame or disappointment. I should be able to handle this better.
- It's all my fault. My kid inherited my stuff. I'm doing a terrible job raising my child.
- My child misbehaves just to get me angry or just to get even. Good kids would do as they are told and appreciate everything they are given and everything they have.

Replacing Distorted Thoughts with Accurate Thoughts

Stressed parents need to recognize when their minds start spinning toward the irrational. Sometimes it helps to think about what you would say if a friend came to you for advice and framed his or her problems in the same way. What would you say to your friend to help him or her think more clearly?

- No child is perfect. No parent is perfect. Everybody falls short sometimes. My children just need to learn from their mistakes, and so do I.
- Positive development is never steady and predictable. Just because there are some steps backward does not mean there can't be steps forward. Spurts and sputters are normal. Change takes time, persistence, and hard work.
- A child needs space to grow. A certain amount of rebellion and noncompliance represents healthy striving for independence.

- I'm not responsible for my child's every success, failure, emotion, or thought. In fact, too much enmeshment is bad for my child—and bad for me.
- Even if my child has an inherited disability, biology isn't destiny. Genetic predisposition does not mean the future is carved in stone. Even if I'm not the world's greatest parent, I can be good enough. My child and I can learn and grow together.
- Just like adults, children do not always feel motivated, especially if they're required to perform in areas of weakness. It's normal to be inconsistent. Everybody has his or her own interests and preferences. Sometimes it's OK to cut my child some slack or use rewards to motivate.
- Children are not just little adults. Skill deficits, lack of experience, and immaturity really do make some things hard. My child's difficulties are legitimate.
- Nobody shows constant appreciation. Sometimes children take their parents for granted, and that's OK. A thank-you would be nice, but I'm not going to hold my breath. My child doesn't really wake up each morning thinking about how to make my life miserable (even though it feels like that sometimes).
- It's normal for children and parents to feel stressed and moody. It's OK if kids sometimes need a break from their parents, and parents sometimes need a break from their kids.
- Not everybody gets what I'm dealing with, and that's OK. I can compartmentalize my relationships. There are those who get it and those who just don't. Some friends and family are good for some things, but not for others. I will take what they can give and look for new friendships and groups to provide the rest. I may need to find "my tribe"; that is, other people who are truly in the same boat.
- Raising a challenging child is really hard work. Any parent would feel stressed, anxious, or depressed. Parents often feel jealous or

alone. More than anything else, it's exhausting. I should accept negative feelings as a normal reaction to a difficult situation. I'm only human. I deserve compassion and support. If I'm struggling, I should lean on friends and family. If I need it, there's no shame in getting professional support. I'll be in a better position to help my child if I make sure to get help for myself. It's the smart thing to do for my family and for myself.

- I shouldn't be so hard on my children. I shouldn't be so hard on my spouse. I shouldn't be so hard on myself. We can all learn to accept, deal with, and even love one another's imperfections.
- My child has developmental differences or a true disability. Other people may not understand. These are not ordinary failures. There may be some very real limits on his or her developmental potential. But maybe a different life can still be a good life. Maybe I need to broaden my idea of success to include what he or she *can* do rather than dwell on what he or she *can't* do.
- Few adults achieve—or even want—total independence. Realistically, my child can achieve greater degrees of self-reliance, stronger self-advocacy, and broader interdependence. And that can be enough.
- Just because my child has developmental delays does not mean that he or she cannot continue to make lifelong progress. The brain continues to grow and develop well past childhood and adolescence. Maybe new strengths and interests will appear in time. Many successful people do not come into their own and find themselves until adulthood.
- Life is about uncertainty: the good and the bad, success and failure. I need to learn to embrace life as it is, not as I wish it could be. A sense of humor, a sense of spirituality, and a sense of responsibility to others outside my family can all help me cope in a more positive and productive way.

Ask yourself: When things are not going well, do I slide into distorted thoughts? What would be a more accurate way of thinking? Would it be helpful to talk this through with somebody I trust so that I don't let my thoughts go too far down the wrong path?

Self-Care

Setting your thoughts straight is very important, but it's never enough. You need to set your life straight too. Do not neglect your own needs. As you work on self-compassion and optimism, also work on self-care. Every day, try to do a little something for yourself. Do not allow yourself to become isolated. Nurture your relationships. Regular "me time" will help recharge your parenting battery and model the importance of self-care for your children. Start small. You may resent well-intentioned but preachy advice, such as: "Don't make excuses. Don't let the perfect be the enemy of the good. Make self-care a priority. Plan and schedule. Think what you can do, not what you can't." Although all of this may feel patronizing, insensitive, or condescending, there's some wisdom in it. Gradually make self-care a regular part of your routine.

As my colleague Dr. Sarah Wayland advises: "Early in the journey, you may think that if you just throw everything at helping your kid, they will get better. Plus, if you take time for yourself, you may find that your children, spouse, and others may spiral out of control while you are gone, making the return more stressful than if you never left. Finding even five minutes to spend on yourself may feel like more than you can handle. Eventually you come to the realization that this is a marathon, and not a sprint. You have to pace yourself. Try to grab even just a few minutes here and there to treat yourself. A cup of coffee alone before everyone wakes up can be a life saver. Learn to appreciate the time alone in the car listening to your favorite music, podcast, or radio station."

What works for you?

- Exercise, swim, walk, bike, dance.
- Read, write.
- Draw, paint, do other arts and crafts.
- Garden, hike, climb, kayak, canoe, boat, fish.
- Sing, play an instrument, listen to music.
- Cook or bake.
- Spend some time alone.
- Go to a favorite place.
- Relax with a movie or TV show.
- Practice yoga, mindfulness, meditation.
- Learn other relaxation techniques.
- Take a bath or shower, get a massage, go to a spa.
- Eat healthy, but allow for a few special indulgences.
- Sleep well.
- Take a break from the phone, e-mails, and computers.
- Be careful about caffeine, alcohol, or other substance use.
- Ask for help from friends and family.
- Get respite care and babysitters for your children.
- Take a trip.
- Have a date night.
- Get physically close to those you love.
- Spend time with friends and family.
- Spend time with your dog or cat.
- Take a class, join an interest or activity group.
- Find a support group or friends who share similar challenges.
- Nurture positive connections with your school and work community.
- Be an advocate, activist, volunteer, or mentor.
- Practice rituals, celebrate holidays, go to religious services, pray.
- See a mental health provider.

This is just a list of ideas. What do you enjoy doing? What are you good at? What do you need to do for yourself? What would represent your best time-in? Make self-care a real priority. You deserve it. And when you feel good, it is easier to be calm and rational as a parent.

Homework for the Second Mile

1. Practice time-in with your child(ren):
    a. Get a plan.
    b. Select an appropriate physical space.
    c. Get one-on-one.
    d. Get relaxed.
    e. Get into whatever your child wants to do.
    f. Give custom-designed, positive attention.
    g. Don't question, command, or teach.
    h. One child and one adult should participate.
2. Practice self-acceptance and self-care:
    a. What phase of emotional adjustment are you in?
        i. Denial
        ii. Anger
        iii. Bargaining and seeking solutions
        iv. Depression
        v. Active acceptance
    b. What are your most common distorted thoughts? How can you replace them with other thoughts that are more accurate and realistic?
    c. Do something for yourself. Try to establish a regular self-care routine.
    d. Ask for help.

Third Mile: Engagement and Understanding (*Bird Calls*)

• • •

The single biggest problem in communication
is the illusion that it has taken place.

—William H. Whyte (1950)

Hawk squawked at Raph, "Time to get back on the boat."

But Raph didn't seem to hear. Raph was too busy kicking pebbles. Hawk squawked again. Nothing. So Hawk tickled Raph's tail tuft.

Raph looked up: "What?"

Hawk squawked to come. Hawk pointed to the boat. Raph looked confused. Finally, Hawk just got on the boat.

"Oh," cooed Raph. "Why didn't you say so?"

• • •

You have reasonable expectations. You assign reasonable tasks, but your child says, "No." You should not lower your expectations. However, to get to the same goals, you will need to modify and customize your approach. In the First Mile, you described your child's profile and explained why some situations don't go well. Here, you will begin to develop and use strategies to turn things around.

Many behavior-management programs focus on what to do *after* a child misbehaves. In later sessions, we will discuss these important reactive strategies. But in the *Parent Child Journey*, we will deliberately start by focusing on how to prevent behavior problems. Isn't it better to set your child up for success rather than just wait for him or her to fail? After all, if proactive strategies work well, there will be less need for reactive strategies.

For proactive behavior management to be effective, you will need to *individualize* your approach. That means coming up with specific strategies that effectively address the underlying reasons for *your* child's noncompliance. In this Third Mile, you will start to fill up your tool kit with behavioral strategies that work for your child. By accommodating your child's developmental profile, you will fix breakdown points. Proactively, you will make sure that your child is "ready, willing, and able."

Fixing Possible Breakdown Points

1. ***Ready:*** There are two parts to readiness: engagement and understanding.
   a. *Engagement:* Overcoming noncompliance or disappointing task performance must begin with engagement. Many parents get frustrated when they think they have their child's attention but don't, or when they know they don't have their child's attention but can't get it. In either case, if you and your child don't have each other's attention, it's hard to expect much cooperation. Similarly, if your child does not have his or her mind on a task, it should come as no surprise when the task is not performed well, if at all.
   b. *Understanding:* Understanding depends on engagement, but engagement does not guarantee understanding. In other words, sometimes your child might be paying attention but still not get what to do. Parents may not be aware of their own ineffective communication or fuzzy directions. If your child does not understand exactly what is required and how to do it, then he or she will not be able to perform or meet your expectations.
2. ***Willing:*** Your child may be engaged and may understand, but still, there might be "nothing in it" for him or her. Sometimes, from your child's perspective, there's just no meaningful incentive to comply or perform. He or she is unwilling because there's no apparent reason to adopt your agenda. To overcome this kind

of inertia or resistance, you might have to use the right kind of reinforcement. Only then, your child goes forward. If the carrot is too small, good luck trying to get the mule to move.

3. ***Able:*** If your child is engaged and understands but does not have the ability to do what is required, then frustration is inevitable. Sometimes parents may not realize when it's just too hard. And just because your child can comply or perform sometimes does not mean that he or she can do it all the time. Inconsistency can be a symptom of relative—but very real—skill deficits.

In this session, we will cover *readiness*; specifically, how to ensure *engagement* and *understanding*. Then, over miles four through six, we will have three more sessions on *willingness;* that is, motivation strategies. After that, we'll cover reactive sessions before turning back to *ability*—and disability—in the last, Tenth Mile, session.

How to Ensure Readiness: Engagement and Understanding

To be ready, your child has to be engaged and clear on what needs to be done. All too often parents and teachers mistake inattention and lack of understanding for low motivation or inability. Children are sometimes assumed to be "lazy" or "incapable" when they really just don't hear it or get it. Parents may puzzle over whether it's "won't or can't" when it may just be poor communication. If your child isn't ready, no way is he or she going to appear willing and able. So, before anything else, make sure you've got your child's attention and understanding.

Tommy is playing a video game. His mother calls him to dinner. She also wants him to help set the table. He doesn't budge. Did he not come to dinner because he "wouldn't" or "couldn't?" Or did he stay glued to the video screen because his mother never really got his attention? Or maybe, he didn't really understand what she expected?

Remember, the best way for you to get your child ready depends on your child's unique profile. Here is a menu of communication strategies. Consider which of the following approaches will work best for *your* child.

"Two-step it"/Separate engagement from instruction: Before you can expect your child to understand and comply, you must have his or her attention. If you start giving directions before you have engagement, you won't get very far. Sometimes it may be as simple as saying your child's name and pausing *before* giving a command. Other times you might need to be more creative, deliberate, and patient.

> *Instead of saying, "Tommy, it's time for dinner," his mother could say, "Tommy, I need your attention." She should not give the command to come for dinner until she is 100 percent sure that he's listening. That means waiting for some verbal or nonverbal acknowledgment, such as Tommy looking up, saying, "Yeah," making eye contact, or turning his body.*

Stop one thing before starting another: If your child is preoccupied, he or she is less likely to register what you are saying. Think about how you feel when you're in the middle of something and someone interrupts you to do something else. Before giving a command, try to wait for a break or the completion of the activity. If you need to interrupt, try to be soft, gradual, and sensitive. Sudden interruption might make your child feel irritated, angry, and less likely to listen.

> *For example, "Tommy, in five minutes you are going to have to stop playing the video game. Then I'm going to need your attention." Or, "Tommy, there's something I need to tell you. When can I have your attention?" Or Tommy's mother could simply wait for a break in the game. As will be discussed, visual schedules and timers can also help children remember routines and wrap-up times.*

Pick the right timing: Respect your child's needs, preferences, and moods. Make requests when your child will be most receptive. If your child is happily engrossed in an activity or upset about something else, he or she will probably not be receptive to shifting. A child who is generally distractible or impulsive will usually be more responsive if instructions or reminders are given just before the task has to be done; that is, at "the point of performance" (Barkley, 2013b). Advance warning or instruction might be forgotten too quickly. On the other hand, a child who is inflexible or slow to transition usually needs extra lead time and preview. In these cases, expectations to respond immediately can cause frustration.

> *Tommy's mother sees that he's in a grumpy mood. She decides to postpone dinner and give him a little extra time to unwind after a rough day at school. Then, when he seems more relaxed, she asks him how long he needs before eating.*

Be empathic: When a child is noncompliant, parents often fall into a trap. They try to explain. They try to teach. They try to motivate. But their child still fails to respond. He or she might even "tune out" more. This can feel like passive resistance or open defiance. But try to put yourself in your child's shoes. Sometimes connecting with your disengaged child might require you to pause and consider how he or she feels. Then show—verbally or nonverbally—that you understand.

> *Tommy's mother says, "Hey, Tommy. Seems like you might have had a rough day at school. How about you take some more time unwinding with your game?" She gives him a quick kiss on the head and a gentle touch on the shoulder.*

Get close: Parents often shout instructions from across the room, across the house, across the yard, or across the playground. If you want to be sure that your child is ready to listen, first—gently—get in your child's space and face. Get up, come near. Bend, kneel, or sit down to your child's physical level. Softly, but deliberately, position yourself directly in your child's line of sight, just close enough but not too close.

> *Tommy's mother resists the temptation to call him from the kitchen. Before saying a word, she stops what she is doing, walks over to Tommy, sits down on the floor directly in front of him, and waits for him to notice her.*

Speak clearly and simply: You may need to modify your volume, pitch, rate, and style of speech. Try pausing to give your child time to think and answer. When offering choices, don't give too many. Don't talk too much or use too many words. Usually, the less said, the better heard. Many children seem more tuned in when parents speak slower and softer. Other children may need their parents to "amp it up." Especially if you are naturally soft-spoken and your child tends to be under-responsive, you might need to talk louder or faster. Experiment and see what style of verbal communication works best for you and your child.

> *Instead of saying, "You're going to have to wrap up the video game now and eat dinner because we've got a very busy night ahead," Tommy's mother keeps it short, slow, soft, and simple: "Game off." (Pause.) "Dinner."*

Use all the senses: For most parents, speech is the most natural mode of communication. But for many children, talking can be a turn-off; like the droning teacher in Charlie Brown's classroom: "Whaa, whaa, whaa." Does your child usually seem attuned and responsive to verbal input? Or would he or she do better with nonverbal and multisensory communication? Which are your child's most reliable listening channels? Does your child register information best through sight, sound, music, smell, taste, touch, or movement?

- *Visual:* Don't underestimate the power of visual engagement and visual communication. What type of visual aid will be most attention-grabbing for your child? What style? Whatever visuals you use, spend time making sure they are attention-grabbing and age-appropriate. Keep visuals clear and simple.
  - Animate what you are trying to say with facial expressions, gestures, body language, and demonstration. Make it subtle or exaggerated, depending on your child.
  - Consider written directions, to-do or checklists, calendars, storybooks, pictures, computer apps, or cartoons. Make chore boards.
  - Try "first-then" boards. (Search for many examples online.) Such as:
    - First, a picture of dinner
    - Then an arrow to the right
    - Then a picture of dessert
  - Visual schedules—usually a series or array of pictures—can be used to clarify morning, after-school, and routines (McClannahan & Krantz, 2010). Visual schedules can break down *macroroutines* (moving from one task or activity to another) or *microroutines* (all the substeps within a task).
  - Include your child in preparing their own visual aids: drawing, coloring, pasting, photographing, or posing.
  - Visuals can be posted right where they're needed, such as over the bathroom sink for teeth brushing, on the shower wall for whole-body hygiene, or on the kitchen cabinet or refrigerator for meal choices (Allen, n.d.). For example, the United States Department of Agriculture's (2016) USDA food plate can teach healthy and balanced daily nutrition.
  - Play or free-time choice menus can be used in the family room to structure up unstructured time and cue acceptable choices.

    - There are many videos available online that demonstrate how to do a wide range of household activities and self-care tasks. Just search online, for example, "video modeling, teeth brushing." Or make your own video, starring you or your child. Make sure that the video clearly focuses on the behavior to be modeled without any background distractions. With a mobile device, run the video where your child can easily see it. Then have your child follow right along.
    - Flash lights to signal the beginning and end of activities.
- *Touch and movement:* Some children do best with hands-on prompting, walk-throughs, or manipulatives. For example, using toy figurines, parents can demonstrate what they want their child to do. For moving from one place to another, your child might be more likely to follow if you're dancing or marching.
- *Music:* Music truly is a universal language. Many children seem more engaged and responsive when words are sung, chanted, or rapped: "Better get up, and ya better get clean, 'cause here comes your dinner, and it's looking mighty mean. Say, here comes your dinner. Here comes your dinner!" Songs that are commonly used in preschools can also work at home; for example, "It's clean-up time." Have fun making up your own songs. To signal the beginning, end, or tempo of certain activities, bells can ring and drums can beat. Music can start and stop, speed up, and slow down.
- *Time:* Many children have a poor sense of time. They might fully understand what to do, but they have no idea *when* to do it or how quickly. To accommodate this "time blindness," there are all sorts of practical timekeepers. Parents can simply prompt by counting out loud or pointing to clocks. Even better, children can learn to independently use schedules, calendars, timers, alarm clocks, alarm watches, and electronic planners. Standard kitchen timers are not very visually engaging. The Time Timer (2016; see timetimer.com) disappearing red wedge has become a very popular time tracking device. Other smartphone timers are

often handy too. Old-fashioned hourglasses can work well. You can also mark time on a regular clock by placing stickies or magnets on the rim or by using erasable markers to shade a "wedge of time" directly on the clock face (Ward, 2016).

Tommy's mother has created a visual schedule and posted it near his play area. It has photographs of him in sequence: playing his video game, setting the table, eating dinner, and then eating dessert. As discussed in advance and specified on the visual schedule, he has set his Time Timer for twenty minutes. She flashes the overhead lights off and on when there's one minute to go. She touches him on the shoulder once with thirty seconds to go. When time is up, the video game turns itself off with a parent control app. She turns on some upbeat Stevie Wonder music, and they set the table together.

Be specific. Break it down: Make sure that your child understands exactly what to do and how to do it. Parents may falsely assume that their job description has been sufficiently clear, and their child "gets it." All too often kids are truly fuzzy or even clueless about expectations. What exactly does it mean to "clean your room," "pick up your toys," "get ready for bed," or "do your homework"? To ensure understanding, break these complex, multistep tasks down into small, simple chunks. Provide details. Be explicit. Clarify specific steps. Assign roles. Again, visuals can be very helpful: pictures, photographs, schedules, sequential instructions, job cards, and checklists.

To help Tommy know exactly how to set the table, his mother has made placemats that show exactly where to put the plate, silverware, and cup. All he has to do is match the items to the placement picture.

Check understanding: Make sure that your child understands your expectations. Ask for repetition of instructions: "I just want to make sure that I did a good job explaining. Could you please tell me what you have to do? What's your starting point? What will this look like when it's all done? What are the steps in between? Any questions?" If your child has difficulty finding the words to demonstrate understanding, showing by doing is even better.

> *Before Tommy begins his video game, Tommy's mother puts her thumb to her ear and her little finger to her mouth, pretending to use a walkie-talkie: "Earth to Tommy. Earth to Tommy. Come in Tommy. Come in. Do you read me? Requesting confirmation. Over." Tommy pretends to use his own walkie-talkie and repeats her instructions.*

Learning by doing: For most children, all the preview in the world does not take the place of practice. For some children, understanding comes only after doing. "Errorless learning" means breaking tasks down into doable chunks and giving whatever level of support is necessary to ensure success. Although we all learn best by making mistakes, some children need this kind of "jump-starting." Depending on your child and the task at hand, consider the following approaches for learning multistep tasks.

- *Forward chaining:* Your child learns step one. Then masters step one. Then learns step two. Then masters putting steps one and two together. Then learns step three. Then masters putting steps one, two, and three together, and so on. In this way, your child learns to complete the chain from start to finish in a multi-step task. For example, when learning a piece of music, the piano student gets help playing the first measure. He or she repeats the first measure, slowly and carefully, before gradually picking up the tempo. Once proficient playing the first measure, he or she practices and tacks on the next measure, and so on, until able to play the whole piece.

> *To help Tommy learn to set the table, his mother thinks about forward chaining. She could have him start by just setting one*

plate at his place only. After he learns to do his plate consistently, she could have him do his plate and hers; then his, hers, and Dad's; then his, hers, dad's, and sister's; then continue adding utensils and cups, one extra piece at a time, until he learns to set the whole table on his own.

- *Backward chaining:* Your child could watch the entire sequence in a multistep task and then learn to do just the last step first. Next, he or she could watch the entire sequence and then learn to do the last two steps, and so on, to complete the chain from finish to start. For example, you can teach children the steps in tying shoes or setting the table by having them do the last step first, then the last two steps, and so on.

  Instead of forward chaining, Tommy's mother decides to set the whole table herself then just ask Tommy to put one fork at his place. "Congratulations," she says, "You just helped set the table." After he masters placement of one fork, she does the whole table except for two forks, then the whole table except for three forks, and so on until he has backward chained all the way to setting the whole table himself.

- *Least-to-most prompting:* This is when you help your child just a little, but if that *doesn't* work, you help a little more. Think about a prompt hierarchy—a level of support—ranging from least to most:
  - Verbal only: "Tommy, set the table."
  - Verbal plus visual: Mom points to each item on the visual schedule and the customized placemat.
  - Verbal, visual, plus physical: Note, there are different levels of physical prompting, ranging from least to most; for example:
    - touch on the shoulder
    - touch the elbow

    - guide from the lower arm
    - hand-on-hand help
- *Most-to-least prompting:* This is when you help a lot; so much that success is guaranteed. Then, when that works, you try helping just a little less. Think about flipping the least-to-most prompt hierarchy (level of support) upside down:
  - Start with verbal, visual, *and* physical prompting. Then fade as much as possible from most-to-least as follows:
    - hand-on-hand help
    - guide from the lower arm
    - touch the elbow
    - touch the shoulder
  - Verbal and visual without physical
  - Verbal without visual and physical
  - Verbal only

Repeat as needed and fade support gradually: Whether you choose forward or backward chaining, least to most, or most to least, one time through is rarely enough. Learning requires successful repetition; especially if you are working toward improved consistency and independence. Generally speaking, you should make sure your child has mastered one level at least 80 percent of the time before fading supports and prompts or increasing expectations.

> *Tommy's mother finds that he does not need her to guide him by the hand, lower arm, or elbow. But he does need a touch on the shoulder, combined with verbal and visual prompts, to put one fork at his place, four out of five days. She sticks with that level of prompting and those expectations for one more week, just to make sure that Tommy again succeeds at least 80 percent of the time. Satisfied, she raises her expectations to more than two forks before further expanding his job description and gradually cutting back on the amount of prompting.*

Be creative. Make it fun: Some children don't like too much joking around. Still, most children appreciate a light-hearted approach. If you're having fun, your child probably will too. But take time to consider your child's unique sense of humor, and try to modify your "shtick" accordingly. Beware sarcasm: many children are either confused by it, resent it, or learn to dish it right back. Think about what good public relations, graphic design, and advertising agencies do to get their message across. In general, the more time and creativity invested, the more effective the communication.

> *Tommy's mother struggles, strains, grunts, and huffs, pretending that one fork weighs five hundred pounds. She challenges Tommy to a goofy fork-lifting competition, which, of course, he wins!*

Establish specific rules, roles, and reasons: A parent without rules is like a teacher without a lesson plan or a builder without a blueprint. If you are clear on your own expectations, you will be much better able to communicate them to your child. Spell out rules of behavior. Use black-and-white distinctions. Make sure that there is no room for confusion about what's "OK" and what's "not OK." Detailed contracts—written and signed, posted or filed—can prevent honest misunderstandings about previous agreements. Tight communication circumvents fruitless repetition. Say it well. Say it once. The techniques reviewed here should lower the chance of power struggles.

> *Tommy's mother made sure that Tommy was 100 percent clear on the rules for video-game use, specifically, "If you don't stop nicely when time is up, then no video games the next day." She made him sign a contract, and she followed through consistently. (More on this in future sessions.)*

Some parents feel that their children should just obey. Your child might resist and challenge your reasons: "Why?" An authoritarian parent can only respond, "Because I said so!" This is usually not a satisfying explanation. True, children may be too young, inexperienced, or immature to understand their parents' wisdom and intentions. Even so, children are much more likely to do what they are told if they understand why. If your commands seem arbitrary or absurd, your child's defiance should not be surprising. Good reasons lead to good behavior.

Tommy protests, "Why should I have to set the table?" Calmly, his mother explains: "In our family, we all pitch in and help one another. Sometimes I help you; sometimes you help me."

Give choices: Children feel more engaged and empowered if they are allowed to exercise some control. Give your child a limited number of choices for play, meals, and other daily activities.

Tommy's mother asks: "What do you want to do first: forks or spoons?"

Anticipate, plan, and communicate in advance: Review your list of problem situations. How many problem behaviors really take you by surprise? Not many. In fact, most challenging child behaviors are pretty predictable. Think about the usual trouble spots. Review a typical day, from dawn to dusk: morning routine, mealtime, classroom, homework, unstructured/free/playtime, TV/video/computer time, chores, evening routine, and bedtime. Although often exasperating, the predictability of these problem behaviors provides an opportunity to anticipate, plan, and strategize. So stop and think. Come up with a very specific and detailed schedule. Write down exactly what you expect your child to do and when. Consider writing a "social story" to help your child preview and prepare. (Gray, C., n.d.) Try to anticipate regularly occurring problem situations, and come up with effective communication strategies for each one. But do not try to solve every problem all at once. Pick one. Solve it. Then forward chain your own efforts…step by step… realistically…effectively.

> *Tommy's mother got out a legal pad and wrote out his schedule. There was quite a list of problems to solve. But first, she decided to focus on the shift from video-game time to dinner. Then she decided to move on to the routine between dessert and bedtime; then the morning routine; then the after-school routine; then dinner-time behavior; then structuring up unstructured time on the weekends; then working with the teachers at school on recess behavior; and so on. One problem situation at a time. This took a while, but at least she felt like she had a realistic plan and was making progress.*

After reviewing this menu of communication strategies, you might be wondering: is all this really necessary? Am I going to be accommodating my child's profile too much? How is my child going to learn to function in the real world? Do I really want to make my house look like some kind of special education classroom?" If you and your child were doing just fine, you wouldn't be reading this book. If you and your challenging child are struggling, these accommodations might go a long way toward fixing significant problems. How else are you going to make sure you have that essential level of engagement and understanding? Don't assume that your child is poorly motivated when you just might need to do some better planning and instruction. Rewards and punishments should never take the place of good teaching and supervision. Basics matter. Experiment with different techniques. See what works. If a strategy is ineffective, modify it or let it go. If a strategy works, tune it up, practice, and stay the course.

Homework for the Third Mile

1. Continue to practice time-in.
2. Figure out the best way to communicate with your child.
3. Choose a simple command, such as, "time for dinner," "cleanup time," "pajamas on," "brush teeth," and so on. Practice individualized and effective strategies for engagement and understanding. Pay careful attention to technique:
    a. Separate engagement from instruction.
    b. Stop one thing before starting another.
    c. Pick the right timing.
    d. Be empathic.
    e. Get close.
    f. Speak clearly and simply.
    g. Use all the senses.
    h. Be specific, break it down.
    i. Check understanding.
    j. Promote learning by doing.
    k. Be creative, make it fun.
    l. Establish specific rules, roles, and reasons.
    m. Give choices.
    n. Anticipate, plan, and communicate in advance.

Fourth Mile: Motivation through Positive Attention (*Raph's Song*)

• • •

Attention is the rarest and purest form of generosity.

—Simone Weil, *Gravity and Grace* (1952)

But Raph was never eager to leave the shore and get back on the boat. Raph always wanted to kick "just one more" pebble. Hawk tried different ways to get Raph back onboard. Sometimes Raph came if Hawk sang and danced in the air.

• • •

Let's say your child is paying attention and understands what to do. Your expectations are reasonable. The task isn't too hard, but there's a motivation deficit. He or she resists, avoids, or acts out simply because there's insufficient gratification. Your child is ready and able—but not willing.

This is the first of three sessions on the important subject of motivation. In this Fourth Mile, we will review how to give positive attention in a way that's meaningful and effective for your child. In the Fifth Mile, you will learn how to motivate by using natural consequences and logical sequences. In the Sixth Mile, we will cover use (and misuse) of rewards. But before diving into specific motivation-boosting strategies, let's cover some terms, controversies, and general principles.

Training a Killer Whale

In the book, *Transforming the Difficult Child*, Glasser and Easley (1999) describes how to train a killer whale to jump out of the water over a high bar (think Sea World). First, the trainer puts the bar at the very bottom of the pool, actually resting on the concrete floor. With an oxygen tank and a very large bag of fish, she gets herself into position and patiently waits until the whale accidentally swims at a perfect right angle over the bar. At that moment, she stuffs a fish in the whale's mouth. Yummy. The whale swims around some more. Again by accident, over the bar at a perfect right angle. Instant fish! It doesn't take long for the whale to figure things out. Swim over the bar, get a fish. Once the whale is swimming across the bar to get fish four out of five passes, or 80 percent of the time—mastery at that level—the bar gets raised just one inch off the floor. The process is repeated. Eighty percent success at one inch from the bottom, and then two inches and so on, until the whale is clearing the bar resting on the water's surface. Then one inch above, and then one foot, and then many feet, until finally, the whale is jumping over the bar high in the air. Deliberately, incrementally, and patiently, the trainer raised the bar, achieving success at each level before going up again. At first, the bar was raised so incrementally—and the fish reward was provided so immediately—that success at each level was virtually guaranteed. Once the whale "got it," the bar could be raised more and the fish treat provided less regularly. This way, the trainer kept the learning process challenging and phased out the reward. If the bar was set too high, raised too much or the reward was not immediate and frequent enough, then the whale would become frustrated, and so would the trainer. The trainer might question the whale's ability to make progress or even her own ability as a trainer.

Internal versus External Motivation

Left alone with a set of blocks, a toddler named Sally easily builds a tower. She squeals with delight as she stacks the blocks higher and higher.

Naturally, children enjoy success. Given certain expectations, clear commands, or reasonable tasks, they want to please. If a child is attentive, understands what to do, and is able to do it, she will likely be propelled forward by some degree of "internal motivation." Do this, *feel* that. Do it again. This kind of behavioral reinforcement comes from *within* the child.

Another toddler, Joe, has problems with fine motor coordination. He tries to build a tower, but it keeps falling down. After the third try, he gets frustrated, throws a block against the wall, and gives up. His

> *dad offers reassurance and encourages Joe to try again. Joe resists. Dad stacks two blocks for Joe and tickles Joe's tummy. Joe loves tickles. Together they place the third one. Dad gives Joe a huge smile and tickles his tummy again. Joe stacks the fourth block on his own and lifts his shirt for more tickles.*

In some situations, there's just "nothing in it" for the child. Skill deficits or task difficulties can create a real disincentive. When there is a gap between expectations and ability, "external motivation" might be necessary to help your child overcome success deprivation, self-doubt, and anxiety. Consequences can powerfully modify a child's willingness to try. Positive reinforcement may be natural or manufactured, real or anticipated. Whatever form it takes, your response matters. External motivation can mean either rewards or punishments. Rewards mean: Do this, *get* that, do it again. Punishments mean: Do this, *get* that, don't do it again. The behavioral reinforcement comes from outside the child (Kalat, 2013).

Classic behavioral theory, as put forth by Skinner (1976), holds that internal motivation is really just a myth, that all behavior is modified by external consequences, that we are all the products of our environment. Whether or not you buy into this view of life, behavior modification clearly works. Standard behavior management has improved the lives of many who had previously been considered beyond help. Lovaas (1987) first used applied behavior analysis to show that children with autism really could make progress. Sundberg, Partington, Carbone, and others used behavioral principles to teach nonverbal children how to speak (2010). Feuerstein and Rand (1998) used reward systems to help adults with severe intellectual disability secure employment. Barkley (2013b) has emphasized the importance of immediate rewards to motivate children with ADHD. Azrin and Foxx (1989) developed effective behavioral strategies for helping children with delayed toilet training. From severe impairment to more ordinary challenges, external reinforcement systems have become an important staple of behavior management in homes, schools, and workplaces around the world.

Risks of Using External Motivation

Despite strong evidence of effectiveness, standard behavior management remains controversial. It seems that behaviorism has as many critics as advocates. In his work with inflexible and explosive children, Greene (2014a) has warned against authoritarian-style parenting. He champions a respectful, empathic, and collaborative approach. Kohn (1999), a provocative educator, writes that children are actually "punished by rewards." He disavows the use of sticker charts, treats, prizes, and grades—even praise (Kohn, 2006). Greenspan, Wieder, and Simons (1998), focusing on children with autism, cautioned that behavior modification produces dependent and scripted "robots." He felt that the emphasis should shift from behavior to relationships. These concerns deserve serious consideration. So before we look at the appropriate and effective use of external reinforcement, let's be mindful of three potential pitfalls.

1. ***Missing the root of the problem:*** Before jumping to rewards and punishments, we should carefully consider the source of a child's behavior problems. Remember, your child's apparent lack of motivation is probably *secondary* to underlying problems with engagement, understanding, and/or ability. Sometimes parents think that children need a system of rewards when all they really need are clear and appropriate expectations. The first thing is to figure out *why* your child is having difficulty. What is it about his or her profile that causes the behavior problem? Maybe it's the job description that needs modification, not the child's behavior.
2. ***Undermining natural drive:*** External motivators can undermine a child's internal motivation or natural drive. If your child is already able and willing, he or she doesn't need a "better

reason." We should never use rewards or punishments when a child would be sufficiently self-motivated. We do not want to raise children who are conditioned to ask, "What will you give me?" Children can become conditioned to negotiate for higher rewards or think of relationships as just a means to a material end. As written by Reischer (2016): "Offering children tangible rewards in exchange for caring behavior can erode their innate tendency to help others." In a family that leans on behavioral economics, "social norms" can be replaced by "market norms." How do we help children learn that some things should be done even when there is "nothing in it" for them? Dweck (2007) writes: "We've created several generations now of very fragile individuals because they've been praised and hyped and feel that anything but praise is devastating." If the challenge, pleasure, or rightness of a task is self-satisfying, parents should consider leaving their children well enough alone.

3. ***Prolonging dependence:*** Overuse of external motivators can interfere with the development of self-reliance and the formulation of an internal moral code. Even if rewards and punishments are necessary to jump-start a child's development, how long should parents maintain this kind of dependence? Scaffolding may be necessary to erect a building, but no one would suggest that it's part of the final plan. Crutches may be crucial to healing bone but harmful to long-term recovery. When and how do we withdraw help so that children can learn to succeed on their own? And beyond the acquisition of independent life skills, how does a child develop his or her own sense of right and wrong?

The Ethics of Behavior Management

Recently, Sea World decided to stop capturing and training killer whales for the purpose of entertaining humans. Animal rights activists successfully argued that captivity and behavior modification were not in the whales' best interest. Neither was this practice consistent with a modern view of civilization. Children are not whales, but what about the ethics of child behavior modification? What's the difference between rewards and bribes? Are the external motivation techniques discussed here really just sugarcoated blackmail?

The difference is clear. Bribes and blackmail are not in the child's best interest. They represent selfish attempts to coerce and harm. In sharp contrast, ethical rewards are in the child's best interests. These strategies are used by loving adults to help a child move toward developmentally appropriate goals. Years later, the child (and other objective observers) would all agree that the goals and techniques came from a place of compassion and unselfish concern. Although there might be room for disagreement about whether rewards were necessary or effective, there should be no doubt about the positive intent.

Internal and External Motivation

Parent Child Journey is based on one guiding principle: there is no "one guiding principle!" I will never understand why so many experts make so many generalizations about what's right for all children. Nowhere is this tendency more apparent than in debates about internal versus external motivation.

Different children need different approaches for different situations at different phases of development. Parents of children with developmental differences are especially attuned to the fact that internal motivation is not always sufficient. Sometimes there's just not enough wind in the sails. For some children, sometimes standard behavior management can make all the difference. This does not mean that we have to use rewards and punishments for all children, all the time. When external motivation is necessary, we can avoid the pitfalls discussed. With careful attention to strategy, rewards and punishments can be used in ways that do not miss the root of problems, undermine natural drive, or prolong dependence. An individualized developmental approach means using the right tools, at the right time, in the right way. The pros and cons of behavior modification are well known. To reap the benefits of behavior science but avoid the risks, we just need to know a little bit about normal development and a lot about good technique.

Normal Development: The Shift from External to Internal Motivation

Over time, your child's needs will change. The right balance between internal and external motivation will depend on your child's current phase of development and the task at hand. Just because he or she might need some external motivation now, does not mean that he or she will need you to reward or punish forever. According to Coles (1998), independence evolves through three general phases.

1. ***Dependence:*** Infants constantly refer to their parents for approval or disapproval. Toddlers live for their parents' attention, whether positive or negative. Even as their sense of right and wrong gradually develops, young children do not consistently carry their own behavioral compass. They remain consequence-driven, most powerfully by their parents' or teachers' immediate reaction to their behavior.
2. ***Transition:*** As children grow, they learn what to expect from the adults in their world. Then they begin to internalize this external code. By remembering a long, rich history of parental reactions, they carry inside "the family rule book," sometimes acting in accordance with it, sometimes in defiance of it, but always with reference to it. They are still driven by consequence, but now the consequences are more delayed and more abstract, having to do with internal feelings such as

shame, pride, and guilt. Motivated by concern for what their parents will think, children of this age act *as if* their parents were right there.

3. ***Independence:*** As children develop, they gradually begin to consider the reasons for different demands. Without reference to the reaction of adults, they ponder the difference between right and wrong. They examine their own lives: What is worthwhile? What is necessary? What is beautiful? What brings comfort? Over time, they develop their own internal code. Sometimes their evolving code incorporates many of their parents' values, sometimes not. Sometimes the internally motivated child acts in ways that bring personal gratification. Other times internally motivated children act knowing full well that there may not be anything in it for them. Their decisions might even bring hardship. But these self-driven children do these things anyway, quite simply because it is the right thing to do.

Let's pause a moment to ask a very important question: should independence be the ultimate goal? Moreover, are any of us *truly* self-reliant and *entirely* self-motivated? Especially for those with developmental differences, complete independence might not be a realistic goal. Children have wide-ranging potential. But even for people without skill deficits or significant challenges, isn't it more accurate to speak about degrees of independence? After all, most of us are *relatively* independent in some ways and *relatively* dependent in others. Do any of us want to be 100 percent self-reliant? How about *inter*dependence as a more realistic goal? In different ways, others do for us *and* we do for others.

The strategies discussed throughout *Parent Child Journey*—especially over these three miles on motivation—are designed to help your child achieve *his or her* highest potential and *his or her* right balance of interdependence without missing the root of significant problems, undermining natural drive, and unnecessarily prolonging dependence.

Enough background theory and principles. Let's get down to some specific strategies.

Positive Attention for Compliance and Performance

If your child is sufficiently self-motivated, you should give positive attention here and there to reinforce these healthy tendencies, but don't overdo it. Let his or her natural drive work its magic. If your child needs extra motivation, you can provide positive attention to increase compliance and reinforce desirable behaviors. Everybody needs to be noticed; some more than others. A golden rule of behavior management: try to give more attention to behaviors you want to see more and less attention to behaviors you want to see less. "Catch 'em being good" (Christophersen, 1998). Try to give your child at least five positive comments for every one criticism or redirection (Gottman & DeClaire, 1997). It's far more effective to give attention *proactively* for desirable behavior instead of *reactively* for noncompliance. Here's how:

- ***Simple noticing:*** When your child does not get much of a warm, fuzzy feeling from just doing a task, knowing that you are watching can make all the difference. There are many jobs that children will perform gladly, but only if they don't have to do them alone. Sometimes you simply need to let your child know that you are there. Work alongside, pull up a chair, or pop in and out. Lend your presence. Let your child notice being noticed. You may not have to say a thing.
- ***Individualized positive attention:*** Most children live for their parents' attention, but they don't all notice or seek approval in the same way. Some parents feel as if their children don't care. Some children even say so! But these declarations of apathy should not be taken at face value. You just need to find a way of giving positive feedback that is meaningful to your child. Different strokes

for different kids! Usually, there's overlap between the most effective way to give your child attention for time-in and the most effective way to give your child attention for motivation. A few reminders:

- *Verbal:* Most of us are accustomed to giving verbal feedback. For many children, spoken praise or description is most effective. For example, "I like the way you're picking up those Legos and putting them back in the bucket."
- *Nonverbal:* For many children, multisensory, nonverbal feedback is the better way to register your approval.
  - Visual communication can be very effective. You can give a thumbs-up, wink, or appreciative smile. Checking off items on a to-do list is another way to communicate appreciation.
  - Applause combines sights and sounds of congratulations.
  - Don't forget touch. Consider a high-five, hug, tickle, hand on the shoulder, or rub of the head or back.
  - No matter what the sensory channel, make sure to adjust your "volume" or "intensity" according to your child's preference. Some highly sensitive children react negatively to praise that is too direct, exuberant, or public. Your child might be one of those who even cry or protest, "I did not do a good job!" Generally, such children do better with a more subtle, muted, or private approach. On the other hand, if your child is undersensitive, you might need to be more animated and dramatic.

- ***Praise immediately:*** When a piano teacher wants a student to prepare for a recital, he or she does not say, "Here's a Mozart sonata. Good luck. See you at the concert hall." The piano teacher sits right next to the student on the piano bench. She or he reacts verbally and nonverbally, commenting steadily while punctuating the air with gestures. The effective instructor gives feedback on every measure, perhaps even every note. It's the immediacy of the feedback that makes all the difference. Similarly, you should not withhold attention until your child completes a task. Give positive attention *while* your child is *doing* the task, or even before, to help jump-start the task. Parents often withhold praise during this initiation phase—when it is most needed. To sustain effort, give intermittent strokes of positive attention throughout performance of the task. The child who is complimented early and often is more likely to get going and keep going.

- ***Pay attention to process over product:*** Rather than praising, parents can simply notice, pay attention, and encourage. In doing so, parents should focus on the quality of their child's effort. You should avoid commenting on the perfection of your child's work or worth as a person. Doing a "good job" has nothing to do with being a "good boy" or "good girl." Such personalization—positive or negative—might affect a child's self-image; more likely, it causes confusion about what exactly is being praised. Be specific. Say, "I see you're being very careful lining up the spoons next to the knives" *rather than*, "Mommy loves you!" or "You're such a big girl." Moreover, as Dweck (2007) would suggest, do *not* comment so much on your child's innate or "fixed" ability; that is, his or her "inborn" talent or intelligence, especially in comparison to others. Avoid comments about the final product or perfectionist goals. It is much better to comment on "process" and "growth"; that is, hard work, effort, focus, and perseverance. Parents should highlight their child's grit and flexibility: how the child may have tried many strategies, learned from mistakes, and improved over time. This all means avoiding statements like, "What a great job! You're such a smart kid!" Instead, give positive attention with process-oriented comments and questions such as, "How did you do that? Tell me about it." In a nutshell, focus on "how," not just "what."

Spacing and Fading Positive Attention

With all this discussion about positive attention, how can you avoid making your child prompt dependent? How can you give support that's needed but still promote self-reliance? If you help too little, your child may become frustrated and lose motivation. But if you help too much, your child may not learn to do for him- or herself. Beware of generalizations about what level of support is right for all children. As if they're all the same! Your child is unique. His or her needs are different from those of other children. Your child's necessary level of support will continue to change, over time and across tasks. So you will need to stay on your toes. Assess and reassess. Don't expect too much, but don't expect too little. Spacing and fading techniques will help you get it just right.

With spacing and fading, you start with the level of support that your child needs to succeed. Then you gradually dial down. In this way, supported success can lead to greater independence. By helping a lot early, you can help less later.

To demonstrate how to fade and space, I'd like to introduce you to my dog, Natty (named for my beloved Washington Nationals baseball team). She and I had three sessions with a dog trainer. For the two-step command, "sit/stay," the trainer showed me how to ensure initial success; then, I was told to tone down, delay, and stretch out my positive support. I am not suggesting that children should be treated just like dogs; however, the same behavior management principles do apply. For teaching Natty "sit/stay," here's one way to space and fade prompts, rewards, and positive attention. Consider the following three steps:

1. ***Ensure initial success:***
   a. Give a loud verbal command. ("Natty! Sit! Stay!")
   b. Bold gesture. (Arm and finger forcefully pointing to the ground for "sit" and then arm extended with palm forward like a traffic cop for "stay.")

c. Tactile input. (Push down on Natty's rear end while pulling up on her collar.)
d. Give immediate multisensory positive feedback. Verbal ("good sit, good stay"), tactile (tummy rub), and gustatory (doggie treat).
e. Deliver all this feedback very frequently and from very close range Make it immediate, close up, and clear.

2. ***Gradually fade the intensity of the command and reward:***
   a. Gradually lower the volume of the verbal command and even fade out altogether.
   b. Gradually tone down command gestures to just a quick point of the finger for "sit" and a subtle hand sign for "stay."
   c. Gradually soften the tactile input until hands on rear and collar plus tummy rub are phased out entirely.
   d. Incrementally, provide fewer doggie treats until discontinued and just verbal praise suffices.
3. ***Gradually space the reward immediacy, distance, and reward ratio:***
   a. Gradually space out the immediacy of positive attention after compliance, from no delay to slight delay (more seconds) to extended delay (more minutes).
   b. Just as gradually, deliver positive attention across greater distances of physical separation: from face-to-face and touching, to inches, to more and more feet, to many yards.
   c. Gradually give positive reinforcement with less and less regularity. The ratio of compliant behavior to reward goes from 1:1, to 1:2, to 1:3, and so on. Also, move from fixed ratios to variable ratios; that is, from 1:3 to 1:1 to 1:2. The reason: once a reward becomes expected, variable ratios work better to keep the exercise lively.

Once you've faded out nonverbal positive attention and rewards, here's how to space out verbal praise:

> Step one: *"Natty. Sit. Stay." She complies. Immediately, without leaving her side, "Good sit. Good stay."*
>
> Step two: *"Sit, stay." Compliance. Take one step away. Then, after just a few seconds and one step back, come back and say, "Good sit. Good stay."*
>
> Step three: *"Sit. Stay." Compliance. Take two steps away. Then, after ten seconds, come back and say, "Good sit. Good stay."*
>
> Step four and maintenance: *Move from praise after compliance for every sit/stay to praising every other time, and then every third time, and then more randomly. Feel free to throw in a treat or tummy rub here and there just to remind her of the good old days.*

After a few training sessions using spacing and fading, Natty sits and stays in response to subtle hand gestures and intermittent verbal praise. After giving the command, I can walk all the way across the yard and hide behind a tree for five minutes. She dutifully waits for my return. I come back and say, "Good sit. Good stay"—even though I didn't need to.

Levels of External Reinforcement

Intensity, Immediacy, Frequency and Distance

In the Third Mile on engagement and understanding, we talked about errorless learning, forward-chaining and backward-chaining, and prompting from least-to-most and most-to-least. Similarly, in this session, we ask, "How much external reinforcement does my child need to successfully meet expectations, perform tasks, and comply with commands?" Your child's need for support will vary from one situation to another, and it will change over time. Think about one type of command. You have your child's attention. He or she understands exactly what you want done. It is well within your child's ability. But how about motivation? At this point in your child's development, how much external reinforcement is enough? A little, a lot, or none?

Across different situations, you can describe your child's need for external reinforcement in four ways: *intensity, immediacy, frequency, and distance.* I'll explain what each of these terms mean. Joey, our frustrated tower builder, will help make it all clear.

Intensity of external reinforcement refers to the type or amount. If your child is internally motivated or driven by natural consequences, then you might not have to give or do anything. (See Fifth Mile.) However, you might have to give various types and amounts of positive attention; verbal or nonverbal; subtle or amped. If all of this is insufficient, you might have to motivate with material rewards. (See Sixth Mile.)

> *Joey quickly lost internal motivation for tower building. The natural consequence of building on his own was failure and frustration, not inspiration to try again. But with a little hands-on help to ensure success, his father combined relatively low-intensity reinforcement (smiles) with higher-intensity reinforcement (tickles). This was enough motivation for Joey to try again. Joey did not need a material reward, such as a favorite treat.*

Immediacy of the external reinforcement refers to how quickly it is delivered. You can measure and describe the degree of immediacy as the time between expectation met and external reinforcement delivered; that is, seconds, minutes, hours, or days.

Joey's father provided the smiles and tickles immediately after Joey placed a block. If Dad waited for even a few seconds, Joey seemed to lose interest.

Frequency of the external reinforcement refers to the time between positive strokes. How often do you have to deliver the incentive? For example, every two seconds or every ten minutes? Frequency can also be described in terms of the "reward ratio"; the number of times you provide reinforcement per times your child meets expectations. For example, every time (1:1), every other time (1:2), or every third time (1:3). You can stick to this ratio ("fixed") or change it up ("variable") as described in the discussion about spacing.

At first, Joey's father smiled and tickled him after placement of each block. After a few blocks, Joey did not pause to look at his father. On his own, Joey just went right ahead with another block. However, if Joey's father did not smile or tickle after two blocks, Joey would not place a third one. So, for the time being, Joey's father settled on a 1:2 fixed ratio of positive reinforcement. He would stick with this awhile before trying to space Joey out to 1:3 or variable ratios.

Distance of the external reinforcement refers to the degree of physical separation between parent and child during performance of the task. After issuing a command, can you travel inches, feet, or yards and still expect compliance before returning to deliver the positive stroke? How about going to another room in the house or, eventually, across the playground, neighborhood, or city? These days, for older children and adolescents, positive reinforcement might be communicated—far and near—by cell phone, video, or text message.

At first, Joey's Dad had to sit right next to Joey. But after a while, his father could go across the room and pretend to get a fistful of tickles out of the tickle box. Dad would wait for Joey to place another block before returning to deliver a tummy tickle.

Pick a problem situation for your child, and use this chart to describe his or her necessary level of support.

Necessary Level of External Reinforcement

For (*specify expectation, task, or command*):				
Date	**Intensity**	**Immediacy**	**Frequency**	**Distance**
current	*type/amount*	*lag time*	*per unit time or reward ratio*	*feet, yards or location*

By quantifying *intensity*, *immediacy*, *frequency*, and *distance* of positive reinforcement, you can determine your child's current level of dependence, clarify the next level up, and track progress toward greater independence.

- ***Dependent:*** *High intensity, immediate, frequent, and close.* Your child needs very substantial positive reinforcement, delivered right away, after every response, with you right there.
- ***Transitional:*** *Faded, delayed, irregular, and distant.* Your child needs a lower level of positive reinforcement, delivered less immediately, less regularly, and less nearby.
- ***Independent:*** *No external reinforcement is needed.* Your child is internally motivated or self-driven by natural consequences.

At this point in his development, Joey is still quite dependent on external reinforcement.

Try thinking about your child's need for positive reinforcement. It won't be the same across different tasks. For now, pick just one challenging situation in which your child does not seem sufficiently motivated. Use this chart to determine your child's current level of reward dependence. And then use the same chart to monitor progress.

Fading and Spacing

Once your child has experienced consistent success at one level of support, you can gradually help him or her through a transitional phase to higher levels of independence.

As a general rule, if your child is successful four out of five times, then it's time to try cutting back just a bit on your level of support: not too much, not too fast. In this context, success means that your child does what's expected about 80 percent of the time and does not experience too much anxiety or distress in the process. Before raising the bar, you want your child feeling fairly relaxed and confident. Then, just like my dog Natty learning to sit and stay, you can gradually fade and space your external reinforcement.

> *After every two blocks, Joey's father gave him immediate smiles and slightly delayed tummy tickles. He collected the tummy tickles from the tickle box across the room. Joey's dad continues to offer blocks for building. With this level of external reinforcement, Joey is relaxed and successful with at least four out of five blocks. Joey's dad decides to start fading and spacing external reinforcement; gradually and incrementally. He varies the ratio of tickles delivered to blocks placed between 1:1, 1:2, and 1:3. He lets a little more time pass after each block before smiling and tickling. Tickles become less prolonged and less vigorous. Joey's dad has to fetch more tickles from a closet even farther across the room. He does not fade or space to the next level before Joey demonstrates sufficient motivation and 80 percent success at the old level.*

Fading and Spacing Positive Attention for Independent Work and Play

Let's see how external reinforcement with positive attention works—especially fading and spacing techniques—for promoting self-reliance. Suzie's mom is frustrated:

> *Every time I try to do something, Susie interrupts. She seems to demand my attention right when I'm least able to give it. She just can't play by herself. She always needs me right next to her. If I walk away for even a minute, she calls for me or comes crying, "Mommy, I need you to play* with *me!"*

Does this sound familiar? Commonly, when parents most need their children to function independently, they seem to demand the most attention. There's an obvious reason. From a child's perspective, the expectation to work or play independently means withdrawal of parent attention and no external reinforcement. When kids feel neglected, they learn all sorts of ways to get attention. Consequently, instead of getting your attention for independence, your child just might get attention for interrupting. If kids could speak for themselves, they might say:

> *Every time you try to do something, it means I'm not getting any attention. Of course I'm going to seek your attention when I'm not getting any. And playing by myself is OK for a little bit but not for long. I don't see what's so great about this independence stuff. Looks like the only way I get some attention around here is by calling or crying. In fact, interrupting or demanding attention works like a charm. I guess that's the trick!*

As described by Barkley, spacing and fading techniques can work beautifully to help your child unlearn these expectations (Barkley, 2013b). First, using engagement and understanding techniques from the Third Mile, make your expectations clear. After securing your child's attention, clearly communicate a ***two-part command:***

1. I want you to do ____________ and
2. I do not want you to interrupt (call, get, cry for, etc.) me while I ____________.

For example,

I want you to ____________:

- Go to sleep.
- Do your homework.
- Play with your toys.
- Read your book.
- Practice piano.
- Choose something to do from your activity menu.

And I don't want you to interrupt while I ___________:

- Talk on the phone.
- Do my work.
- Talk to these people.
- Rest.
- Make dinner.

Here's the key: once you've got your child set on doing something specific, then you're in a position to give positive attention to that non-disruptive behavior instead of feeling forced to give attention to the disruptive behavior. First jump-start, then gradually space and fade to promote independence.

- *Jump-start:* You might have to linger and take some time to get your child settled. Give your child plenty of positive attention for doing the preferred activity. Once he or she is jump-started, gradually space and fade your positive attention—but not too quickly.
- *Spacing and fading:* Give a steady stream of positive attention for not interrupting. Pop back and forth between your child's activity and yours. Gradually space out the frequency and distance of

your external reinforcement. For very dependent children, you might have to start spacing by just standing briefly then coming right back down to their level. After success at that level, you can try taking just one step away before returning, then two steps, return, and so on. Meanwhile, stretch out the time interval. Gradually, be less immediate about your return. At first, pop right back. Then return after just a few seconds, then after ten seconds, and so on. By interrupting yourself, preemptively providing enough positive attention then gradually spacing and fading, you can reinforce your child's independent behavior—not their interrupting!

Whenever her mom tries to answer work e-mails on her desktop computer, Susie interrupts. Her mother decides to try some spacing. At first, for training purposes, Mom just pretends that she's got work to do.

- Two-part command: *"Susie, I'm going to do some work at my desk. You play with your toys here while I answer my e-mails—and no interrupting."*
- Jump-start: *One second later, without taking a step away, Mom comments, "Oh look Susie, you're getting out your Jasmine figure!" Mom walks over to her computer but maintains good eye contact with Susie. As she pretends to answer her first e-mail, Mom gives Susie a smile and a wink. Quickly, Mom comes back to Susie and gets down at eye level. Mom says, "Susie, I see you've got Jasmine playing with Aladdin. That's great, and thanks for letting me do my work." Mom lingers a moment to ensure compliance.*
- Spacing and fading: *Mom returns to her desk for more pretend e-mails. She sits at a forty-five-degree angle to maintain frequent visual contact with Susie. While typing on her computer, Mom gradually decreases the frequency of nonverbal signs of approval. After a minute, Mom wanders back over to Susie to give her some more nonverbal and*

> *whispered praise for playing so well and not interrupting. Then she goes back to her desk. This time, just for a moment, she deliberately breaks off visual contact. Then, as Susie acclimates, Mom's visual contact and nonverbal positive attention become even more intermittent, brief, and subtle. During this pretend work period—and real ones that follow over the next few months—Mom's preemptive positive strokes continue, but they are progressively subtler, fewer, and farther between. In this way, Susie makes progress toward more independent play—even when her mom has to withdraw attention.*

This kind of proactive positive attention can be used to reinforce all sorts of activities where self-reliance is at a premium. You can use this technique to promote independence for:

- sleep
- homework
- morning routines
- evening routines
- play
- chores
- self-care

Try applying these principles and techniques to some common problem situations. Give positive attention for compliance. Then space and fade.

Homework for the Fourth Mile

1. Keep up time-in.
2. Keep up good technique for ensuring engagement and understanding.
3. Practice giving frequent, immediate, individualized positive attention:
   a. "Catch 'em being good."
   b. Attend to "process/how," not just "product/what."
   c. Customize how you give positive attention according to your child's unique profile.
4. Promote independence by giving sufficient positive attention and then spacing and fading.

Fifth Mile: Self-Motivation and Learning through Experience (*Hawk Flies Off*)

• • •

The only source of knowledge is experience.

—Albert Einstein (Howard, 2000)

Sometimes Hawk squawked and sang, but Raph still wouldn't stop playing on the shore. So Hawk just flew to the boat and waited.

Raph kept on playing. But suddenly, Raph looked up and thought, *Where's Hawk?* For a moment, Raph was scared. Raph ran fast back to the boat. There was Hawk, patiently perched.

• • •

The Fourth Mile strategies require you to step forward and reinforce your child's behavior by giving positive attention. In this Fifth Mile, you're going to learn about the importance of taking a step back. Your child does not have to learn everything from you. In fact, children often learn best from their own experience. *Sometimes* parents just need to give children opportunities to appreciate the consequences of their *own* actions and learn from their *own* mistakes. Here you will decide when it's not necessary to jump-start with errorless learning because it's sufficient to hand over the steering wheel for error-full learning.

Mogel (2008) chose a wonderful metaphor for the title of her insightful book, *The Blessing of a Skinned Knee: Using Jewish Teachings to Raise Self-Reliant Children*. A child falls down and skins a knee. One of two things can happen. An adult can rush to help: "What happened to *you*? Does it hurt? Let me make it better *for you*." Or the child can be left to fend for him- or herself: "What happened to *me*? It hurts. How can I make it better *for myself*?" Depending on your usual response, your child learns helplessness or self-reliance, vulnerability or resilience.

"Skinned Knee" or "Broken Femur?"

This is *not* an across-the-board case for "tough love" or "the school of hard knocks." Parents should not allow their children to experience *every* natural consequence. You should never stand idly by and allow your child to experience serious harm or suffering. Selective exposure to natural consequences does not mean putting kids in "sink or swim" situations and letting them drown. Parents should protect their children. After all, Mogel's book is called *Blessings of a Skinned Knee*, not *Blessings of a Broken Femur!* But when is it a "skinned knee" and when is it a "broken femur?" When should you take a step back, and when should you take a step forward?

Throughout *Parent Child Journey*, we try to avoid sweeping statements about what's right for all children across all situations. Yet magazine articles and playground conversations swing from one generalization to another. Channeling Mogel, some argue that parents are doing too much. They sound warnings about "helicopter parenting," "micromanaging," "spoiling," and "enabling." Others say that parents are not doing enough. Moms and dads across the land are reprimanded for being too "free-range," "hands-off," or "oblivious to the achievement gap." There are even parenting stereotypes about whole ethnic groups and nations! Loudly, parents may accuse one another of being either "too soft" or "too tough." Perhaps more softly, parents may accuse themselves of the same tendencies. All this generalizing is unproductive, harmful, and beside the point. True, some parents may "overhelp" some children some of the time. But the very same parent may also "underhelp" the very same child at other times. Generalizations are not at all useful. The key is deciding *when* to do more and *when* to do less.

Natural Consequences

Ignoring Your Child's Inappropriate Demands

Children often make demands that are inappropriate, unreasonable, or unhealthy. Parents may give in to these demands or get sucked into arguments.

- If you give in, you might unintentionally reward your child's demands. As a result, he or she learns to demand more.
- If you "stand your ground" but engage in a lot of back and forth, your child's demands may not be granted, but he or she still get a lot of attention. By being overly responsive and reactive, you may unintentionally reinforce your child's demanding behavior.

Whether you are too permissive or too authoritarian, child demands + parent response = more child demands.

By ignoring your child's inappropriate demands, you can avoid reinforcing this kind of "entitled" behavior and give your child essential opportunities to learn some important life lessons:

- You cannot always get what you want.
- Sometimes you need to help yourself.
- Very unreasonable or inappropriate demands will not be reinforced (or dignified) with a response.

If parents exercise restraint and ignore unreasonable demands, children can learn to "do without" or "do for themselves." Here are some common ways that parents might give in to inappropriate demands:

- providing pacifier, bottle, or breast to your child or on-demand (when it's not the right time or it's no longer age-appropriate)
- giving in to unhealthy or impulsive eating and drinking
- rocking, lying down, or staying with a child to help them fall sleep
- fetching things for your child on-demand
- transporting your child on-demand
- buying things for your child on-demand

Sometimes your child may learn best if you simply ignore these kinds of inappropriate demands. It's easier to be consistent if you establish clear rules and expectations.

Ignoring Your Child's Noncompliance

The same principles apply when your child won't follow appropriate directions. Let's assume that you are making reasonable suggestions on matters of comfort, health, and success. Your child may resist. If you insist and repeat, your child may ignore you or become more defiant. As discussed, once this kind of power struggle begins, it can only end with you overpowering or giving in. Instead, give the direction: calmly, clearly, and once and only once. Then back off and let your child experience the natural consequences of his or her decision. Sometimes backing off is not a good idea: Broken femur. But other times, experience may be the best teacher: skinned knee. For example, if you ignore noncompliance, your child might learn to answer the following questions for him- or herself:

- What happens if I don't eat? (hunger)
- What happens if I don't sleep? (fatigue)
- What happens if I don't put on a warm coat? (cold)
- What happens if I don't try to work out problems with siblings and friends? (no one to play with me)
- What happens if I don't do my homework or study for a test? (failure)
- What happens if I don't clean up my room? (lost stuff)
- What happens if I don't put my laundry in the basket? (no clean clothes)
- What happens if I don't help myself? (nobody else will)

If given the opportunity, children can learn from hunger, fatigue, cold, loneliness, teacher reaction, lost toys, and smelly socks. It's not all up to you. Think about specific situations where your responsiveness might interfere with your child's self-education. You don't want to reinforce your child's demanding or helpless behavior. You don't want to undermine self-motivation. We cannot prepare our children for all of life's contingencies. We need to resist the temptation to help our children over every little bump in the road. Look for opportunities to teach your child to deal with minor disappointment and distress. By selectively ignoring, you give your child the chance to learn for him- or herself.

Consider the following examples of learning from natural consequences.

Example #1: Homework

Some children, especially those with learning disabilities or attention problems, might need more structure and more support to do homework. For them, backing off to let them "sink or swim" means sinking. Allowing them to flunk or fall hopelessly behind is not OK: broken femur. However, other children need less parent involvement. For them, backing off to let them "sink or swim" means struggling but swimming: skinned knee. But let's beware of generalizations. The same child may require different levels of support for different subjects and different types of assignments. Parents need to figure out when to give more support and when to let the child work through problems independently. Sometimes less is more.

Sometimes more is less. Let's take a deeper look at the danger when parents provide too much oversight. These parents might insist on homework completion or perfection. They might even end up doing their child's homework themselves. In these cases, failure to cut the umbilical cord results in a dependent, resentful child. The parent burns out too. The parent-child relationship suffers. The teacher has no clue about the child's true abilities or the appropriateness of the homework assignments. These parents need to take a step back. Maybe a dip in grades and a bit of stress is just what the child needs to turn things around. In sorting this out, try to be honest and objective about your own anxiety. Sometimes failure is a prerequisite for success. Your child might need to fall two steps backward before he or she can learn how to take three steps forward. Again, this does not mean allowing your child to flunk out of school or slide into a deep depression. Allow for skinned knees, not broken femurs. Or as Mogel (2011) says through the title of her second book, grant *The Blessing of a B Minus*.. The result: a healthier parent-child relationship and a more self-reliant student.

An important digression about too much homework: The skinned knee/broken femur dilemma is often not about getting children to do homework, it's about getting them to stop! Some children are too anxious, perfectionistic, or competitive about their schoolwork. I've heard third-graders say, "If I don't get good grades, I won't get into a good college!" Some teachers assign homework that's too hard or too much. A growing body of research shows that homework in elementary school is more harmful than helpful. Too much homework has a negative impact on long-term educational achievement. Health suffers—emotional and physical. Children need time to play, socialize, and relax. Overworked children suffer anxiety and sleep deprivation (Kohn, 2007). The value of homework in middle school and high school is more controversial. Certainly, the risk-benefit ratio depends on the quantity and quality of the assignments.

The National Education Association's (2016) guidelines seem reasonable; that is, no more than ten minutes of homework per grade per night. So the *maximum* daily homework time for a kindergartner would be zero; for a second grader, twenty minutes; for a fifth-grader, fifty minutes; and for an eleventh-grader, 110 minutes. Whatever your child can get done in that time, fine. If there's still more to do, maybe kids should learn to shut it down. Parents can send a note: "Dear Teacher, Jimmy put in his max homework time, and this is what he finished. Thanks for your support and understanding." How else do teachers know about the appropriateness of their assignments? How else do teachers know how their assignment load adds on top off work from other classes? How else do they know how much time it takes and how hard it is for each student? Moreover, your child learns that the sky doesn't fall if he or she practices good self-care. It's very important for parents and teachers to synchronize expectations, communicate regularly, and work together.

Example #2: Eating

The distinction between skinned knee and broken femur sometimes requires expert input. Some infants born extremely premature—with breathing problems, heart disease, or other serious medical conditions—need tube feedings to grow. This might be the only way for them to get crucial calories. Otherwise, there would be serious repercussions for growth and recovery. This would be worse than a "broken femur." However, tube feedings over an extended period may interfere with the development of normal oral-sensory and oral-motor abilities. Medical necessity during early life can have a negative effect on later self-feeding and mealtime behavior. These tube-fed children just might not have enough opportunity to learn naturally. They can become "tube dependent" and refuse to take any foods by mouth.

In these situations, pediatric gastroenterologists might recommend stopping the tube feedings and letting the child lose some weight. Only when they are allowed to experience enough hunger do they gradually become motivated to feed themselves. This can take many weeks. If too much weight loss would seriously threaten the child's health and recovery, then the tube feedings might have to continue awhile longer. Obviously, parents should not make these serious medical judgments on their own.

An important digression about eating: Let me emphasize, there are some children who would rather starve than eat. For them, a natural consequences approach would backfire: broken femur. However, when there is no serious health threat, parents may effectively ignore undereating. If the kitchen is closed in-between meals, then poor eating at one meal can lead to better eating at the next one. The child's natural hunger—not the parent—drives better eating. This way, there is better habit formation and no parent-child power struggles over food. The same principles apply to children who eat too much. To make overeating ignorable, parents could simply limit or deny access to food. Then the child has to learn self-control and delayed gratification (Satter, 1987).

Logical Sequences ("First-Then")

Noncompliant behavior is often the result of illogical sequencing. What does this mean? Most children do not easily shift from preferred activities to nonpreferred activities. For example:

- "George, I want you to stop playing that video game (preferred activity) and do your chores (nonpreferred activity)."
- "George, stop playing with your friends (preferred activity) and do your homework (nonpreferred activity)."

George is naturally reluctant to stop doing something he likes and start doing something he does *not* like. Analyze a typical day: hour by hour, from wake-up until sleep time. Consider morning routines, after-school routines, and evening routines. Ask yourself: what problem situations and behaviors might be due to illogical sequencing? When do my child's preferred activities come *before* nonpreferred activities? When do niceties come *before* necessities?

If there's a problem with motivation because the carrot is behind the mule, the fix is simple: move the carrot in front of the mule. Logical sequencing, also called "first-then," means switching things around so that preferred activities come *after* nonpreferred. Simply adjust rules and routines to set the order right. All you need to do is withhold what your child prefers until *after* he or she does what is required. A logical sequence. The child learns: "to get that, I must first do this."

Here are some common examples of logical first-then sequences:

- Get out of bed, go to the bathroom, and get completely dressed, then you can have your breakfast.
- Brush your teeth and get your backpack ready, then I'll be waiting for you in the car with your favorite song on the radio.
- Do your chores, then you can have a friend over.
- Clean up all your toys, then you can have a snack.
- Finish all your homework, then you can watch TV or use the computer.
- Eat at least three pieces of each food on your dinner plate, then you can have dessert.
- Put your dish in the sink and come upstairs, then we can play a game of cards.
- Brush your teeth, get your pajamas on, and pull out your clothes for tomorrow morning, then we can have story time.

First-then for parents:

- First set rules and lay out logical sequences, then take a step back and enjoy watching your child learn on his or her own.
- First tune your technique regarding ignoring and limit access to preferred activities, then let the system run itself.

Technique Pointers

Natural consequences and logical sequences work best when parents use excellent technique. Let's review some pointers for ignoring, controlling access to preferred activities, and communicating clearly.

Ignoring

When employing natural consequences or logical sequences, you will probably have to ignore some demands and noncompliant behaviors. Good ignoring technique means *immediate, nonverbal, and nonemotional withdrawal of attention.* Just turn away, create some distance and find something else to do. If you delay, talk, or show any emotion, you are not really ignoring. Proper ignoring creates physical and emotional distance when there would otherwise be physical and emotional intensity; that is, a power struggle. Be ready for a burst of protest, disbelief, or testing. Stay strong. Keep ignoring. Your child will learn that increasing the intensity or duration of tantrums still fails to get your reaction. Strategic ignoring compels your child to deal with the natural consequences of their behavior. (For a more detailed discussion about ignoring, go to the Eighth Mile.)

"Walk and wait"

For overcoming resistance to transitions, "walk and wait" is an effective variation on the ignoring strategy. When a child won't get moving, parents often repeat their commands: "I said it's time to get upstairs. How many times do I have to tell you?" The child doesn't budge. This is largely because the parent continues to provide an audience. But what if the audience walked out? Would the performer continue with an encore? Would the show of defiance still go on? When trying to motivate your child to move from one place to another, you can simply move to the destination and wait. This way, you withdraw attention from the resistant behavior and give attention for compliance. Instead of pushing from behind, you lead from the front. The natural consequence of failing to follow: your child is left alone. The logical sequence: first come, then get attention.

For example, if your child needs to:

- Leave the house or leave a public place, wait just outside the door or in the car.

- Go upstairs and get ready for bed; just go upstairs and wait in the bedroom.

If your child does not like separation, this "walk and wait" technique works very well. A little bit of controlled separation anxiety can be viewed as a skinned knee, not at all a broken femur. Obviously, "walk and wait" won't work if your child doesn't mind being left alone.

Controlling Access to Preferred Activities: "Birthrights" versus "Earned Privileges"

Natural consequences or first-then strategies may require parents to withhold "this" until the child does "that." For some children, simply stating the rule is sufficient. "Do this, then you can have that." However, if your child is not so rule bound, you will need to employ some effective environmental controls. If you don't control your child's access to preferred activities, logical sequences won't work. Some things that your child has previously considered "birthrights" may have to be reclassified as "earned privileges."

For example:

- *Screens:* Screens include TV, movies, video games, computers, cell phones, and entertainment centers. If your child has to do X before screen time, then you will need a way to block screen access. You can make the device physically unavailable. Or use parent control features such as passwords and automatic log-off timers. To learn how, just do an Internet search on the device and "parent controls."
- *Food:* Your child might eat too little at meals or too much in between. He or she might eat when it's not the right time or place. Or you might want to use food as a first-then motivator.

Under any of these circumstances, you will need a way to block the availability of food. For younger children, this might mean moving preferred items up and out of reach. For older children, it might mean getting a lock for the pantry. For the whole family, it's never a bad idea to just get rid of all the junk food.

- *Money:* Children and teens might demand money or spend impulsively. They should simply not have easy access to cash or credit. Free allowance can become 100 percent earned income. For older children, debit or store-specific gift cards work to limit the amount of money available for frivolous spending. Online credit card purchases should always be blocked by not sharing parent passcodes. (More on material rewards just ahead in the Sixth Mile.)
- *Transportation:* Rides can be earned or restricted. Requests for parent taxi service must be placed at least twelve hours ahead. For teens, parents can control money available for public transportation or confiscate the family car keys.

Visual Communication

First-then strategies work best when you communicate clearly. Use the visual communication strategies reviewed in the Third Mile. To ensure understanding, keep expectations front and center. Use checklists, visual schedules, or "first-then" boards. For example, put a photo of your child getting on pajamas, followed by an arrow, followed by a photo of you and your child reading a book together. Place this "first pajamas → then story time" board in your child's bedroom so it's easily seen. Written words, pictures or photographs can make your child less dependent on your spoken reminders; otherwise known by children as "nagging" and by parents as "having to repeat myself."

Putting It All Together

We are building a behavior management tool kit. It's important to learn *how* to use each tool. But it's just as important to learn *when* to use each tool. Which behavioral strategy is best for which problem situation? In some situations, you will need to take a step forward with positive attention. In other situations, you will need to take a step back and use natural consequences or logical sequences. In the next session, we will cover the use and misuse of material rewards. Sometimes it's hard to guess which approach will work best for which situation. However, with good technique, you can try and see. The whole idea is to choose a strategy ahead of time, use it well, and then see how it works. Often techniques work better in combination than they do one at a time. For example, you might be using some regular time-in with targeted engagement and communication strategies plus first-then motivation. Mile by mile, you will continue to layer one strategy on another. The order of presentation is designed to help you combine these strategies effectively.

Homework for the Fifth Mile

1. *Practice natural consequences:* Pick one problem situation when you should take a step back and "help your child more by helping your child less." Give your child the chance to learn from natural consequences. Prepare for some protests and distress, but hang in there with good ignoring technique.
2. *Practice logical (first-then) sequences:* Pick another situation—usually a morning, after-school, or evening routine—where there's been a problem because preferred activities have come before nonpreferred. Flip it around so that your child is motivated to do nonpreferred activities *before* preferred. Consider using visuals, such as a first-then board.

Sixth Mile: Motivation through Rewards (*The Tambalacoque Fruit)*

• • •

For we cannot tarry here,
We must march my darlings…

—Walt Whitman, "*Pioneers! O Pioneers!*" (1959)

Sometimes Raph just wouldn't get back on the boat at all-unless, of course, Hawk promised Raph a tambalacoque fruit.

• • •

Why Give Rewards?

Some behaviorists think that rewards and punishments should be front and center in any behavior management program. Not necessarily. In the Fourth Mile, we discussed how inappropriate use of rewards might miss the root of the problem, undermine natural drive, and prolong dependence. If you can use other proactive strategies effectively, why give rewards at all?

Michelle is a quiet toddler. She tends to sit and focus on one thing at a time. She seems fascinated by lines, shapes, and shadows. Michelle might find a toy or a household object and hold it in front of her eyes, carefully examining the angles and edges. She can peacefully entertain herself like this for long periods. Michelle's dad has learned to get her attention by squatting down to her level, gently touching her face, and waiting for eye contact. However, Michelle is generally inflexible and has a high intensity of reaction. When he asks her to come to the table to eat, she just sits there. Instead of smoothly shifting gears, Michelle derails. She screams and throws herself to the ground. To help her transition, Michelle's dad has tried showing her a photo of herself at the table. She might glance at it, but still doesn't budge. He has tried taking away her toy and physically carrying her to the table, but then Michelle has a tantrum. He has tried just waiting until she gets hungry, but then she doesn't eat. He has tried an if-then board with a picture of the meal then dessert, but she's just not interested.

Like Michelle's dad, let's say you've done a "pretty good" job using proactive behavior management strategies:

- time-in and parent self-care
- engagement and understanding
- positive attention
- natural consequences and logical sequences

But your child still lacks motivation, especially for tasks that are unpleasant or difficult. Consider Michelle's problem transitioning from play to dinner; or specific situations with your child when there just may not be enough "gain to justify the pain" or enough "will for there to be a way". Parents may feel that rewards *should not* be necessary. But sometimes they just are.

> *Ricky is a rambunctious and enthusiastic older child. He is very active and has a short attention span. Except for sports and video games, he has trouble sticking with any one activity for long. School is not really his thing. Monday through Friday, he has a lot of trouble with the morning routine. On weekends, whenever he has a soccer game, there's no problem getting out of bed. When the soccer field beckons, he gets dressed, eats breakfast, and beats his mom out to the car. But when the school bus threatens, Ricky gets easily distracted. He starts doing one thing, and then another. His mother has done a great job with time-in, visual schedules, timers, and positive attention. Ricky moves a bit more purposefully if she stands right next to him and prompts him through every little step. Even then, Ricky is usually late for school. And his mom is usually frustrated and late for work too.*

In this last of three miles on motivation strategies, our discussion of rewards will be based on one fundamental idea: **reward systems modify a child's behavior by first modifying adult behavior.** How so? Well, if you're going to use a reward system effectively, you have to do a lot more than just put a sticker on a chart. Good reward systems address the following key issues:

1. ***Clarity:*** Children may not always understand exactly what they are supposed to do. Parents and other involved adults may not be in sync about expectations. Different adults may work at cross-purposes, undermining one another's efforts. Creating an effective reward system requires the adults to reach a consensus and

draft a very detailed job description. Exactly what are you rewarding? What are your specific expectations? Your child can't be clear about the details unless you are first. Your child can't understand exactly what to do unless you map it out. Reward systems compel parents to "structure up" rules and regulations. Good reward systems ensure that the principles and techniques from the Third Mile, about communication and understanding, are put into practice.

2. ***Preparation:*** Effective reward systems require adults to think ahead and prepare carefully. It is always better if parents clarify expectations and determine consequences proactively. We all do our best thinking in advance, when calm and clear-headed, rather than in the moment, when high emotion or urgency clouds our judgment. The best reward systems take a lot of anticipation and attention to detail. By sharing the reward system with your child in advance, you give him or her something to work for. Coming up with reward systems "on the fly"—in reaction to noncompliant behavior—can feel like "marketplace bargaining". Good contracts are drafted, reviewed, and signed before the first "workday" or "paycheck."
3. ***Custom design:*** Every child is different. Why would we think that every child should be given the same job or feel motivated by the same rewards? When designing an effective reward system *for your child*, consider the appropriateness of your expectations and the effectiveness of specific rewards. When individualizing the job description and the payoff, make the job developmentally "doable," and use rewards that are uniquely motivating. If there is a gap between your expectations and your child's abilities, you have to deny the reward. Frustration follows. It's like saying: "Want it? Sorry, can't have it!" Reward systems only work if your child is set up for success. If you think certain rewards should be motivating but they're really not motivating *for your child*, then the reward system won't

work. One-size-fits-all reward systems for whole families or whole classrooms rarely work. What motivates one child may be meaningless to another. Good reward systems appeal to each child's unique desires.

4. ***Feedback:*** Good reward systems require parents to give regular feedback. You should customize a feedback system to fit your child's developmental profile. Your mode of providing effective feedback should depend on your child's preferred communication pathways. The frequency and immediacy of feedback should also be individualized. Some children need more feedback, more consequences, more often. For these children, reward systems work when adults structure up their communication in a manner that is clear, consistent, and timely.
5. ***Monitoring:*** Good reward systems should reinforce performance consistency and lead to steady improvement, not just isolated minivictories. It is hard sometimes for parents and children to tell whether they are making progress. Quantitative reward systems are very useful for tracking and highlighting performance trends. The number of rewarded checks, points, chips, or coins help mark your child's overall progress. In addition to documenting moment-to-moment success, good reward systems monitor trends over time; week by week and month by month.
6. ***Responsibility:*** Some children do not naturally appreciate the consequences of their behavior. Reward systems can help parents teach children the connection between cause and effect. By enhancing awareness of consequences, reward systems can promote self-awareness, self-ownership, and self-control. Reward systems can also help children learn to accept responsibility, work hard, and spend wisely.
7. ***Independence:*** Some children become too dependent on adult attention and prompting. A reward system can help parents be more effective in spacing their feedback and fading their

support. Rewards can serve as a "parent surrogate," helping to motivate children without so much immediate and direct adult involvement. Thoughtfully designed reward systems can serve as a bridge to delayed gratification and self-reliance.

So much for general principles. Let's get down to specific techniques. How can you implement reward systems that are effective but do not miss the root of the problem, undermine natural drive, or prolong dependence?

Michelle's father needed to find something that would motivate her to shift away from playing and come to the meal table. Ricky's mother had to figure a way to motivate him through the morning routine more efficiently and independently. They both decided to try using rewards.

How to Reward Effectively

The Job

- ***The job list:*** First, decide what requires a reward.
    - *Do not put something on the job list if you can fix it otherwise.* Could this problem resolve with more time-in or better parent self-care? How about more effective engagement and communication? Maybe better motivation through positive attention, natural consequences, or first-then strategies? For any of these strategies, does your technique need a tune-up? Are your expectations appropriate for your child's developmental level? Does the task just need to be modified? If you answered "yes" to any of these questions, then maybe you don't need to use rewards. Try fixing fundamentals first.

- *Create a job list.* Let's assume that you've answered "no" to all of the questions in the preceding paragraph, and your child really needs a reward system to promote specific behaviors. Think about your child's day, from morning through night. Go back to the First Mile and review your original list of problem situations and behaviors on the Behavioral Topography Survey. What situations are not getting better with the strategies you've tried so far? What are the regular behavioral breakdown points? What are the greatest sources of family tension? What expectations remain unmet? Where does your child need to do better? Some children need short job lists, just one or two items. Others need much longer lists. Some children have different job lists for weekdays versus weekends and vacations. The number of behaviors up for rewards depends on your child.
- *"Start" and "stop" behaviors:* It is easiest to reward children for doing something; so-called start behaviors. For example, clean up your room, do your homework, get through the morning and evening routines, do chores, etc. *Do this, get a reward.* It is a bit trickier, but also possible, to reward children for *not* doing something; so-called stop behaviors. For example, don't interrupt, don't say mean things, don't hit, don't swear; don't pick, pull, or bite; don't sneak food, and so on. *Don't do this, get a reward.* In a bit, we will talk in detail about different techniques for rewarding "start" versus "stop" behaviors. But here, I would like to sound a word of caution. You can include "stop" *behaviors* on your child's job list. Just don't try reward systems to stop your child's negative *emotions*; for example, don't get angry, don't cry, or don't get frustrated. In sessions to come, we will cover better ways to react: ignoring, empathic responding, and problem-solving. These strategies are always more effective and appropriate than reward systems for helping your child with emotional self-regulation.

Better yet, look at what led to your child's distress in the first place and proactively address these issues at their source.

- The job description: For each behavioral goal on the list, parents should clarify their expectations. Exactly what needs to done? Where? When? How? The job description should be detailed and specific: airtight, black and white, spelled out, no wiggle room. A good job description makes it easier for your child to succeed. Sometimes this clarity is the essential missing piece. You might want to review the Third Mile strategies for ensuring understanding.
  - *The job manual:* It is not enough for you to understand the job. You need to communicate your expectations to your child: effectively and explicitly. Job specifics should be broken down, demonstrated, illustrated, scheduled, written down—whatever it takes to make the job clear and doable for your child. The time you invest mapping out expectations will pay good behavioral dividends.
  - *The job understood:* Your child should be able to recite or—better yet—demonstrate exactly what it takes to do the job and earn the reward. What does it mean to be "done" or "meet expectations"? If your child is not able to show or tell, then you might need to do a better job of explaining and teaching. Make sure that you are not expecting too much. If your child does not understand the job description, he or she will not be able to do it.
- ***The job manager:*** You are the job manager, not your child. Once your child gets used to the idea of being rewarded for certain behaviors, he or she might want to increase profits by adding to the job list: "What are you going to give me? I'll do this if you give me that!" This kind of talk is against the rules. You should nip it in the bud. No negotiating. Once and only once, calmly remind your child: "If you do these jobs and mind these rules, then you get a chance to win rewards. But we don't make up jobs just to

win rewards." Consider ignoring any persistent demands. If necessary, put "not asking for more rewards" on the job list. Or, if your child refuses to accept this relationship, consider suspending the whole reward system. Parents and not children determine whether to use rewards and what has to be done. You may decide to enhance motivation by adding some easy jobs or giving some degree of choice. Still, you control the job list.

For Michelle's father, the job list was short and simple: come to the table to eat.

For Ricky's mother, the job list for the morning routine was longer and more elaborate:

- *Wake up to alarm clock at 6:45 a.m.*
- *Use the toilet.*
- *Take off pajamas; fold and place them at the end of the bed.*
- *Get dressed, including shoes on (clothes selected and put out the night before).*
- *Come downstairs.*
- *Feed goldfish.*
- *Eat breakfast.*
- *Brush teeth.*
- *Choice time: Legos, iPad, TV.*
- *Put on jacket and backpack (both placed by door the night before).*
- *Leave for school (out the door by 7:30 a.m.).*

Note that Ricky's mom only put specific times down for waking up and leaving for school. Each step in between is fixed regarding sequence, but with wiggle room regarding completion time.

We'll come back to Michelle and Ricky's reward systems after reviewing a few more important concepts.

Tracking Job Performance

Good behavior management depends on measurable outcomes. That means knowing exactly how you will track progress toward very specific goals. A running record of your child's response to the reward system ensures good communication between adults and children. Recording behavior provides a way to objectively evaluate how well the system is working. Data collection about your child's behavior also promotes self-awareness and independence.

- ***Record:*** Whether offering rewards for "start" or "stop" behaviors, adults need a way to record performance that's simple, reliable, and practical. The recording system should be easy to use and readily available. Depending on the job and personal preferences, your child's response to the reward system can be measured in many different ways; for example, clip boards, charts, check marks, tokens, poker chips, coins, index card tears, report cards, or marbles. There are many electronic apps that allow performance with smartphones, tablets, and computers. Choose a recording medium that appeals to you and your child. Make it as easy as possible to document job performance on a regular basis. This usually means recording number ratings or marking success/failure without much delay.
- ***Recording for "start" behaviors:*** For start behaviors, it's easy. Do this, get that. For very young or impulsive children, the reward—or at least documentation of progress toward a reward—should be shared immediately. Older children are usually better at remembering how they did and accepting delayed gratification. You may be able to record their success when it's more convenient; for some things, this may be at the end of each day. However, even for older children, if you wait too long to record, you miss opportunities to give meaningful feedback and it's harder to ensure accuracy, and the reward system may not work as well.

- ***Recording for "stop behaviors":*** For stop behaviors, it's a bit more complicated. How to track a child's success for *not* doing something? There are two ways:
  - *"Trial period" or "ready-set-stop":* Pick a period. How long do you think your child can inhibit the unwanted behavior? Two minutes? Twenty minutes? Two hours? To increase the chance of success, set a timer—just *less* than that! Then challenge your child *not* to do the stop behavior for that period. Ready-set-stop. If your child goes the whole time without doing the behavior, you record his or her success. For example: "Congratulations, you just went fifteen minutes keeping your hands to yourself."
  - *"Cost-response" or "yours to lose":* Another technique for rewarding stop behaviors is called "cost-response." In other words, "If you do that, it's going to cost you." With cost-response, parents give a predetermined number of tokens or points at the beginning of an observation period. The observation period can be a full day or just the time for a specific activity. The tokens or points are your child's to keep or lose.
  - *Baseline probe:* To determine the starting number of tokens or points, do a baseline probe. Observe for one week and see how many times your child does the "stop" behavior on average each day. For example, if your child gets too physical with his or her siblings about seven times per day, start each morning with ten coins in a jar. Or you could use marbles, chips, points, etc.
  - *The cost of failure to stop:* Tell your child that you will take one coin from the jar each time he or she touches another child inappropriately. Be consistent and vigilant. Every time your child fails to stop the targeted behavior, you need to make it cost. When removing a coin, let your child know, but this is not the time for talking or teaching. Don't be dramatic,

preachy, or emotional. Keep it all very matter-of-fact. This simple act of accounting gives you something to do without getting upset.

- *Measuring success:* The number of coins left at the end of the day are your child's to keep. Make your child's success matter. Coins earned go toward rewards. I will talk about bonuses for improvement over time—specifically, extra points for breaking daily and weekly records. Each day is a new day. If you started with ten coins yesterday, then you start with ten coins again today. They are yours to lose. As with all behavioral strategies, this should all be discussed with your child in advance. Otherwise it can feel arbitrary or confusing. If your child is too young to understand the system, then don't use it.

- ***Communication:*** All this quantifying and recording behavior facilitates communication between teachers, parents, babysitters, and consulting professionals. Behavior charts structure up direct communication between adults and children. For younger children, it's usually best for the adult on the scene to give immediate feedback. Older children may be able to deal with delayed feedback. At the end of the day, behavior charting allows other adults to easily share data and let you know how things went. By backpack or (preferably) Internet, teachers can communicate with parents by using a daily behavior report card. Points earned at school could roll into points and rewards earned at home.
- ***Tracking:*** Reward systems allow parents and children to track progress and critically evaluate the effectiveness of the program. Totals or tallies can be made at the end of each day, week, and month. You can graph results and analyze trends. Tracking creates opportunities to teach your child self-assessment. Parents can ask: "How did today compare to yesterday? How about this week compared to previous weeks? This month? Better, worse,

or same? What do you think explains the trend? What seems to be working? What needs to change?"

- *Responding to poor progress:* Generally speaking, behavior management is working if your child is tracking toward at least 80 percent success. If that's not happening, don't ignore your data. Data are only useful if we look at them and respond accordingly. Most behavior management systems do not work perfectly. There's always a need for some fine-tuning. Tracking gives you a chance to recognize breakdown points and make repairs. Sometimes the reward system has been poorly designed. For some children and some goals, reward systems just prove to be inappropriate. Other times the goals need to be modified to improve chances for success. Or the rewards are not sufficiently motivating. In any case, data collection allows parents and children to critically evaluate the effectiveness of the program and make any necessary adjustments. If the program isn't working, don't keep doing the same thing. In addition to promoting self-awareness, data tracking represents an important opportunity to teach your child some problem-solving: Why isn't this working? What can we do about it? More on all that in the Seventh Mile.
- *Promoting consistency and progress:* Too often reward systems fail to promote progress over time. We should take care not to reinforce *inconsistent* performance, *intermittent* success, or the same *old* basic skills. Why offer your child rewards for staying at the same level? Tracking is crucial for motivating children toward greater performance consistency and real developmental gains. Tracking allows children to move beyond transient goals and intermittent success toward longer-term and more durable gains. Tracking creates opportunities to recognize and reward positive trends. How else do you know if your child is moving forward or staying stuck? How else does your child know? The best reward

systems encourage children to recognize and work toward true progress.

- Measuring progress: Performance consistency and forward development can be measured over time by comparing percentages (20 percent to 40 percent to 80 percent success) or fractions (one out of five to two out of five to four out of five positive trials).
- Breaking personal records: Once you have a tracking system in place, your child can work toward "breaking" hourly, daily, weekly, and/or monthly records. Personal bests can be rewarded more than isolated success at previous levels: "Each time you break your daily record or get a perfect score (100 percent of possible points), you get ten bonus points. Each time you break your weekly record or get a perfect score, you get fifty bonus points. Each time you break your monthly record or you get a perfect score, one hundred points!"
- Raising the bar: Once your child consistently achieves at least 80 percent mastery at one level, the amount of prompting or support can be faded and/or expectations can be raised. "Pay" should also be raised accordingly. (See "job promotions" later in this section.) In this way, trend tracking shifts the goals of the game from short-term success to long-term progress.

- *Rewarding independence and self-responsibility*: Another piece often missing from reward systems is the promotion of greater self-reliance. Properly implemented, reward systems can relieve parents and children of the need for hovering and micromanaging. A welcome goal for all parties involved! A good reward system should lead to less prompt-dependence. More carrot should mean less stick. The goal: your child learns to independently consider the job description, anticipate the possible rewards, and then just do what needs to be done—all on his or her own.

- For younger children, fading and spacing techniques can work just as well for rewards as they do for giving positive attention. As described in my dog-training example, rewards can be initially coupled with positive attention and then faded gradually, such that positive attention alone becomes sufficiently motivating. (Eventually, positive attention can be faded as well.)
- For older children, greater rewards can be tied explicitly to greater degrees of independence. For example, two (or more) points for compliance with no reminders, one point for compliance with one reminder, and no points for more than one reminder (even if there is eventual compliance). The reward for true independence is bigger. If you have to repeat yourself more than once, there is no reward at all.

The Rewards

Employers set expectations and decide what work needs to be done. Employees decide how to spend their paychecks. Similarly, you decide what goes on your child's job list, but your child should be encouraged to determine the type of reward. Children will not be motivated if rewards reflect *parent* preferences. Go with rewards that are selected by your child. Try to match the rewards to your child's individual style, likes, and needs. Beware of one-size-fits-all rewards. For example, some children may be labeled "unresponsive" or "noncompliant" when a "whole class" reward just isn't as motivating to them as it is to others. Just because standardized rewards work for some does not mean that they will work for all. As with everything in the Journey, customization of rewards is key.

Ask your child: You want your child to feel invested and motivated. How you ask your child about rewards depends on his or her developmental profile.

- *Verbal:* If your child is able to answer, go ahead and ask. A good way to start: "I've got some rules and some jobs that need to be done. I'd like to have a way to show you how much I appreciate your efforts. Maybe there are some things you'd like to have. Maybe there are some things you would like to do. Let's make a reward list. What do you want to work for? What would make this job worth the effort?"
- *Nonverbal:* What to do if your child is not able to answer these kinds of questions directly? If your child is too young or language impaired, you might have to come up with rewards on his or her behalf. But you know your child's preferences. What does he or she like to have? What does he or she like to do? Some parents might say, "My child is so hard to read. There's nothing that my child likes." You might have to pause, observe, or experiment. What does your child naturally gravitate toward? If necessary, put out an array of possible rewards and see what he or she chooses. Test one thing and then another to see what seems most motivating to your child. At any age, every child can communicate in his or her own way. We just have to stop, look, and listen.

Different Kids, Different Rewards

There are many different types of rewards. Rewards can be:

- Perishable (edible treats) or nonperishable (prizes).
- Material things (Lego pieces, toys) or favorite activities (blowing bubbles, going to the park).
- Quiet, intellectual stimulation (books, puzzles) or adrenaline rushes (trampoline, video games).
- Simple and immediate or more elaborate and complicated.

Let's explore these different types of rewards in more detail. Consider the following variables and issues when matching rewards to your child's profile.

- ***Immediate rewards:*** For younger or more impulsive children, rewards are most motivating if there's no delay between doing and getting. Delayed fulfillment of a promise—one month, one week, one day, one hour, or even thirty seconds later—might be too late to motivate. For these "here-and-now" children, the behavioral consequence must occur in the moment to provide immediate gratification at the point of performance. You did it now, you get it now. Such immediately gratifying rewards include snacks (crackers, sweets), physical stimulation (tickle time), or here-and-now entertainment (video clips, songs).
  Parents should not drop everything and run to the store. If it's not practical to provide a reward as immediately as your child would like it, you can give tokens, coins, or stickers; checkboxes on a list, tears on index cards, or marks on a hand. You can use these types of placeholders to tally intermediate steps or subtasks. These very short-term IOUs are like quickly accumulating liquid credit, available for spending without too much delay. There's some immediate gratification even if the actual reward requires a bit of waiting. Like having a paycheck in your pocket, it feels good even before you cash it.

  For example, "You get one ticket for each of these steps. As soon as you get three tickets, you get your treat. (Child does first problem.) Way to go. Here's your first ticket!"

  The positive feedback is one step away even if the reward is around the corner. For these children, school grades might *not* be motivating because they are too abstract and far removed from daily requirements. Instead of schoolwork, they would rather play—and right now! As a counterweight, in-class and homework might have to be rewarded sooner instead of later.

- ***Delayed rewards:*** Other children may actually prefer delayed gratification. This is generally true for older or very persistent children. For them, feedback that is too frequent and immediate might be distracting or demeaning. They might feel better about working long and hard to get something really special. They might enjoy tracking gradual progress toward their reward; for example, with cool computer graphing software. They might care more about tokens, stickers, stars on calendars, and checks on charts. A picture of the reward can be cut up and used as a puzzle with each piece won representing one step closer to the pictured reward. Or the picture of the reward can be placed at the top of a column of blocks, a staircase, or a ladder, with each substep toward the pinnacle represented by each block, step, or rung. Using such customized media, you can enhance your child's growing sense of excited anticipation. Some children seem to enjoy the process more than the prize. They seem to favor collecting and accumulating over consuming or exchanging. They just want to keep growing their pile. They cling to symbols of success—without necessarily cashing them in. They enjoy saving and counting money in their piggy bank more than spending it. In school, this kind of child might be very motivated by cumulative grades.
- ***Novel and varied rewards:*** Some children crave whatever is fresh, new, and different. It doesn't matter so much what it is, they just don't want to get the same old thing. These novelty seekers might like grab bags full of ever-changing surprises or a large menu of rewards from which to choose. Perishables and special activities may work best. For children who tend to change their minds, try money, points, or tokens that allow for flexible spending or saving. These children sometimes choose cheap and easy rewards; other times they choose rewards that

are more expensive and hard to get. If money is the reward, shopping malls or Internet stores provide bottomless treasure chests. For some of these children, the act of shopping might be the true reward, not so much the item purchased. If so, perhaps a scheduled "shopping date" is what goes on the reward list. It's the freedom, excitement, and control that's motivating.

- ***Familiar and predictable rewards:*** Some children are motivated by rewards that are familiar favorites. They like what they know. They feel better working toward a clear and stable goal. Their reward list might be relatively short. They would rather collect ten of the same thing than one hundred different things.
- ***Turn assumed rights into earned privileges:*** Children have the right to essential food, clothing, shelter, safety, education, friendship, love, and affection. In addition, parents may choose to bestow certain privileges unconditionally. It is our pleasure to give our children some things they want but don't really need. However, children should not take these gifts for granted. Some things that your children assume as rights should perhaps be moved to the reward list; that is, as privileges to be earned. Consider some of the privileges that your child currently considers rights, especially those that you would not regret withholding; for example, time on TV, video games, cell phone and other electronics, expensive activities or outings, and allowance and other money. You may have already established some expectations, but precedents can be broken. At a family meeting, you could announce: "I'm afraid we've gotten into some bad habits. From now on, you're going to have to earn some things that you used to get for free. You will have the chance to earn everything you used to get—maybe even more—but no more freebies."
- ***Should some types of rewards be avoided?*** Do not make your children earn things that you would regret denying, for example, play dates or books. Time-in should be unconditional. If you are

worried about nutrition or eating disorders, should you avoid using edible rewards? Similarly, would screen time rewards attach too much value to unhealthy electronic habits or even predispose children to gaming addiction? Can money rewards fuel excessive materialism? It is important to consider these possible repercussions. However, be careful not to let your own concerns get in the way of responding to your child's individual needs. As emphasized throughout this *Parent Child Journey*, let's beware of generalizations about what's right for all children. These may be serious concerns for some children—a true slippery slope, black hole, or forbidden fruit—but not for all. One could even argue that it's a good idea to include such items in a reward system to structure up and limit availability. Perhaps reward systems can be designed in a way that even promotes self-regulation. For example, reward systems that compel children to earn money through hard work and careful spending may do many kids much more good than harm. In just a bit, we will talk more about using reward systems to teach responsibility.

Home Economics for Older Children

For young children, you should create reward systems that are very simple. For older children with longer and more complicated job lists, things can get complicated. Some parents feel comfortable tackling more elaborate reward systems. Others may have difficulty. This is not for everybody. Although the reward system should be designed primarily around your child's needs, it's always a good idea to consider your own profile, preferences, and possible limitations. Many parents find it useful to consult other parents, teachers, or specialists for help with reward system design, implementation, and management. So if you need help, get it. (See Tenth Mile: Who Ya Gonna Call?) But if you feel motivated and able to tackle more complicated systems, let me try to help with the following general guidelines and personal biases.

At the end of this discussion, I will follow up on our examples so that you can see how to put all this into practice. If you like, feel free to skip ahead to the end of this chapter and read Ricky and Michelle's stories now.

What is each job worth? Take a good look at the job list. How should you set the pay scale? Although your child should be encouraged to help develop a reward list, you decide how hard it will be to earn those rewards. It would otherwise be like an employee deciding his or her own salary. To custom-design incentives, your child could earn more for relatively difficult jobs and less for easy ones. For example, A child who has a great deal of trouble getting dressed on time might be given three points for that job. If brushing teeth is not so difficult, then just one point for that. What is easy for one child might be difficult for another. For the sake of simplicity, you might want to just set one point for each job.

Bonuses and job promotions: Previously I made the case for bonuses. As mentioned, bonuses can be offered for performance consistency and progress. This can be done by awarding extra points for breaking previous (daily, weekly, monthly) performance records. Extra points can also be offered for greater degrees of independence. As discussed: zero points for needing more than one prompt, one point for responding to just one prompt, and five points for independent success without any prompts. I also mentioned the importance of recognizing when your child has mastered expectations at one level and "raising the bar" to a next level. This means requiring even greater degrees of independence, responsibility, or skill. Human nature is such that your child will reasonably expect greater pay for greater work. This amounts to a job promotion. If you want to keep your employee motivated and on the job, give a pay raise. This is usually as simple as giving additional points for each additional job or for higher levels of performance.

The family budget: Parents may be concerned that base pay and potential pay raises will allow their child to amass great wealth and maybe even drain the family budget. Let's head this off. First, consider shifting more items from the list of assumed rights to the list of earned privileges. That should help a lot. Reward systems require parents to spend energy, time, and money. Make sure to keep weekly rewards within your affordable range. However, you should probably provide at least as much payout for earned privileges as you used to spend on your child when the rewards were unearned rights. If you were "spoiling" your child a bit, you may actually come out ahead. Furthermore, your child's spending will now be limited by his or her earned income, not by your bank account or patience. Decide how much time, money, and energy to budget per week and make that amount available for earning. If you are serious about teaching self-responsibility and promoting independence, your child should be able to earn some meaningful rewards.

Daily and weekly maximum possible wages: For each *day*, add up the maximum possible number of points for each job plus the maximum possible number of bonus points. Then for each *week*, add up the maximum possible number of points for each day plus the maximum possible number of bonus points. Now you have your child's maximum possible number of weekly points. If your child has earned 80 percent or more of this maximum possible, that's a pretty good week!

What does each reward cost? Now examine the reward list. To be sufficiently motivating, rewards must be special enough and not too hard to earn. On the other hand, parents can spoil their children if rewards are too special or too easily won. Children often want rewards that are unaffordable, unacceptable, or undesirable. That's fine—in fantasy. They can wish for anything they want: a pet chimpanzee, a $3,000 guitar, electronic gaming equipment, a Ferrari, a nose ring, or a trip to Tahiti. You say, "Great! Let's write it all down." But then, it's time for some reality. You might say, "Let me take some time to figure out what you will have to do to earn those rewards. Then let's sit down and talk it over another day. I'll let you know." (Spoiler alert: Your child could win the trip to Tahiti in about 5,247 years.) In setting the cost of each reward, there are two general considerations:

1. What's the relative value of each reward? Carefully consider your own time, convenience, and feelings about each reward—plus, of course, the actual cost. Also consider how badly your child wants each reward. Then assign each reward to one of the following three categories.
   a. *Easy:* Your child should have some opportunities for relatively immediate gratification. These rewards should be attainable within less than one week; even just one day. Cheap and easy rewards are usually necessary for younger children, but may also have appeal for some older children. Such rewards might include special treats, knick-knacks, or daily privileges. For these "easy" rewards, you set the price low.
   b. *Hard but possible:* Your child may *really* want some new electronic device, but you have serious reservations. You might be willing to give in, but only if your child works very hard over an extended period. He or she must truly earn it. For these "hard but possible" rewards, you set the price high but within reach.
   c. *No way:* Your child might want some rewards that you are unable or unwilling to provide; for example, the trip to Tahiti (unable), the nose ring (unwilling), or the pet chimpanzee (both!) However, by including these items on the list, you can grant these rewards in fantasy but deny them in reality. The lesson for your child—strike up the

Rolling Stones—"You can't always get what you wa-ant." For these "no way" rewards, you set the price impossibly high.

2. How long should it take to win each reward? Consider what it means to do well. If 80 percent or more of your child's daily or weekly maximum possible points is "good" (worth a lot), then let's call 50 to 80 percent "fair" (worth just a little) and less than 50 percent "poor" (not worth much). Consider your child's age and profile. Consider each item on the reward list. Then ask yourself: "If my child does a good job each day and each week, how long should it take to win that? What if he or she does just a fair job or a poor job? How long should it take then? For example, if your child could win one hundred points each week, then a good week would be 80 percent of that, or eighty points. Let's say he or she really wants that new electronics item, and it costs $100 for actual purchase. You decide that if he or she really does well for twelve weeks, then you'd be happy to get it. That means twelve times eighty, or 960 points, equals the cost of that reward. If he or she only does fair, it would take a longer time. If he or she does poorly, it would take many months. (By the way, that degree of failure should prompt you to reevaluate the whole system.) In this way, you set the cost for each reward.

Consistency: Reliable employees need reliable employers. Reward systems usually don't work if parents are inconsistent about recording, tracking, or paying. It is crucial for parents to set a schedule and stick to it. When will I record? When will I sit down with my child and review his or her earnings? When will my child be able to exchange points for rewards? It's often helpful to set very specific times and places for these administrative tasks.

- *Follow-through:* The reward system schedule should be clearly communicated and consistently honored. Parents who are not prompt and punctual in keeping their promises can hardly expect children to uphold their end of the deal either. Reliable follow-through is crucial to motivation.
- *Planning:* Only give points for jobs on the list. Children should know in advance what they're working for.
- *No takeaways:* Once earned, don't take away points, rewards, or privileges. If pay is docked or workers are fined, employers should not be surprised if their employees go on strike. You don't want to undermine your child's faith in the system. Trust works both ways.

So what happened with Ricky, the lively and distractible boy who had trouble getting through the morning routine? His mother created a daily tracking chart. Thinking ahead, she added afternoon and evening routines as well.

Ricky's Job Chart

Ricky's Job Chart	Mon	Tues	Wed	Thurs	Frid	Sat	Sun
MORNING	*******	*******	*******	*******	*******	*******	*******
Toilet	0 1 2	0 1 2	0 1 2	0 1 2	0 1 2	0 1 2	0 1 2
PJs	0 1 2	0 1 2	0 1 2	0 1 2	0 1 2	0 1 2	0 1 2
Dressed	0 1 2	0 1 2	0 1 2	0 1 2	0 1 2	0 1 2	0 1 2
Fish	0 1 2	0 1 2	0 1 2	0 1 2	0 1 2	0 1 2	0 1 2
Eat BF	0 1 2	0 1 2	0 1 2	0 1 2	0 1 2	0 1 2	0 1 2
Teeth	0 1 2	0 1 2	0 1 2	0 1 2	0 1 2	0 1 2	0 1 2
Choice	0 1 2	0 1 2	0 1 2	0 1 2	0 1 2	0 1 2	0 1 2
Jacket	0 1 2	0 1 2	0 1 2	0 1 2	0 1 2	*******	*******
Backpack	0 1 2	0 1 2	0 1 2	0 1 2	0 1 2	*******	*******
Car	0 1 2	0 1 2	0 1 2	0 1 2	0 1 2	*******	*******
AFTERNOON	*******	*******	*******	*******	*******	*******	*******
Jacket	0 1 2	0 1 2	0 1 2	0 1 2	0 1 2	*******	*******
Backpack	0 1 2	0 1 2	0 1 2	0 1 2	0 1 2	*******	*******
Snack	0 1 2	0 1 2	0 1 2	0 1 2	0 1 2	*******	*******
Homework	0 1 2	0 1 2	0 1 2	0 1 2	0 1 2	0 1 2	0 1 2
Choice	0 1 2	0 1 2	0 1 2	0 1 2	0 1 2	*******	*******
EVENING	*******	*******	*******	*******	*******	*******	*******
Set table	0 1 2	0 1 2	0 1 2	0 1 2	0 1 2	0 1 2	0 1 2
Dinner	0 1 2	0 1 2	0 1 2	0 1 2	0 1 2	0 1 2	0 1 2
Clear table	0 1 2	0 1 2	0 1 2	0 1 2	0 1 2	0 1 2	0 1 2
Backpack	0 1 2	0 1 2	0 1 2	0 1 2	0 1 2	*******	*******
TV	0 1 2	0 1 2	0 1 2	0 1 2	0 1 2	0 1 2	0 1 2
Pajamas	0 1 2	0 1 2	0 1 2	0 1 2	0 1 2	0 1 2	0 1 2
Clothes out	0 1 2	0 1 2	0 1 2	0 1 2	0 1 2	0 1 2	0 1 2
Teeth	0 1 2	0 1 2	0 1 2	0 1 2	0 1 2	0 1 2	0 1 2
Toilet	0 1 2	0 1 2	0 1 2	0 1 2	0 1 2	0 1 2	0 1 2
Game	0 1 2	0 1 2	0 1 2	0 1 2	0 1 2	0 1 2	0 1 2
Bed	0 1 2	0 1 2	0 1 2	0 1 2	0 1 2	0 1 2	0 1 2
Read	0 1 2	0 1 2	0 1 2	0 1 2	0 1 2	0 1 2	0 1 2
Lights out	0 1 2	0 1 2	0 1 2	0 1 2	0 1 2	0 1 2	0 1 2
DAILY TOTAL							
DAILY BONUS							

2 POINTS IF NO REMINDERS
1 POINT IF ONE REMINDER
0 POINTS IF MORE THAN ONE REMINDER

DAILY BONUS 10 POINTS
WEEKLY BONUS 50 POINTS

WEEKLY TOTAL	
WEEKLY BONUS	
WEEKLY GRAND TOTAL	

For school days:

- *There are ten jobs in the morning, worth a maximum of twenty points.*
- *There are five jobs in the afternoon, worth a maximum of ten points.*
- *There are thirteen jobs in the evening, worth a maximum of twenty-six points.*
- *The maximum possible earned for each school day is fifty-six points; plus ten possible bonus points per day = sixty-six possible points per day.*
- *The maximum possible for each school week is sixty-six x five days = 330 points per week.*

For weekends:

- *There are nineteen possible jobs per day, worth a maximum of thirty-eight points. (Not all weekday jobs are necessary on weekends.)*
- *Plus ten possible bonus points per day = forty-eight possible points per day.*
- *The maximum possible for the weekend (Saturday and Sunday) is forty-eight points per day x two days = ninety-six points per weekend.*

For the entire week:

- *There are 330 possible points per work-week + ninety-six possible points per weekend = 426 possible points for the whole week.*
- *Add fifty possible bonus points per week = a maximum possible grand total for the week of 476 points.*

Success means:

- *Good: 80 percent of 476 points = 380 points per week or 1,523 points per month or 18,278 points per year*

- *Fair:* 50 to 80 percent *of 476 points = 238–380 points per week or 952–1,523 points per month or 11,424 to 18,278 points per year*
- *Poor: less than 50 percent of 476 points = 238 points per week or 952 points per month or 11,424 points per year*

Separately, Ricky and his mother came up with a list of rewards. She assigned points to each reward depending on how long she thought it should take him to win each one, by getting 80 percent of his maximum possible number of points per week.

Ricky's Reward List

- *Dog: eighteen thousand points (roughly one year)*
- *Weekend trip to amusement park: three thousand points (roughly two months)*
- *One hour on climbing wall: 380 points (roughly one week)*
- *Saturday night choice of movie: 380 points (roughly one week)*
- *Favorite restaurant for dinner: 380 points (roughly one week)*
- *Trip to baseball card stores; buy one pack: one hundred points (roughly two to three days)*
- *Thirty minutes of screen time (TV, video game, iPad) to be used during weekday choice time or on weekends: fifty points (roughly one day)*
- *Two s'mores: twenty-five points (roughly a half a day)*
- *Money: one penny per point (maximum possible earned weekly income $4.76)*

Ricky and his mom meet every Sunday before dinner to review his job performance chart, count up points, track weekly trends, add bonus points, and discuss how he wants to use his points. Every now and then, Ricky adds items to his rewards list, and his mother assigns point values. Over time, she drops some items from the job list and adds new ones. Despite some bad weeks here and there, Ricky gradually makes progress overall. He is able to earn more points. He likes being able to exercise more control over his spending.

• • •

For younger children, reward systems should be kept much more simple and here-and-now.

Back to Michelle, the toddler who refused to come to the table to eat. Michelle is too young to tell her father what she'd like to win. But he knows that she loves time on the iPad. Michelle's father decides to reclassify iPad time as an earned privilege, no longer a right. He even goes one step further and temporarily makes it a forbidden fruit. He does not allow her to use it for one week. Then he creates a first-then board. It has a picture of Michelle sitting at the kitchen table and then an arrow pointing to a picture of the iPad. He is ready to put this system into action.

Michelle is busy playing with Legos. Her father sets a Time Timer (2016), presents it at eye level, and touches her on the shoulder. He waits for eye contact then says, "Two minutes to dinner." The timer alarm beeps. Michelle doesn't budge. He goes to the table, turns up the volume on her favorite iPad game and starts playing by himself. Immediately, she recognizes the tune. She comes over and cries for the iPad. He keeps playing, pretending not to notice her. She cries louder. Ever so casually, he shows her the first-then board and pats the chair with his hand. She cries again. Again, he plays the iPad by himself. After a minute, desperate for her iPad, she climbs up on onto the seat next to him. Immediately, without saying a word, he gives her the iPad. She smiles broadly and enjoys her game. With a parent control app, the iPad turns off after three minutes. She gets upset. He shows her another first-then board with a picture of her eating and then the iPad. Eager to get more time on the iPad, she eats her food.

Michelle's father tracks her success on a chart. It takes one week for Michelle to consistently come to the table and eat: calmly, without distress, anticipating her reward. Her father raises the bar: Time Timer alarm, come to the table (no iPad yet), eat, and then *get the iPad. After success at this level, he withholds the iPad until she comes to the table, eats,* and *clears her plate. Gradually, Michelle's father adds more items to the job list and more iPad privileges. This is his way of giving Michelle job promotions. For more work, Michelle gets more pay; more time on the iPad, and he offers a broader choice of electronic games. In this way, a reward for simply coming to the table gradually motivates her to assume even more responsibility and independence.*

Michelle needed a simple and immediately gratifying reward system. Ricky needed something much more elaborate and comprehensive. If your child is developmentally somewhere in between Michelle and Ricky, then you can target an in-between slice of the motivational pie. Set up a system that's more involved than Michelle's system but simpler than Ricky's. For example, you could set up rewards for several steps of the morning routine but not the whole thing, and not the afternoon or evening either. What you target and how you reward should change as your child develops. In other words, if needed, you could start relatively simple but gradually expand your reward system over time.

Common Issues

Siblings and fairness: Parents might feel torn if their children don't have equal access to rewards. Siblings often complain, "That's not fair!" It's even more complicated when a brother or sister has special needs or behavior problems and may already get all kinds of extra attention. The squeaky wheel needs more grease—but the nonsqueaky wheels need some too. Still, if a child is old enough to protest a lack of justice, they are usually old enough to learn that "fair" does not mean "equal." True fairness should be determined by individual need, not arbitrary rules about symmetry. Because every child has different needs, fairness requires parents to treat children *un*equally. You can explain, "In our family, we treat one another as unique individuals. We do different things for each of you because you are different people with different needs." If one child needs rewards and another child does not, that's OK. You should not feel compelled to use unnecessary and potentially harmful reward systems just for the sake of "fairness." You can counter your guilt and your other child(ren)'s jealousy by deliberately increasing their time-in (see Second Mile) and positive attention (see Third Mile). If you decide to make rewards a whole-family affair, just be sure to individualize the expectations and the rewards. For example, one child might get customized rewards for overcoming problem behaviors or skills deficits. His or her typically developing sibling could get different types of rewards for assuming more responsibility around the house. Different children; different approaches.

Children and money: You might decide to make each point worth a certain amount of money. If you do use money as a reward, establish a set "payday," but don't just hand over the cash. Take full advantage of this opportunity to teach your child about money management, responsibility, and family values.

- *Spending and carrying:* A significant percentage of earnings should be available for spending. A small chunk of spending money should be for carrying. Without money for spending and carrying, your reward system probably won't be sufficiently motivating. You will need to teach your child how to keep spending money in a secure place. You will also need to teach about carrying money safely: when, how, and how much. Sometimes children will want to buy things that cost more than they are allowed to carry. However, with clear carrying limits placed in advance, your child will not be able to make these purchases without thinking and planning ahead. Debit cards are an option for mature adolescents.

- *Saving:* A small and specific percentage of earnings should be set aside as savings. Teach your child how to use a home piggy bank, safe, or real bank account. Help your child learn about interest and how to track their savings. You can have them use computerized systems or old-fashioned bank books. Parents and children should develop clear rules and guidelines about when it is OK to dip into savings. Your child should understand use of savings is always contingent on parent approval.
- *Charity:* Set aside a specific small percentage of earnings for charitable giving. Children are never too young to think about how to help those in need, compassionately and effectively. Some children actually want to give all their earnings away. To them, this is more rewarding than anything they could buy for themselves. Families can discuss the pros and cons of contributing to various organizations. A family tradition of giving can be incorporated into seasonal or holiday rituals.

Money and natural consequences: Your child should have enough purchasing power to enjoy the fruits of his or her labors. Things are expensive. If your child cannot earn enough money, he or she will quickly lose motivation for the reward system, and you will lose an opportunity to let natural consequences teach some important life lessons. If your child is not careful with his or her own money, he or she should not be shielded from experiencing the results.

> *Ricky and his mom are at the mall. He impulsively demands a cheap toy. He had been saving points for the trip to the amusement park, but he'd also redeemed a portion of his points for cash. Over time, Ricky has exchanged enough points to have about ten dollars. This "toy of the moment" is probably going to break in just a few days. In the past, his mother might have responded with a long-winded lecture on the virtues of self-control and prudence. Or Ricky might have sucked her into an embarrassing argument at the toy-store counter. But now, calm*

and cool, she simply replies, "OK." Ricky looks up, pleased but a bit bewildered. Casually, his mother asks, "How much does that cost?" Ricky says, "I don't know." She shows him how to find the price tag. Then she asks, "Do you have the money?" No answer. She waits for the person at check-out to ask for payment. She turns to Ricky.

If Ricky had left the money at home, it would do him no good now. If he had brought the money but lost it, a lesson would have been learned about carelessness. But this time, he had thought ahead. Before leaving, he asked his mom about bringing some extra carrying money: "Just in case I wanna get something." Safely and carefully, he brought along an approved amount. His mother gave him some positive feedback: "Good planning." Then, a moment of doubt. Ricky thought twice about spending his hard-earned money on this little toy. Did he really want it after all? He faced a tough choice. His mother started to make a suggestion, but then she decided to stay quiet. Ricky looked up and asked, "Mommy, do you think I should get it?" If he made a poor choice, he would learn from his mistake. If he made a good choice, he would feel a greater sense of pride. She answered, "Ricky, it's your money. Your decision. I like the way you're thinking about things so carefully."

• • •

Whatever happens on this sort of shopping trip, you—like Ricky's mom—can relax and enjoy watching your child's self-education. The shopping mall becomes a place for learning and shared pride. No more anger and arguing. If children earn enough money to achieve some degree of financial independence, they will learn to exercise more caution. In this way, reward systems can teach some important lessons about independence and responsibility.

This discussion of rewards is so long because there are so many potential pitfalls. The length of this section should not be misinterpreted as some general endorsement. To the contrary, it is an extended note of caution. You should only use rewards if necessary. If you do use rewards, make sure to customize both the job list and the rewards themselves according to your child's developmental profile. Continue the reward system; modify and phase it out according to your child's evolving needs. Remember, rewards are never the whole answer. However, if done well, rewards may be an important part of a comprehensive behavior-management strategy.

This concludes the last of three miles on helping your child with motivation. Our behavior management tool kit now includes the following strategies to promote your child's willingness:

- positive attention, including spacing and fading
- natural consequences
- logical (first-then) sequences
- rewards

Next, we will be shifting gears to discuss one of my favorite topics: how to teach your child problem-solving. But first, some homework.

Homework for the Sixth Mile

1. Which situations or behaviors are still problems because of your child's unwillingness? For each, decide which of the motivation strategies (alone or in combination) is probably going to work best:
    a. positive attention
    b. spacing and fading
    c. natural consequences
    d. logical (first-then) sequences
    e. rewards

    Remember, not all children need reward systems for all their problems. Don't forget to keep up time-in. Stay mindful of securing your child's engagement and understanding. Integrate and layer these strategies according to your child's unique needs.
2. If you need to use rewards for some of the items on your list, start with a problem behavior or situation that's relatively simple. You can always add more later.
    a. What jobs or behaviors do you want to target first? Create a very clear job description.
    b. What rewards will be most motivating for your child?
    c. Set up a reward system. Only implement after you've prepared carefully. Make it tight.
    d. If it's a complicated system, consider getting some help or at least running it by someone else.
    e. Then, see how it works. Modify as necessary.

Seventh Mile: Problem-Solving *(Navigating the River)*

• • •

Human freedom involves our capacity to pause between the stimulus and response and, in that pause, to choose the one response toward which we wish to throw our weight.

—Rollo May, *The Courage to Create* (1994)

And then there were times when nothing
seemed to work. Hawk wanted to get going,
but Raph could be a stubborn bird.

Hawk would say, "Let's go."

Raph would say, "I want to stay on
shore and kick more pebbles."

So they talked and worked out a compromise; like, five
more pebble kicks, and then Raph gets to help steer.
OK? OK. And so they'd go, back up the river. Together.

• • •

Problem-Solving

Problem-solving is the last proactive strategy for your behavior management tool kit. Sneak preview: based on a very large body of cognitive-behavioral therapy literature, here's what we're going to be covering (Beck & Beck, 1995; Burns, 1999; Kendall, 2007; Seligman, 2007):

STEPS to problem-solving:

1. ***S***ay what the problem is.
2. ***T***hink about all possible solutions.
3. ***E***xamine each possible solution.
4. ***P***ick the best solution.
5. ***S***ee how it works.

As you will see, these problem-solving STEPS can be applied across a broad range of situations: at home, in school, and with friends, in work and play. Before getting down to the "how to," let's review some important background principles.

Problem-solving can be done by—and for—anybody:

- Parents for their own problems
- Parents on behalf of their very young or developmentally limited children
- Parents in collaboration with developmentally ready children (or other adults)
- Children for their own problems
- Children for other people's problems (including their parents!)

Notice that this list is arranged in a developmental sequence. Depending on the nature of the problem and your child's abilities, at first you may have to serve as a surrogate or model problem-solver. But once your child is developmentally ready, you should coach him or her to solve problems more independently. Start by helping your child with problems that are relatively simple. Then gradually move your child toward more complicated challenges. Meanwhile, shift from problems that are self-centered to problems that are other-centered. If you see problems as teaching opportunities, your child can learn better self-determination and collaboration. Over time, you can help your child grow more resilient and confident.

Setting the Stage for Problem-Solving

Problem-solving works best if you match your approach to your child's level of readiness; psychological, developmental, emotional, and social.

Psychological readiness: Seligman's (2006) work on "learned optimism" provides some important foundational concepts. Across different settings, he studied how people respond to failure. Seligman discovered two self-explanatory styles: optimistic and pessimistic.

Pessimists tended to make self-defeating generalizations. They used words like "never," "nobody," and "nowhere." They viewed themselves as helpless and hopeless. Pessimists were guilty of committing "three Ps" of negative self-talk:

1. Pessimists took their failure ***p***ersonally. ("I'm no good.")
2. Pessimists assumed that failure in one situation meant failure would become ***p***ermanent across all future situations. ("Things will never get better.")
3. Pessimists assumed that failure in achieving one goal meant that failure would be ***p***ervasive across all goals. ("Nothing ever goes right for me.")

In sharp contrast, when *optimists* faced failure, their self-talk was remarkably positive. Optimists tended to see problems as specific, situational, and solvable. They were more self-forgiving and hopeful. They avoided the "three Ps" of pessimism. They did not take their failure personally, permanently, or pervasively:

1. They did not blame themselves; rather, they blamed an unlucky situation. ("Just a tough break.")
2. They did not assume that failure was inevitably carved in stone; it was just a temporary setback. ("Nobody said this was going to be easy.")
3. They did not assume that failure in reaching one goal meant failure across all goals. ("Well, nobody's perfect.")

Seligman did an experiment in which dogs could learn either optimism or pessimism. The dogs were placed on an electric grid and conditioned to expect a shock every time a light dimmed. The dogs learned: dim light equals danger!

Some dogs were taught to escape the shock and control their fate. These dogs learned optimism. They were happy dogs. Other dogs were not taught to escape the shock. They had no control. These dogs learned pessimism. Over time, when the light dimmed, these dogs did not bother moving at all. Clearly, they felt helpless and depressed.

Like these dogs, parents of challenging children can feel like they are on an electric grid: a light dims in our lives; we anticipate a shock. No matter which way we turn, it seems that there's no escape. Whatever move we make, it feels like the grid will shock us again. Children with developmental differences can feel the same lack of control over their lives. Especially for those who face extra challenges, it's easy to understand why some children might learn pessimism. But Seligman wondered: even if there are real limits to how much control any of us can have, maybe we can still exercise some control over how we deal with adversity.

The MetLife Insurance Company hired Seligman to improve its hiring practices. The company had invested substantial resources training new hires. But too many salespeople were quitting. Call after call: "Hello, can I interest you in buying some life insurance? No?" (Sigh.) Seligman interviewed the salespeople and found that quick quitters took rejection personally, permanently, and pervasively. So he advised the company to administer his test of self-explanatory style. Deliberately, MetLife identified and hired only optimists. As a result, employee retention rates and sales performance improved substantially.

Heading into the 1988 Seoul Olympics, Seligman turned his attention to swimmers at the University of California–Berkley, among them superstar Matt Biondi. Seligman conducted a fascinating experiment. After a first swim, he lied to the swimmers; adding a second or so to their real practice times. He asked them how they felt about their "disappointing" performance. Then he had them swim again. In the second swim, athletes who reacted with pessimism swam slower. Biondi, an optimist, did not take disappointment personally, permanently, or pervasively. ("Just a one-off swim. No big deal.") In his second trial, he swam faster! True to form, when the Olympics rolled around, Biondi rebounded from a disappointing first race to one of the greatest overall performances—and demonstrations of hopeful resilience—in Olympic history.

Along the same lines, Dweck (2007) has described two different "mind-sets." People with a *fixed mind-set* believe that abilities, intelligence, and talents are inborn, permanent traits. According to this viewpoint, we all have just a certain amount of smarts. For such people, the goal is to look smart all the time and never make a mistake. On the other hand, people with a *growth mind-set* believe that abilities, talents, and intelligence can be developed through effort, practice, and persistence. Not that everyone has equal potential or that anyone can be an Albert Einstein or a Michael Jordan, but everyone can get smarter and become more successful. You just need to work at it, take some chances, and see mistakes as opportunities for learning.

For parents and children, psychological readiness for problem-solving requires an optimistic attitude and a growth mind-set. As we will discuss, this starts with stating problems in specific and solvable terms and avoiding pessimistic generalizations and distorted thoughts. The best way for you to cultivate optimism in your children is to model a growth mind-set yourself.

Developmental readiness: As mentioned previously, the degree to which your child will be able to participate in their own problem-solving depends on his or her developmental profile and the complexity of the problem at hand. You will need to modify your expectations accordingly. As you will see, relatively undeveloped cognitive and language skills need not preclude children from thinking about their own problems and having a say regarding possible solutions. You just need to include your child in a way that's consistent with his or her developmental profile. As with other proactive strategies, refer to your child's Gander as a guide to individualizing your approach. More on this to follow.

Emotional readiness: There's a right time and a wrong time for problem-solving. Parents and children do their best problem-solving well before or well after action is required. While rumbling, raging, or recovering, big brains and little brains alike are flooded with emotion. For effective problem-solving, everyone should wait until their rationality switches are fully back "on." In the next two sessions, we will discuss reactive strategies for avoiding power struggles and helping cooler heads prevail. You will learn when and how to use time-out, ignoring, and pausing. During difficult moments, these reactive strategies minimize emotional intensity. Whichever reactive strategy you use, it is important to wait for the restoration of emotional readiness before prematurely plunging into problem-solving. Depending on your child and the nature of the problem, the recovery phase may range from seconds to minutes, hours, or even days. Wait until your child is most teachable and you are a most able teacher. Then and only then you can make the most effective pivot toward problem-solving.

The *pivot* from reactive management to proactive problem-solving represents *an invitation to problem-solve* (Greene, 2014a). Parents should understand that this invitation might be accepted, declined, or left dangling, and that's OK. After all, we are looking for emotional readiness, not coerced participation. Problems should be framed in such a way that motivation for problem-solving comes from within the individual (Miller & Rollnick, 2012). Why problem-solve if goals feel imposed? It's much better when the "will to change" flows naturally from recognition of a gap between the world as it is and the world as one would like it to be. As a motivational strategy, we deliberately "create cognitive dissonance." This means that we highlight the discrepancy between an individual's future goals and his or her current path. You can help your child feel internally motivated by asking a few key questions: "What are your short-term goals? How about your long-term goals? Is that the direction things seem to be going now? How do you want this situation to turn out?" Whether young or old, acknowledging a discrepancy between wishes and choices can represent a pivotal step toward considering alternatives.

Think about three steps in the pivot toward problem-solving:

1. Delivering the invitation: *Wait for the right moment and say, "Hey, remember when you wanted such-and-such?" (Empathic pause.)*
2. Creating cognitive dissonance: *"I guess that didn't turn out the way you wanted?" (Another empathic pause.)*
3. Pivot to problem-solving: *"Well, I bet if we put our heads together, we can solve this problem. Is now a good time for you, or should we do it sometime later? What would work for you?" (Invitation to problem-solve.)*

Be prepared for the possibility that your child might decline your invitation. As your child considers your respectful tone, the sincerity of your offer, and his or her own dissatisfaction with the status quo, the RSVP will hopefully be a "yes." But if your child doesn't come around emotionally, you might have to wait for a better time. Or if he or she is just not developmentally ready, you might have to do the problem-solving on his or her behalf.

By the way, parents should practice inviting themselves to problem-solve. Is there a discrepancy between your life as it is and your life as you'd like it to be? Don't be a pessimist. Don't decline your own invitation. If you need some help with your own problem-solving, go back to the Second Mile on self-care and check out the Tenth Mile on Who Ya Gonna Call?

Social readiness: Parenting style can make some parent-child relationships too lopsided (Baumrind, 1966). *Authoritarian parents* simply impose their will. The child's perspective is not considered or taken seriously. *Permissive parents* cave to their child's will and the parent's perspective is not taken seriously by the child—or even presented. Neither of these unilateral arrangements ever proves satisfactory or sustainable. Whether the "control arrow" is pointing toward the parent or toward the child, authoritarian and permissive problem-solving are both one-sided processes. Social problem-solving cannot take place within the context of relationships marked by power, fear, and resentment.

But there is a third—and better—way of raising children. *Authoritative parents* practice mutual respect. The relationship arrow between parent and child points in both directions. These parents take their child's perspective, but the child must take the parents' perspective too. With authoritative problem-solving, parents put their child's issues on the table, but they put their own issues on the table too. Everyone's view matters. When problems involve more than one child and one adult, there's plenty of room on the table for additional perspectives as well. The problem-solving is multilateral and collaborative. These families operate on one central principle: for any solution to be durable, it must be mutual. Parents put themselves in their child's shoes. But the child must look beyond their own selfish needs and consider the needs of others as well. In this kind of prosocial problem-solving, there is no room for unbridled egocentricity. Together, parents and children work through compromise and democracy rather than power and autocracy. If anyone's needs are not met, then the solution will not last.

Shuttle diplomacy: You need to make a judgment about whether your child is socially ready for face-to-face collaborative problem-solving. Especially with siblings, emotions can flare, and any chance at compromise flies quickly out the window. But just because siblings might have difficulty coming to the peace table does not mean that war is inevitable. Sometimes it is easier to consider other people's thoughts and feelings from a distance and with the help of a mediator. If necessary, parents can talk separately with conflicting parties. This way, each can be on the receiving end of an empathic response. In addition, each party can get help stating the problem from his or her perspective. Each can get some coaching on seeing the problem from the other's perspective. And each can state his or her ideas about possible solutions. Just like a secretary of state jetting between hostile countries, parents can go back and forth between brothers and sisters, presenting, negotiating, and working toward compromise. Diplomatic parents should try to bring warring siblings together for the entire process. But in the short term, if needed, a peace treaty signed separately is better than no peace process at all.

Truly collaborative problem-solving might come more slowly for some children (and adults) than others. But you should never underestimate your or anybody's ability to learn and grow. Neither should you underestimate your own ability to teach and model. Even if your child is not yet fully able to participate in his or her own problem-solving, he or she can begin to learn. With practice, your child can become more skillful and independent.

How to Problem-Solve

As mentioned, all cognitive-behavioral approaches have a common sequence of problem-solving STEPS. These simple STEPS can be applied to a broad range of issues. Children and parents can learn to use the STEPS to solve problems at home, school, work, or play. Remember, STEPS to problem-solving

1. ***S***ay what the problem is.
2. ***T***hink about all possible solutions.
3. ***E***xamine each possible solution.

4. ***P***ick the best solution.
5. ***S***ee how it works.

To learn these problem-solving STEPS, first choose a relatively simple problem. For example, you can use the STEPS to decide what's for dinner, what to do this weekend, or what move to make in a game of tic-tac-toe. Once you and your child have the STEPS down for simple problems, then you can tackle more complicated problems, including socially-emotionally loaded problems, such as what to do about sibling conflicts, academic difficulties, and lack of social success. Pretty much any problem can be plugged into this "stop and think" template. This problem-solving process can be very simple or—as you will see—very involved. Obviously, you won't have time to go through the STEPS for every problem that arises, but your investment of time and energy will be worth it for problems that are regular and persistent.

> *Moe is an eight-year-old boy. On his Gander, he has low motor activity level, short attention span, negative initial reaction, low adaptability, high intensity of reaction, sensory under-reactivity, below-average expressive and receptive language, and poor time awareness and organization skills. Given all that, of course, Moe had some difficulty with school. But he also had trouble with morning transitions. Just getting out of bed was a major source of tension between Moe and his schedule-driven mom.*
>
> *Every morning, Moe's mom went in to wake him. She turned on the light and opened the shades. As pleasantly as she could, she said, "Moe, time to get up." But every morning, he just groaned, turned over, and pulled the blanket over his head. She left him and checked on his brother, who, as usual, was already dressed and downstairs eating breakfast. She grabbed her coffee, took a deep breath, and went back upstairs. There was Moe, still dead asleep as she had left him.*

Mom: "*Come on, Moe. Don't make me do this again.*"
Moe: (No response.)
Mom: "*You're gonna miss the bus again!*"
Moe: (Nothing.)

Exasperated, Moe's mom ended up doing what she always did. She pulled off his pajamas.

Moe (still half-asleep but suddenly screaming): *Leave me alone! I'm up!*
Mom: "*You are not up. The second I walk out of this room, you'll be back in la-la land!*"

As usual, the yelling escalated. Somehow, she got him dressed. She didn't even try to get him to eat breakfast or brush his teeth. Moe's mom had given up on all that long ago. So she marched him down the stairs. She handed him his coat and backpack, then she led him out the door. Moe's mom reminded him about the extra snack in his lunch box. At least he might eat something on the bus. As Moe scuffled off, his mom thought, This can't keep on. When is he going to learn to take care of himself? Who's going to wake him up when he's twenty years old? *She'd tried everything. Maybe it was time for him to think about this problem at least half as much as she was. She decided that they had to just sit down and talk it out. She called a friend, who told her about the problem-solving STEPS.*

That night, after dinner, Moe's mom asked him if he'd like some ice cream. "Sure," he said. She made two bowls and they sat down together.

Mom: "*Ya know how you don't like me waking you up and nagging you every morning?*"
Moe: "*Yeah?*"

Mom: *"Well, I don't like it either. How about we come up with a plan so that I can stop nagging, and we can both have better mornings? Want some more ice cream?"*
Moe: *"OK."*
Mom: *"OK, no more Mom nagging, or OK more ice cream?"*
Moe (grinning): *"OK both."*

How to Do the STEPS:

1. ***Stop and Say*, "What's the problem?"**
   - *Avoid pessimistic generalizations:* When children are asked, "What's the problem?" they often answer as if the situation is hopeless. They might use words that make problems seem unsolvable, words such as "never," "forever," "always," "everywhere," "nowhere," "everybody," "nobody," "no way," "every way," "everything," and "nothing." Parents can be unnecessarily pessimistic too, maybe because of their own previous failures, exaggerated worries, unrealistic expectations, or simple lack of knowledge. A sense of helplessness can be paralyzing, self-perpetuating, and contagious. Parents and children can amplify one another's feelings of being stuck.
   - *Avoid irrational thinking:* A "can't do" attitude is often the product of exaggerated or distorted thinking. Children and parents can fall into a bad habit of overstating problems. They catastrophize. They make mountains out of molehills. They think everything is a big deal. Black or white. All or none. Perfection or disaster. Heaven or hell.
   - Define the problem situation in specific, solvable terms: Pessimistic generalizations are avoidable. Words like "*never*" should never be used in a problem description. Instead, parents and children should *do the five Ws:*

- What is the problem?
- Where does it happen?
- When does it happen?
- Who does it happen with?
- Why is it a problem for you? (Or, in other words, how does it make you feel?)

Parents and children should get in the habit of using the word "some." After all, most problems are about *some* specific situation, not all of life. Most problems happen in *some* specific places, not everywhere. Most problems happen at *some* specific times, not always. Most problems involve *some* specific people, not everybody. Framed this way, most problems are more solvable than people think. *Five Ws = specific and solvable.*

- *Think in shades of gray:* Irrational and distorted thinking *is* avoidable if parents and children stick to using vocabulary that describes the middle ground. For younger children: "big deal, little deal, medium deal," or "red light, green light, yellow light." Nonverbal children can point to a smiley face, neutral face (straight mouth), or frowning face. Or they can signal with thumbs-up, thumbs-down, or thumbs sideways. For older children, if zero is disaster, ten is perfection, and one to nine is everything in between, they can pick a number that more finely reflects the relative degree of difficulty. They can say the number, write it, or point to a number grid. (A tangential question: "Is the number for how this problem *makes* you feel different from the number for how you think it *should* make you feel?" If so, "Why?")

> Mom: *So I want to make sure I understand. Each morning, when it's time to get up, what's the biggest problem for you?*

Moe: *You're always telling me what to do about everything. It's like all the time!*
Mom: *Well, I guess I wouldn't like someone telling me what to do either. How big is this morning problem? Zero means no problem and ten means huge problem.*
Moe: *Ten!*
Mom: *Well, which is a bigger problem: me nagging you to wake up or me nagging you to do homework?*
Moe: *Homework is the worst.*
Mom: So I guess they can't both be a ten?
Moe: *Yeah. Homework is a ten and waking up is a nine.*
Mom: *How about me nagging you about video games?*
Moe: *Now that's a ten!*
Mom: *So…*
Moe: *Yeah, so video games is a ten, homework is a nine, and waking up is an eight.*
Mom: *So waking up is still a pretty big problem, but there are some other big problems too. Let's start with just fixing the morning, then we can fix the other stuff too. What's the worst thing about me waking you up?*
Moe: *I just want to sleep.*
Mom*: Because you don't want to go to school?*
Moe: *Yeah.*
Mom: *So I think I understand how you feel in the morning. If we're going to solve this problem together, I want you to understand how I feel too. I don't much like mornings either. I really don't like nagging. It makes me feel bad, and it's not the greatest way to start a day. If I knew that you would get up and get to school on time, I'd be really happy to just leave you alone, stay downstairs, and enjoy my coffee. So let's fix this. Then we can both be happy. OK?*
Moe: *I guess. But how?*

2. **Think about all possible solutions.**
   - *Developmental constraints:* Younger children and those with more significant developmental disabilities will need more help generating possible solutions. Some children might be relatively limited in their ability to consider a large number of complicated alternatives. If so, you might need to present just a few simple choices. In so doing, you still empower your child to problem-solve to the best of his or her current abilities. Even if your child is very dependent on adult scaffolding, you can still lay down a solid foundation for more independent problem-solving in the future.
   - *Brainstorm:* In a way that respects your child's current level of development, you and your child should make a list. Take turns offering possible solutions. Children and parents often make suggestions that neither would have been able to think of on their own. Take out a piece of paper and write down all the possible solutions. Be sure to give your child a chance to suggest his or her own ideas first. After your child runs out of suggestions, you can say, "Ya know, I think I might have a few ideas too. I'm not sure if they would work, but let's see how long we can make our list." To keep the brainstorming fun but also productive, feel free to balance your suggestions with some ideas that are ridiculously silly and others that are seriously workable.
   - *Teamwork:* If necessary, after you and your child run out of ideas, consider "getting a consult" or "phoning a friend"; that is, ask for input from another parent, sibling, teacher, or coach. This is especially important if it looks like you haven't been able to come up with enough good solutions or if other "players" are directly involved in the problem. It's not a bad idea to make "getting a consult" a standard part of this brainstorming step. This gets children into the healthy habit of seeking advice from others.

- *Anything goes:* In this brainstorming step, accept good ideas, bad ideas, silly ideas, serious ideas, simple ideas, complicated ideas, selfish ideas, and compromises. Give positive reinforcement for just participating in the brainstorming process. Keep your child invested and engaged.
- *No comments:* Up front, you and your child should agree not to endorse or criticize any solutions as they are being proposed. That would shut down or sidetrack the brainstorming process. Gently catch your child (and yourself) skipping ahead to examining possible solutions. This step is just about generating the list. Skipping a step is a problem-solving no-no! Solutions should be discussed and evaluated only *after* all possibilities have been listed.
- *Always consider the status quo:* It is usually a good idea to list "doing nothing" or "just keep things the way they are" as a possible solution. This is always an option, but probably one worth rejecting or at least critically reevaluating. After all, if the status quo was so great, you wouldn't be having the whole problem-solving discussion in the first place. This maneuver comes in handy when some children refuse to participate in the problem-solving exercise altogether. For example, your child might just shut down and say nothing, or scream, "I don't want to talk about it!" Without sarcasm, you can respond, "Well, that's one possible solution."

> Mom: *I bet we can come up with some ideas. I'm gonna get out some paper and a pen so that we write them all down. Good ideas, bad ideas. Let's think about anything that might work. There have to be one or two good solutions we can think of. Do you have any ideas?*
> Moe: *Nope. Nothing's gonna work. You just have to leave me alone.*

Mom (resisting the temptation to comment): *OK. I'm writing that down. Leave Moe alone. That's one possible solution. Any other ideas?*
Moe: *Nope. If you just left me alone, that would solve everything.*
Mom: *Well, maybe. But I think I might have some other ideas too. (Pause.)*
Moe: *Nothing else is going to work.*
Mom: *You might be right. Some of my ideas might be terrible. But maybe? Hmmm...*
Moe: *What?*
Mom: *You could drop out of school. (She writes this down.)*
Moe: *MO-om!*
Mom: *I could pay you one million dollars every morning that you got up and got to school on time. (She writes it down.)*
Moe (smiling): *Come on Mom. Cut it out!*
Mom: *But seriously, how about some other kind of reward?*
Moe (suddenly looking interested): *Like what?*

Back and forth they go, generating a list of possible rewards and other practical solutions. Mom suggests some. Moe suggests some. During the brainstorming step, they agree not to say whether the ideas are good or bad. That will come next. They fill up a whole page.

3. Examine each possible solution.

- *Predict outcomes:* After your list of possible solutions is complete, it's time to talk it through, one solution at a time. Children often need help considering future consequences: "Look into your crystal ball," or, "Climb into your time machine." For each of the possible solutions listed, "What would happen if you tried this? Then what would happen? Then what would happen? How would that make you feel? How would that make other people feel? So thinking ahead about all of that, how well do you think this solution will really work?"

- Rate each possible solution using an individualized system: As you did with rating the severity of the problem in STEP 1, individualize your approach to rating the effectiveness of each possible solution. Infants and toddlers—or others at a very early level of language development—can simply point to whatever object or picture they prefer. As discussed previously, young children who can understand simple symbols can point to a picture of a smiling face, neutral (flat mouth) face, or frowning face. Or they can use thumbs-up, thumbs sideways, or thumbs-down. Some children like using green light, yellow light, or red light. Older children, who are capable of more abstract thinking, can use a numerical rating system: 0 = stinks, 1 = bad, 2 = OK, 3 = good, 4 = very good, 5 = excellent. Musical children can use low notes, medium notes, and high notes or even minor chords, seventh chords, and major chords. Nature lovers can choose animals or weather to represent different degrees of favorability. Use whatever mode of self-expression is meaningful and practical for your child.
- *Be realistic:* Just like we need to avoid black-and-white thinking about problem statements, we also need to rate possible solutions in shades of gray. Parents and children should remember that most solutions are one through four, not just zero or five. They should not reject imperfect solutions. Say: "Just because it's not a five doesn't mean it has to be a zero." Sometimes a solution that is just OK is the best one possible: "What if two or three is the best we can do? That's still better than a zero." If your child is jumping to all-or-none

thinking, you can ask, "Are you just zero-and-fiving? Aren't there any solutions that get an in-between number?"

- *Accept different opinions:* You can respectfully ask your child to explain his or her ratings and make sure that consequences have been considered. However, don't challenge your child's choice. If the problem involves parents or siblings, each "player" should rate possible solutions from his or her perspective. Parents should rate possible solutions honestly. But parents and children should not debate, denigrate, or defend one another's ratings. Everyone should understand and respect one another's varying needs and opinions. Parents and children sometimes would have made wrong guesses about one another's ratings. This is a chance for everyone to speak for themselves and be heard. You're probably not going to change one another's minds. This exercise is all about acknowledging different perspectives, and then moving past all that to find some common ground.

Moe and Mom go down their list of possible solutions. At first, Moe's mom catches him giving just 0s and 5s. Otherwise, she respects his ratings, and he agrees to respect hers. They just give each possible solution a number—without any discussion at all. Moe's ratings gradually become more thoughtful and nuanced. Sometimes he wants to change a rating on a previous item. His mom reassures him, "That's fine."

Possible solution	Moe/Mom
Just leave Moe alone; if late, "So what?"	*5/1*
No electronics for twenty-four hours if late	*1/5*
Flashing lights, musical (super cool) alarm	*3/4*
Pull out clothes the night before	*2/5*
Go to bed earlier so less tired in morning	*1/5*
Keep fighting every morning	*0/0*

Rewards for being up and ready on time

• *One million dollars*	*5/0*
• *Twenty-five cents*	*0/3*
• *One dollar*	*0/2*
• *Two dollars*	*3/1*
• *Five dollars*	*4/0*
• *Video game (when ready) until it's time to go*	*4/3*
• *Friday night movie/popcorn if five good mornings*	*5/5*
• *Pancakes for breakfast*	*3/3*

4. *Pick the best solution.*

- *Encourage self-determination and self-education:* Some problems don't require family consensus, for example, what to eat for breakfast, how to win a game, or how to approach a problem at school. If it's your child's problem, it should be your child's solution. The best fix will be the one(s) that your child rates highest. Using a word processor or old-fashioned markers, highlight in green those solutions rated 3, 4, or 5 (good, very good, or excellent); highlight in red those solutions rated 0 or 1 (stinks or bad); and highlight in yellow solutions rated 2 (OK). Children should accept that there may not be a 5, but there's still some solution better than the status quo. Parents should accept their child's choice; even if—especially if—you would have given a different rating. This way, your child will have a chance to learn for him- or herself.
- *Seek consensus and compromise:* If the problem involves more than one person—such as, siblings and parents—then the solution must be satisfactory to all. If not, the fix won't last. The best solution should not receive a very bad rating from any one person. Look down the list of possible solutions with everyone's ratings written next to each one.

- 0–1, not worth trying: Highlight in red any solution rated 0 or 1 by any person. Even if others rated it well, somebody's going to be unhappy.
- 3–5, worth trying: Find possible solutions rated 3 or better by everyone. Highlight those in green.
- 2, maybe. If the lowest of the ratings is a 2, highlight it in yellow.

If your child sabotages the whole process by rating everything 0 (including the status quo), then it's back to the drawing board for more possible solutions. Be gentle but relentless in your pursuit of common ground. Using this collaborative and mutually respectful approach, every interpersonal problem is an opportunity to teach the art of consensus and compromise.

> *Moe and his mom looked down their list of ratings. Even if one of them put a 4 or five, they crossed out any solution with a 0 or a 1. They needed to find something that would work for both of them. If they didn't find anything better, they'd have to consider some 2s. But fortunately, they both gave 3 or higher to several possible solutions and decided to try them all:*
>
> - *If* all *ready, then video game until it's time to go*
> - *Friday night movie/popcorn if five good mornings*
> - *If on time, pancakes for breakfast*
> - *Flashing lights, musical (supercool) alarm*

5. ***See how it works.***
   - *Anticipation:* After choosing the best solution, you and your child should preview any potential problems. Ask and consider: "Exactly how are we going to pull this off? What could go wrong with this plan? Do we need to talk with anyone

about the plan or put anything in place before starting? Is there any extra problem-solving to do? Do we have to talk about any what-ifs?

- *Experimentation:* Parents and children should remember that plans are always put into action on a trial basis. Before implementing, give a little lesson on scientific method: "Sometimes plans work great. Other times plans don't work at all. In most cases, best solutions never work quite as expected, and that's OK. Let's see how this works. You never really know until you try. Doing an experiment is the best way to see what really works." Teach your child that there's no such thing as a bad experiment, just poor attention to results. In this way, you can normalize and model learning by trial and error.
- *Evaluation, modification, and reevaluation:* After a reasonable and predetermined period, you and your child can sit down to discuss the results of your experiment. If siblings are involved, schedule a family meeting. Ask: "So what was our original problem? How well did our plan really work? How would (each of) you rate our solution now that we put it into action? Is that the same number you gave before; better or worse? If things did not go as expected, why did that happen? What went wrong?" Breakdown points may only become apparent during the trial. Sometimes plans should be continued or repaired. Other times you might have to go back to the drawing board and consider possible solutions all over again. Even when things work well, it's important to schedule periodic reviews. Things change over time. What once worked might need a tune-up. But no matter what happens, this trial-and-error process should be embraced.

Before putting their plan into action, Moe and his mom talked through a few "what-if" *pitfalls. Together, they came up with some more solutions:*

- What if *Moe did not stop the video when it was time to go to school?* Solution: *Moe's mom got an app that just turned it off automatically.*
- What if *Moe demanded pancakes even when he was late?* Solution: *He would lose the chance to have pancakes the next morning.*
- What if *Moe didn't wake up with the loud and fancy new alarm? Or what if he woke up but did not come downstairs?* Solution: *Moe agreed that Mom could try to wake him* once *and remind him to get downstairs* once*—but no nagging after that. If this didn't work, they would have to go back to the drawing board.*

So Moe and Mom launched their plan. They hoped it would work, but they understood that it might not. They agreed to meet again in one week to evaluate results and consider a possible tune-up. The first morning, much to his Mom's amazement, Moe woke to the alarm, jumped out of bed, got dressed, and ran downstairs. He was eager for pancakes and morning video time. His Mom had the batter ready and the frying pan hot. Moe dowsed his pancakes with maple syrup and gobbled them down. He still had twenty minutes to play the video game. Incredible! The video game was set to turn off automatically. When the screen went dark, Moe scowled. He wanted to play more. Anticipating Moe's disappointment, his mom stayed calm and cool. She said, "That's one good morning toward your movie and popcorn. Way to go." Moe shrugged and went to school. Miracle.

The next morning, much to his Mom's disappointment, Moe slept through his alarm. She woke him up by mentioning the pancakes and the video game, but he got distracted and was late for breakfast. No pancakes. No time for the video game. Angrily, Moe stomped out of the house.

Moe and his mom both had the day to think about what happened. Moe's mom called the school counselor. They decided to have a school team meeting. After school, Moe's mom asked him how he felt about the morning. He was mad about not getting his pancakes and his video game. She empathized. They agreed to redo their problem-solving after dinner. In this way, working together, compromising, and learning by trial and error, they modified successive plans until they came up with one that worked. The solution wasn't perfect, but mornings were generally much better than before. As Moe said, "Well, I guess it beats screaming at each other." Meanwhile, Moe's mother and teacher did some serious problem-solving about his academic difficulties. They came up with an individualized education care plan. Gradually, Moe seemed less negative about going to school.

How to Help Your Child Solve Problems with Anxiety

Cognitive-behavioral approaches work especially well for solving problems related to anxiety (Rapee, Wignall, Spence, Cobham, & Lyneham, 2008; Zucker, 2017). If your child is fearful or worried, it's natural to try reassuring or instructing. Any loving parent will want to protect his or child by keeping the child away from the source of fear. But denial or avoidance maneuvers are often the product of a parent's own anxiety. Franklin D. Roosevelt understood that people need to face their fears; famously saying, "The only thing we have to fear is fear itself." Usually, the more you try to protect your anxious child, the more anxious your child becomes. Your child needs to learn how to deal with his or her own worries. Not every stress is avoidable, and you won't always be around to provide emotional shelter.

As with all problem-solving, proactive management of anxiety is better than reactive management. "Worry busting" works best when everyone is calm and not right in the middle of an anxious episode. Using a variation on the problem-solving STEPS, you can teach your child how to "STOP" and face his or her fears (Kendall & Hedtke, 2006).

STOP and face your fears:

1. ***S***cared?
2. ***T***hinking about what?
3. ***O***ther things I can do or think to help myself relax.
4. ***P***at myself on the back for facing my fears.

How to STOP and Face Your Fears

1. **Scared?** Before children can solve their problems with anxiety, they must learn to recognize when they are feeling anxious. Each child can be taught to notice his or her own telltale signs, such as muscle tension, fast breathing, fast heart rate, abdominal discomfort, headache, nervous habits, shaky feelings, tearfulness, irritability, anticipatory dread, avoidance behaviors, obsessions, compulsions, and so on. On a deeper level, your child can also learn to recognize his or her own avoidance behaviors as symptoms of anxiety; for example, when school phobia is really about avoiding separation anxiety, when staying indoors is really about avoiding bees, and when perfectionism is really about fear of failure. The earlier your child recognizes these red flags, the easier it will be for him or her to use effective self-help strategies.

Your child should learn to say, "I can tell that I'm beginning to feel scared. I need to *STOP*."

2. **Thinking about what?** After recognizing their anxious feelings, children need to identify the source of their anxiety and then put their anxious thoughts into words. For example, your child might say, "I'm afraid that robbers will come while I'm asleep," or "I'm feeling nervous about flunking my exam," or "I'm worried that something might happen to my parents." It's best to just put these fears right out there. Otherwise, anxiety controls your child instead of your child controlling his or her anxiety. Children need to be aware of their irrational or distorted thoughts. It's normal to have anxiety. Sometimes it's even helpful. But it's not at all helpful to become paralyzed by anxiety that's way out of proportion to the threat at hand. Children can learn to control their anxiety if they frame it in specific and solvable terms; that is, not make a mountain out of a molehill.
3. **Other things I can do or think to help myself relax.** Children can face their fears with confidence if they think ahead about possible solutions, pick the best one, and practice. Initially, most children need parents (and/or professionals) to help them brainstorm "other things to think or do." Such "worry busters" may include positive self-talk, muscle relaxation, breathing awareness, meditation, yoga, physical exercise, positive imagery, self-hypnosis, talking with friends or family, playing favorite games, spending time with pets, music, reading, drawing—any relaxing or distracting activities. After considering all possible solutions, your child should choose the best one(s). Then he or she can look for opportunities to see how it works. By deliberately and gradually increasing exposure to the source of anxiety, you can give your child opportunities to practice using "worry buster" strategies. Then your child can experience a greater degree of control over his or her anxiety. At the same time, you also give yourself

important practice giving up control and letting your child face his or her own fears.

4. ***P*at myself on the back for facing my fears**. Initially, parents and professionals will need to do some coaching and encouraging. They may even need to provide some positive incentives. But eventually, your child should learn to choose and carry out his or her own plan. This way, he or she not only lessens distress and impairment, but gains the confidence needed to conquer future challenges. After effectively overcoming some fears, your child should feel empowered: "If I just STOP and think, I guess I can face just about anything!"

Homework for the Seventh Mile

1. Try using STEPS (or STOP) on a problem of your own.
2. Consider your child's level of readiness for problem-solving. How much can he or she be coached to do his or her own problem-solving? How much complexity can he or she handle? Considering your child's Gander, how should you individualize your approach?
3. Whatever your child's level of readiness, start with a relatively simple problem. Coach your child through the STEPS. You might want to begin with something like, "What should we have for dinner?" Or maybe, "What should we do this weekend?" Once you've both got your STEPS down, you can move on and apply this problem-solving process to more complicated social and emotional challenges. Take it slow.
4. Remember: some solutions don't work as well as expected. At first, the problem-solving process may not work as well as hoped. Try to view setbacks as necessary trials and important learning opportunities; not hopeless situations or incompetence. "Errorless learning" is never as effective as learning from mistakes.

Eighth Mile: Ignoring and Time-out (*Logs and Lightning)*

• • •

You gotta know when to hold 'em
Know when to fold 'em
Know when to walk away
Know when to run.

—Kenny Rogers, "The Gambler" (1978)

Hawk had never been a navigator, but the more they traveled, the better he became. If there were logs, they could just cruise the boat right over the tops of them.

If there was lightning, Hawk carried Raph off the river and onto a safe island.

• • •

Turning to Reactive Strategies

Over the first seven miles, we focused on proactive strategies. You have collected a set of customized tools. You have practiced a variety of tactics for helping your child—and you—experience success. By individualizing, layering, and integrating these techniques, you and your child should have begun to feel a greater sense of control and peace.

Up to this point, we have deliberately postponed discussion of reactive strategies. Why talk about things going wrong before trying to make things go right? I hope that you are now encountering fewer problem behaviors and don't need reactive strategies quite so much as before. However, behavioral strategies never work perfectly. You and your child are going to have good days and bad days. And some children need more than just good behavior management. So in addition to your proactive strategies, you will also need good reactive strategies. What should you do when problems happen despite your best efforts to head them off? How should you handle things when your child doesn't do what he or she is supposed to do? How can you effectively react to noncompliant behavior and unmet expectations?

Way back in the First Mile, we considered the importance of avoiding power struggles. If your child does not comply or perform and you just repeat your commands, he or she is unlikely to become less resistant. All too often the intensity just ratchets up. You end up overpowering or giving up. Either way is no good. Instead of power struggles, I recommend an approach similar to the one first outlined by Greene (2014a), but with some important embellishments and variations.

When your child becomes frustrated or loses control, you might also feel frustrated and out of control. Your child shuts down, rumbles, or rages. Your emotions rise in parallel. Parents do not mean to lose control. It's just hard to stay calm when you're not 100 percent sure what to do or how to do it.

How should you react? Should you be soft or tough? Let it go or take a firm stand? Talk it through or bite your tongue? It doesn't take more than a moment of uncertainty before you and your child are either locking horns or turning tail. You struggle to think, but your emotions race ahead. The irrational brain fires and floods faster than the rational brain can stop and consider. Primitive "fight, flight, or freeze" reflexes kick in before you have time to logically weigh options, come up with a coherent plan, and practice its implementation. You lose control. Anger, anxiety, or frustration quickly fill the void of uncertainty. And even if you knew what to do and how to do it, what if your technique is underdeveloped or rusty? The key to helping your rational brain stay ahead of your emotional brain is to give your rational brain a "head start." This means planning and practicing ahead.

If you take the time to develop a plan, then you don't have to figure out what to do in the moment. Let's get real. When you're busy or stressed or tired or emotional, it's hard to think. You just have to be ready to do. Winging it never works as well as following a carefully developed strategy. After all, how successful is the actor without a script? The builder without a floor plan? The traveler without a map? The coach without a game plan?

In this Eighth Mile, you will review your list of problem behaviors and assign each one to a different category. You will decide whether each problem behavior is a "log" to be ignored; "lightning," which needs a time-out; or a "rock," which requires a pause. You will practice quickly recognizing "logs," "lightning," and "rocks" and then clicking right into your predetermined plan. I will not tell you which behavior goes in which category or which reactive strategy to use. However, I do strongly recommend that you decide what to do and then do it well. First we'll cover some general principles, then we'll get to some specific techniques.

The Importance of Technique and Practice

Whether you choose to ignore, time-out, or pause, technique matters. So often parents report, "I tried that, but it didn't work." This is sometimes because they were using the right strategy but the wrong technique. Ineffective technique may be due to lack of understanding or lack of practice. You may read this book, take a parent training course, talk about these strategies with friends, and feel like you've got it all down. But you never really know how things are going to go until you put your plan into action. You might stumble and have to make adjustments. You hone your approach only through experience. Just like shooting baskets or solving math problems, the more you practice, the more effective and automatic you get. Remember the first time you changed your firstborn's diaper? You probably felt uncertain, clumsy, and inefficient. But the more diapers you changed, the smoother you got. Quite literally, you learned to change diapers in your sleep. The goal with these reactive strategies is to become that natural and skillful. Whether ignoring, using time-out, or pausing, practice is the key. Through repetition and experimentation, you will become more effective and consistent. If a strategy doesn't work right away, it could be the wrong one. But maybe you just need a little more practice.

Log (Ignore), Lightning (Time-out), or Rock (Pause)?

Ignoring or time-out should be used for behaviors that cause physical injury, emotional harm, property damage, or social disruption. You should ignore if your child's behavior is relatively insignificant or inconsequential; that is, "a log" that you can float right over. Use time-out if the behavior is significant, serious, and unignorable "lightning" that requires action to avoid serious harm. Pausing should be used for everything else: "rocks" that you can't float over but you can easily avoid if you just stop and let the current adjust your path.

Why Use Ignoring or Time-out?

Although time-out and ignoring are used for different behaviors, oddly enough, these reactive strategies are used for the same reasons. Time-out is really just a technique for converting the unignorable into the ignorable. Here's what I mean:

1. ***Create physical and emotional distance:*** Both time-out and ignoring *create physical and emotional distance* when there would otherwise be physical or emotional intensity. Parents and children often get "sucked into" increasingly intense and prolonged interactions. Intensity quickly begets counterintensity, and parent-child interactions "turn ugly." Physically, emotionally, or verbally, you may be able to overpower your child. However, the ability to impose your will in the moment is not worth the cost over the long run. Overpowered children learn resentment, anger, and fear. Overpowering parents experience frustration, sadness, and poor self-image. The parent-child relationship suffers. Time-out and ignoring help parents and children immediately defuse explosive situations and avoid harmful power struggles. Time-out and ignoring may cause a minor degree of distress for child and parent, but that's nothing compared to the emotional harm and relationship destruction caused by prolonged battles.
2. ***Avoid unintentionally reinforcing negative or undesirable behavior:*** Both time-out and ignoring allow parents to avoid unintentionally reinforcing negative or undesirable behaviors. Instead of repeating, arguing, yelling, or spanking, parents can use ignoring or time-out to turn their attention away from

behaviors they want to extinguish. When children misbehave, sometimes it doesn't matter what parents say or do: positive or negative, soft or tough. The more words said and the more attention given, the more likely your child is to continue or repeat the misbehavior. A "golden rule" of behavior management: Attend to behaviors you want to see more. Turn attention away from behaviors you want to see less. Controversially, Skinner (2005) taught that thoughts and feelings are behaviors to be modified. You may choose to target some of your child's verbal and emotional behavior with either ignoring or time-out. However, in my view, it's better to respond to your child's negative thoughts and feelings by pausing to reflect, responding empathically, and problem-solving. (See miles seven and nine.)

3. ***Protect persons and property:*** Time-out (for sure) and ignoring (sometimes) can be used to immediately stop dangerous behaviors. Whether the harm is to person, property, or normal family functioning, time-out and ignoring can ensure safety and minimize damage.
4. ***Get off the negative:*** The more time and attention you spend interacting with a misbehaving child, the less positive time and attention you have for that child, his or her siblings, and yourself! Sometimes the squeaky wheel gets too much grease. Who could blame the misbehaving child and well-behaving siblings for wondering if positive behavior gets less parent attention than negative behavior? Who could blame these siblings for resenting unequal distribution of parent resources? Who could blame you for feeling that your relationship with your child, your own self-image, and a disproportionate share of your life are all being defined by these negative behaviors? Don't let your family relations and personal happiness be dominated and usurped. Time-out and ignoring minimize the time you spend on trouble and conserve your family's most valuable resource—you!

Whenever possible, use ignoring instead of time-out. It's easier, and you don't always have to intervene. Many parents feel that ignoring is "doing nothing." They wonder if ignoring leads children to believe that "they are getting away with it." They want to step up as good parents and not miss opportunities to discipline and teach. These are all understandable concerns. However, ignoring is most definitely "doing something." Ignoring sends a strong and clear message—perhaps the most powerful message a parent can send—without saying a word. When you ignore properly, you communicate clearly: "What you did is so unacceptable that I am going to turn away and withdraw the most important thing I have to give—my attention." Ignoring is a far cry from doing nothing. It's just that some behaviors can't be ignored. So when ignoring would have regrettable consequences, you need to do something else. That's when time-out is required to render unignorable behaviors ignorable. In this way, time-out is a *sometimes* necessary step on the way to ignoring, but ignoring is preferred. To overstate the point: you should use ignoring much more than time-out.

Now for some controversial suggestions. In my view, ignoring and time-out should *not* be used to:

1. ***Punish.*** Used effectively, ignoring and time-out *may* cause a child to feel remorse or decrease their problem behavior—*but maybe not.* These strategies are primarily used *instead* of (what most parents consider to be) punishments. For example, spanking can increase animosity and tension. In contrast, with proper technique, ignoring and time-out work better to keep parents from "fueling the fire." Some parents ask, "What if my child does *not* feel remorseful about being ignored or put in time-out? I want them to feel bad and know that they are being punished." Other parents ask, "What if my child feels too bad about being ignored or put in time-out? I don't want them to suffer or

feel like they are being punished." With the modest version of ignoring and time-out advocated here, it doesn't matter whether the ignored or timed-out child feels bad or immediately begins to play happily. The child may suffer or not. Toys need not be removed or provided. All that does matter is creating physical and emotional distance where there would otherwise be intensive conflict. The goal here is simply avoiding reinforcement of negative behaviors and preserving some semblance of sanity at home.

2. ***Make a child feel remorse or say, "I'm sorry."*** It is very important for children to understand how their behavior effects other people. But ignoring and time-out are not designed to instill compassion. You might insist on an apology. But this would represent coercion, not genuine repentance. Or your child might suddenly "see the light" and plead forgiveness. This is often a transparent ploy to regain engagement or win early release. Don't be manipulated. Follow through with ignoring or time-out based on your child's behavior, not his or her miraculous discovery of religion or ethical humanism.
3. ***Teach.*** As a consequence of being ignored or put in time-out, children may learn that harmful behaviors will not be tolerated or dignified. Ignoring and time-out can give some children the time and space they need to think things over. However, your child's failure to learn does not necessarily mean that ignoring or time-out didn't work. In fact, ignoring and time-out are most appropriate and effective precisely during those emotionally charged moments when children are least available to learn and parents are least competent to teach. Children still need to be taught right from wrong—just not as they are whining for cookies or punching their siblings in the nose. At these times, their rationality switch is usually off. If your child learns something as a result of being ignored or put in time-out, that's fine. But

that should not be the goal. Ignoring and time-out are designed: to shorten the power struggle and allow everyone to get their rationality switches back on sooner. Your child will be a better learner—and you will be a better teacher—later.

Logs

When to Ignore

Some undesirable behaviors do not require a time-out or any response at all. In fact, parent attention could result in a power struggle or make these behaviors even worse. You should consider ignoring behaviors that are:

1. Relatively *harmless* and of no significant consequence.
2. Easily *convertible* from unignorable to ignorable without requiring a time-out. (See "converting lightning to logs.")
3. *Self-limiting* and not likely to become repetitive. If you did react and give attention, these behaviors would be more likely to continue or recur.
4. Potentially *maturational;* that is, relatively appropriate for your child's developmental age and no big deal. Sometimes kids just need time to grow up.

"Ignorable logs" include:

1. *Minor injury* to any person, such as nonrepetitive bumping, swiping, or pushing.
2. *Minor damage* to property, such as breaking a cheap toy or crayon or making an age-appropriate mess.
3. *Unkind talk*, such as verbal jabbing, whining, complaining, or demanding.

4. *Minor disruption* to normal family or social functioning, such as interrupting, inappropriate comments or gestures, cheating, or arriving late or leaving early from the dinner table.

Note: Many sibling or peer spats fall into this "ignorable log" category.

How to Ignore

When ignoring (or using time-out), be careful to use excellent technique. This simply means be *immediate, nonverbal, and nonemotional.*

- *Immediate:* Without a moment's delay, slowly turn or walk away. Do not hesitate. But do not rush. Just quietly disregard and retreat. Occupy yourself with something else. Read the paper. Do the dishes. Sometimes it's enough just to rotate your body. Ignoring is all about immediate withdrawal of attention. Simple as that.
- *No words:* Effective ignoring immediately puts a lid on all verbal interaction. Don't say a word. Zero. No commenting on the misbehavior. No sarcastic, "You've got to be kidding." No self-contradictory, "I'm ignoring you now." Just go 100 percent mute.
- *No nonverbal communication:* Parents should stifle any disapproving facial expressions. Your body language should be neutral, not transparent. No exasperated scowls. No eye-rolling. No weary sighs. No angry posturing. No stomping off. No "acting as if you don't care," like whistling or singing. These and other nonverbal messages do not constitute true ignoring. Your nonverbal language should only convey, "Whatever. It just doesn't matter to me. What you just did is of no consequence. Like a soft wind in the trees. Not even worth noticing."
- *No emotion:* The key to staying cool is having confidence in your plan. You have already decided what to ignore. You know how. Your technique is simple and effective. You are clear and

confident. All you have to do is do it. You say to yourself: "My child may be out of control, but I am in control. All I need to do is follow the script. It isn't so complicated. I've got this."

- *Be ready for the extinction burst:* To stay cool, calm, and on-course, you should anticipate the possibility of a so-called extinction burst; that is, a burst of misbehavior before the strategy works to render it extinct. Like the last few flares of embers in a dying fire. Extinction bursts happen with time-out too. Whenever you take control and set limits, expect an even bigger spike of misbehavior. Your child might not quite believe what is happening. When you withdraw your attention, your child might not quite understand what just happened; especially if he or she is used to getting a reaction. He or she might do just about anything to regain your attention. He or she might just turn up the volume or intensity of the behavior you're ignoring or try something new and more extreme to break through the wall you've erected. If you are ready for the burst and stay true to good ignoring technique, your child will not get reinforcement. If you hang in there and keep ignoring, there's a good chance that the behavior will be extinguished. You just have to be ready and stick with the plan.
- *When logs become lightning:* Some behaviors that start out as "insignificant and ignorable" logs might become "serious and unignorable." Minor behaviors might become major if they escalate or continue.
    - Escalation: Despite excellent ignoring technique and extinction burst preparation, your child might escalate beyond safe or reasonable limits. Ignoring does not mean allowing yourself or other family members to become physical or emotional punching bags. Ignoring does not mean allowing significant property damage. If your child escalates beyond ignorable, you say to yourself, "Hmmm. That's not a log any more. It shape-shifted into lightning." Quickly use time-out

instead of ignoring. It just happens sometimes. If "lighting strikes a log," you will be ready.

- Continuation: Despite excellent ignoring technique, your child might just continue to misbehave. Not that the behavior got worse, it just didn't stop. Your child's behavior might have been ignorable for a short time, but it has become unignorable via repetition. Some behaviors just can't be ignored forever. Ignoring should not mean allowing prolonged disruption of normal family or social functioning. Children need limits. If it was a log, it would have floated by. Parents should not ignore low-intensity but persistent misbehavior ("little but long-lasting lightning storms").

- *Converting lightning to logs:* Whenever possible, parents should seize the opportunity to convert potentially unignorable behaviors into ignorable ones. Who wouldn't prefer logs to lightning? For all these minimizing maneuvers, make sure to use good technique. Be *immediate, nonemotional, and nonverbal.*
  - Removal: For inappropriate use of toys, food, utensils—or baby siblings!—simply remove the "object(s)" from your child's reach.
  - Distraction or redirection: For the relatively minor behavior problems of younger children, it may be especially appropriate to just distract or redirect. Matter-of-fact. No big deal. Keep it calm. With this technique, you are not truly ignoring your child, but you are ignoring your child's misbehavior.
  - De-escalation: If your child inflicts *minor* injury on you, just walk away. For minor injury to siblings or playmates, quickly get your body between the two children. Then distract or redirect. If one child is being aggressive toward another, you can deliberately turn your back on the perpetrator and attend to the victim.
  - Retreat: If ignoring is difficult because your child is *very* persistent, try calmly relocating yourself to another

room. If there is a sibling involved, bring him or her along too. If necessary, you can retreat behind a locked bedroom door. This represents a slightly different spin on the "reverse time-out" described later. Whatever you call it, the bottom line is rendering the unignorable ignorable. Of course, this is not an option if leaving the misbehaving child unattended in the rest of the house raises safety issues.

Lightning

When to Use Time-out?

Time-out should be used for behaviors that are *serious, very harmful*, and *unignorable*. This includes behaviors that cause:

1. *Severe injury* to any person, such as, hitting, biting, kicking, or throwing dangerous objects.
2. *Serious damage* to valuable property, such as, destructive acts that would require expensive repair or replacement.
3. *Lasting emotional harm*, such as, verbal assaults. These behaviors should not be tolerated in homes any more than they would be tolerated in schools. This includes persistent, recurrent, and relentless bullying or teasing of siblings. Parents should not allow themselves to be abused by their own children.
4. *Significant disruption* to normal family or social functioning, such as might occur at the dinner table or in the classroom.

How to Do Time-out

If you've learned about time-out elsewhere, you might notice some differences in the technique described here.

- *Immediate, nonemotional, nonverbal:* When putting a child in time-out, just like ignoring, a parent's mantra should be: *immediate, nonemotional, and nonverbal.* When time-out fails, it is often due to poor technique; that is, delay, loss of self-control, or too much talking. If your child's behavior justifies a time-out, then don't give extra warnings or second chances. Be stern and serious, but cool and matter-of-fact. The message should be: "You, my child, are out of control, but I, your parent, am not." If the behavior warrants a time-out, there should be no explanation, discussion, or back and forth. It is too late for apologies or negotiations. Talking or admonishing just prolongs the interaction. If parents delay implementation, talk too much, or get emotional, then the vicious cycle of intensity and counterintensity is perpetuated. *Remember: immediate, nonverbal, and nonemotional.*
- *Counting out for gathering storms:* Some behaviors are hard to ignore, but they might fall short of needing an immediate time-out. "Tweener" stuff. Not just a log but not quite lightning. This includes socially disruptive or inappropriate behaviors, for example, unkind talk, annoying mealtime behaviors, potentially unsafe activities, or persistent whining. Phelan's (2010) *1-2-3 Magic* is a popular approach. I recommend it specifically for this kind of refractory noncompliance, as a kind of warning shot. With this technique, parents are instructed to firmly issue a short series of numerical warnings: "That's one!" (Pause.) "That's two!" (Pause.) If the child still does not stop, "That's three—you're in time-out." I do not recommend this kind of counting out as a global behavior management strategy. It should not be used when an immediate time-out is necessary and certainly not to the exclusion of other proactive and reactive strategies described throughout this Journey. However, counting out can be useful in these borderline situations. For behaviors that lie somewhere between ignoring and immediate time-out, this relatively immediate, nonverbal, and nonemotional script can function as an effective stopgap.

- *Safety first:* If other young children are present, first see to their safety. Get physically in between perpetrators and victims. Control any objects that could inflict further harm. Attend to any serious injuries. A baby can be moved to the floor. Triage and *then* time-out should take place so quickly that you can return attention to other children without compromising their safety.

GETTING YOUR CHILD INTO TIME-OUT

In advance, think about the quickest, most efficient, and most reliable way to get your child into time-out. Whatever is necessary—no more, no less. Your child's room is usually the best place. (More on that in a bit.)

- *Point or tell:* Parents can just point to the time-out room or say, "Time-out." Nothing more. A minority of children will turn contrite and immediately put themselves in time-out. (But usually not children of parents who would read this book!)
- *March*: Some parents need to escort their child to time-out. Immediately get behind your child, put a firm hand on each shoulder, and march.
- *Carry*: Size, strength, and age-permitting. If your child is going to resist, immediately get behind and bend at the knees. Circle one arm firmly around his or her waist and your other arm around the chest. Keep your back straight. Use your knees and lift. Through the lift and carry, no words and no emotions. Ignore screams and protests. Just secure and go. Deposit your child in the time-out room. The goal is simply to get your child in time-out as quickly and efficiently as possible. Then you will have successfully converted the unignorable into the ignorable.
    - About arms, legs, and head: Your child's back and head should be tight against your chest. Prevent reverse head-butting by

leaning forward slightly to flex your child's neck. Just focus on controlling the head and trunk. Don't try to restrain arms or legs. Kicking and flailing into the air can be ignored.

- Be ready for Spiderman: At doorways, some children "go wide" with arms and legs to prevent passage. If you see this coming, just do a quick 180-degree spin, clear the door by taking a few steps through while facing backward, and then spin another 180 degrees to proceed forward again.

- *Deposit:* After marching or carrying your child into time-out, just turn, walk out, and shut the door immediately, nonemotionally, and nonverbally.

DURING TIME-OUT

Remember that the purpose of time-out is to convert unignorable behaviors into ignorable ones. When your child is in time-out, there should be no interaction at all. Do not linger outside the door. Your child can sense whether you're there or not. And besides, why torture yourself?

- *Prevent escape:* If you know your child might leave the time-out room, secure the door. Do not invite secondary battles with a defiant escapee. That would defeat the whole purpose. "Emotional trauma" and "psychological scars" are much more likely caused by out-of-control parents and prolonged power struggles than inanimate doors. Holding the door from the outside avoids direct contact, but this does not create enough emotional and physical distance. Instead, lock the door from the outside by reversing the doorknob or installing a heavy sliding bolt. (For safety in the very rare event of a fire, never keep a child's door locked if you might fall asleep.)
- *Anticipate an extinction burst:* Just like ignoring, time-out may trigger an "extinction burst." Not quite sure what's happening, your child may test the system. He or she might increase the

intensity or outlandishness of their behavior. Some children don't just turn up the volume of their screams, they trash their rooms or try anything to get you to react. Be ready. Stick with the plan. Don't cave. Your child will give up this type of behavior once he or she learns what time-out really means.

Ending Time-out

- *How long?* Depending on the severity of the behavior and your child's average recovery time, time-out should last about one to two minutes per year of age. Decide on the time in advance. As soon as you close the door, look at your watch, use an alarm, or set a timer.
- *Prolonged lightning storms:* What if it is time to end time-out, but your child is still screaming and carrying on? Through the door and one time only, you could say: "You can come out of time-out when you are calm and ready." You may want to listen at the door for the moment your child quiets. Then, right away, open the door and end the time-out to reinforce this "glimmer of sun showing through the clouds." However, if it's still not quiet in there, and immediate relapse is likely, do not release your child! You would just have to put him or her right back in anyhow. This is not to say that a good mood is required. To end time-out, do not insist on a smile or expressions of contrition. You just don't want your child to come out swinging, cursing, or repeating the same behavior that landed him or her there in the first place.
- *Clean slate:* When time-out is over, simply open the door. At most, say, "You may come out now." Proceed with your day as if nothing happened. In my view, there should be no discussion about the incident or requests of apology. Not right away anyhow. He or she has done the time. It is now time for everybody to hit the emotional reset button. Let the embers

die all the way down. Don't kick the fire one last time. If appropriate, there will be plenty of time *later* for postmortem analysis, teaching, and relationship repair. If you would like to talk about the incident, wait awhile—even the next day—until everyone is calm. Then you can go back to the Seventh Mile and do some problem-solving.

Where to Do Time-out

The child's bedroom: Safe and away, the child's bedroom is usually the best place for time-out. The bedroom is out of the mainstream of traffic. The door is effective and secure as a visual, auditory, and physical barrier. Parents can easily control this small environment and head off any safety issues. Some windows may need to be secured. (If you're not sure, consult your fire department on how to do this safely.) Property damage is usually less of a concern in a child's room than elsewhere. Although "bursting" children may turn destructive, any dangerous or valuable items can be removed in advance. Allowing a very volatile child to trash his or her own room beats the alternatives. It's all his or her "stuff" anyway. By preparing the room, parents can eliminate the need to check on the child, render even extreme behaviors ignorable, and avoid undermining the time-out altogether. Some parents are concerned that using the child's bedroom for time-out will create unpleasant associations, pollute the child's emotional "safe harbor," or cause nightmares. I have not seen this happen.

Your child's bedroom may *not* be usable if it is:

1. *Unavailable:* If the bedroom is shared, time-out might require suddenly relocating and disrupting a sibling. Also, time-out in a shared room might cause unfair damage or displacement of the sibling's possessions.

2. *Inaccessible:* Sometimes the child's size and strength plus the parent's own physical limitations create an unfavorable balance of power. In these cases, getting a child into the bedroom might prove unsafe, inefficient, or impossible.

Alternative time-out places and techniques: Although the child's bedroom is the most commonly used place for time-out, there are other options. Given your physical limitations, choose a place that works best for you and your child.

1. *Other rooms or places:* Some parents use bathrooms or other closer or more accessible rooms. A chair or bottom step might suffice; that is, if it's out of the mainstream of traffic and your child will actually stay put. Just be sure to anticipate and prevent any potential problems with insufficient isolation, lack of ignorability, safety, property damage, or escape.
2. *The "roomless" time-out:* If your child has a knack for suddenly going limp and transforming into immovable dead weight, or if you have your own physical limitations, it sometimes works to just point and declare: "You are in time-out!" The spot the child is on magically becomes the time-out place. Of course, this will only work with a child whose temperament is such that he or she is unlikely to leave time-out. Unfortunately, most children who need to be put in time-out also need walls and doors to stay there.
3. *The "big bear hug":* If you are unable to lift and carry, you might still be able to sit and hold. This might be the best option when failure to immediately restrain would result in very serious injury. Without a moment of hesitation, get behind your child. With his or her back to your chest, wrap your arms around and sit down on the floor so your bodies are like two stacked chairs. Lean slightly forward. If necessary, encircle your legs too. Be strong and firm, but do not cause pain or injury. Restrain

without saying a word or showing any emotion. Release as soon as the danger has passed. The "big bear hug" should not be used if it might result in a "big bear fight." For this to work, you have to be 100 percent calm, cool, and in control.

4. *The reverse time-out:* If you can't move your child to the other side of a door and wall, maybe you can move yourself. Just go to your own room and lock the door. This can work well. However, it is not always wise given potential problems with safety, property damage, or other people. After all, your angry child will be free to do anything. He or she will have access to all other rooms in the house and perhaps the great outdoors. Remember, safety first.
5. *The car and public places:* If you are in the car and your child's backseat behavior requires a time-out, drive to the nearest safe place and pull over. Get out. Remove any other children. Turn your back to the car and ignore your child for the allotted time. Do not threaten to leave your child alone in a locked car. Don't let your body language imply possible abandonment. You may want to lean back against the driver's door and do some reading. Child-safety settings and remote control locks can prevent dangerous escape. If you are in a public place, you can use this same technique to quickly convert your car into a portable time-out unit. Just pick up your child, carry, open the door, and deposit in the backseat. Remember: immediate, nonverbal, and nonemotional.
6. *School and time-out?* If there is truly a safety issue at school, a time-out place can be prepared and used according to the principles outlined previously. However, school time-out is rarely necessary, often counterproductive, and sometimes harmful. Teachers and administrators should beware that time-out in school usually backfires. Humiliation, misunderstanding, animosity, and unenforceability often make this behavior management strategy

much more difficult in the classroom setting than at home. Moreover, the most common causes of misbehavior at school are learning and social difficulty. Struggling children may act out to escape tasks or situations that make them feel frustrated or anxious. Special attention should be paid to identifying underlying causes and patterns of behavior that suggest an escape function. The school team and other professionals can be helpful. Some children need individualized accommodations and interventions, perhaps a proactive break instead of a reactive time-out. A teacher might gently suggest a quiet place to relax. Better yet, children can be taught when and how to ask for help. Although detailed discussion of classroom behavior management is beyond the scope of this book, the Seventh Mile presentation of collaborative problem-solving is certainly relevant to teacher-student relations (Greene, 2014b). Remember, whenever possible, proactively troubleshoot and avoid the need for time-out altogether.

7. *For older children and adolescents:* For some large and strong children, time-out may prove impractical. As children get older, time-out should not be used at all. As children grow up, parents can usually rely more on ignoring, empathy, and proactive problem-solving. However, for older children and adolescents, the stakes can be higher. Little kids, little problems; big kids, big problems. Although this book focuses on children from preschool through early adolescence, this may be the place to digress and offer a few words about more complicated issues: What to do about drug and alcohol use? Truancy, academic failure, or severe school misbehavior? Property damage, parent abuse, or severe disruption of family functioning? Stealing or other illegal activities? Parents in these serious situations should seek professional help. When considering reactive options, it is always best to think things through and spell out terms in advance. Behavior contracts should include very specific penalties.

Instead of time-out, delineated behaviors could result in more age-appropriate and effective restrictions and loss of privileges. For example:

- Restricted use or loss of Internet access, cell phone, or other electronics
- Restricted use or loss of car keys
- Social restrictions, including curfews, banned places, or approved escort
- Monitoring, including GPS cellphone tracking, drug testing
- Grounding (but not too long): for hours to days, not weeks

In the most serious situations of all, some parents of teenagers may face very painful decisions regarding change of school (including boarding schools), residential or wilderness mental health treatment, or the juvenile justice system. Again, for these very complicated situations, parents should always seek professional support.

Why Time-out and Ignoring Don't Always Work

Parents commonly complain that they have tried ignoring or time-out, and it does not work. There are a number of possible reasons:

1. ***Overuse:*** Ignoring and time-out are often used for the *wrong behaviors* or the *wrong reasons.* Sometimes people use time-out when it would be better to ignore or pause and reflect empathically. Ignoring and time-out should not be used for every behavior problem.
2. ***Poor technique:*** Many parents do not do time-out right. Usually this means not being immediate, nonverbal, and nonemotional. Review your "how-tos."
3. ***Not enough proactive problem-solving***: An ounce of prevention truly is worth a pound of cure. Why wait to react with ignoring or time-out when good proactive behavioral strategies

would head off the problem altogether? If you use all your proactive strategies—do regular time-in; give positive attention for compliance; ensure engagement, understanding, ability, and motivation—then the need for ignoring and time-out should lessen. Especially if your frequency of time-outs is not steadily declining, it is a sure sign that more work needs to be done on the front end. Ultimately, we don't want to need any time-outs at all.

4. ***Not enough "time-in":*** Some parents might focus too much on their children's misbehavior. They find themselves giving their children too much negative attention. These children might actually welcome ignoring or time-out as a reprieve. Some boys and girls misbehave just to get any kind of reaction out of their parents. Children need to know that they will get regular love and acceptance just for being who they are. This is why we implement time-in before time-out.
5. ***Allows escape from negative environment:*** Unless adults are giving a lot of positive attention and a child is feeling safe, time-out will not just be ineffective, it might even backfire. This point is worth repeating. If a child is struggling with unappreciated learning problems in the classroom, he or she might get negative feedback from the teacher. Frustration and anxiety mount. The child acts out and is sent to the principal's office. There, he or she gets some attention and is spared further humiliation. To such a child, time-out represents an effective escape to safe harbor.
6. ***Parent, family, and other care-provider factors*:** Sometimes parents and other involved adults have a hard time deciding what to do. They are confused about which reactive strategy to use. They find it difficult to follow through consistently and use good technique. This is often due to their own stress and exhaustion. Raising any child is hard work—especially so if your child is challenging and you have competing responsibilities. It's impossible

> to always be at your best. Some parents may be wrestling with their own feelings, perhaps projecting onto their children leftover guilt or anger about their own upbringing. Your spouse, your extended family, and other care providers as well might bring their own emotional history or cultural tendencies to the complexities of choosing and implementing effective reactive strategies. You might be a single parent. Your marriage might be strained or broken. Some parents or providers have their own mental-health challenges. Some might not "believe in" having a behavior management plan at all. Some might resist talking through strategies and differences. They might get defensive or feel uncomfortable. All of this makes it very difficult for the involved adults to reach a consensus and support one another's efforts. Parents, grandparents, nannies, and teachers can feel in conflict with one another and/or alone in their struggles. With all these mixed messages, inconsistencies, and tensions, it is no wonder that reactive strategies do not always seem to work.

If, for whatever reason, you are having trouble choosing or implementing behavioral strategies, try to talk things through with your spouse, partner, trusted family member, or friend. You may want to consider some professional help. Take care of yourself. (Go back to the Second Mile.) At the very least, consider the following general guidelines for breaking stalemates.

Log, Lightning, or Rock?

Resolving Uncertainty and Disagreements

Every parent has a different temperament, skill set, and threshold for tolerating certain behaviors. Different parents will reasonably assign the same behavior to different categories. Grandparents, other relatives, care providers, and teachers will sometimes have different values, cultures, or biases. Within a family, it is important to try to resolve these differences. It just works better if the adults can reach a consensus about which strategies to use in which settings for which behavior. Children should not be on the receiving end of mixed and confusing messages. Children do best when adults act consistently and predictably. Over time, across settings and across people, children should know what to expect. Parents and other involved adults should put themselves in a position where they are able to support one another's efforts. If adults are uncertain or divided, then children will seek rocks (empathy) over logs (ignoring), and anything before lightning (time-out). In this way, deliberately or subconsciously, children can "triangulate" so that one adult is pitted against another. Tension and conflict ensues. Behavior problems escalate.

Playing the "log, lightning, rock" game: How can the adults form a unified front? How to resolve uncertainty or disagreement? How to "break logjams," avoid "getting caught between a rock and a hard place," and make sure that your family is not "struck by lightning?" When adults can't decide on reactive behavioral strategies, kind of like the old "rock, paper, scissors" game, you can just play a game of "log, lightning, rock." For each problem behavior, adults can resolve uncertainty and conflicts by following these simple rules:

- rock (pause) always beats lightning (time-out) and log (ignore)
- log (ignore) always beats lightning (time-out)
- lightning (time-out) always loses

When in doubt or disagreement, the least desirable strategy is time-out, next least is ignoring, and you can always play it safe by pausing to reflect. In other words, err on the soft side.

When in doubt, try it out: You never really know what works best until you try. Don't speculate or argue. Just set up an experiment. Pick a behavior. Consider the baseline frequency, duration, and severity. Decide: "log" (ignore), "lightning" (time-out), or "rock" (pause). Run the experiment. If your educated guess is right, and you do a good job implementing the strategy, then the frequency, duration, and severity of the problem behavior should decrease week by week. If, on the other hand, you guess wrong, and the behavior does not improve or gets worse, then you should consider a technique tune-up or a different strategy. Either way, you will learn what works and what doesn't. Adults come together more reliably when they share data and experience, not opinions. Using time-limited trials, you will arrive at the most effective strategy for your child. Along with your proactive strategies, these reactive strategies will help you fill out your behavior management tool kit. Different children, different situations, different approaches. Choose what's best for you and your child.

Shape-Shifting

You may have the opportunity to shift the shape of your child's behavior to a more easily managed form.

- *"Lightning to logs":* Whenever possible, parents should convert unignorable behaviors into ignorable ones. As discussed previously, try to avoid having to use time-out by removal, distraction, redirection, de-escalation, or retreat. For example: *Freddie, looking hostile and aggressive, threatens to punch his baby brother. Calm and quick, his mother swoops in, picks up the baby, turns her back, and takes a few steps away. Simple as that.*
- *"Lightning or logs to rocks":* When appropriate, as discussed in the Ninth Mile ahead, parents can use a reflective pause, instead of ignoring or using time-out. For example: *Trudy screams at her father: "I hate you more than anything in the whole world!" He pauses and takes a*

deep breath. With genuine concern and compassion, he says, "I guess you're feeling pretty angry." She talks. He listens. Trudy gradually calms down.

As you implement one reactive strategy, your child's behavior might shift and require you to make a midstream adjustment.

- *"Rocks to logs or lightning"*: Depending on the child's reaction, an empathizing (rock) parent might have to "unpause"; that is, stop reflecting and use either ignoring or time-out. For example: *Despite Mom's best efforts to show compassion and validate Maude's feelings, Maude is relentless in her verbal assault. Maude's mother shifts to ignoring and walks away. She lets out one little extinction burst: "I said I really hate you!" Mom goes into the kitchen to make dinner. Then, with slightly less intensity, Maude adds, "I really mean it." But then, Maude notices some crayons and decides to work on her coloring book.*
- *"Logs to lightning"*: Children may compel parents use time-out by turning potentially ignorable behaviors into unignorable ones. For example: *Lucy's father ignores her complaining. This makes her angry. He walks away. She gets even more upset and follows him into the kitchen. Lucy starts hitting her father in the back. Immediately, nonemotionally, and nonverbally, he puts her in time-out.*

This discussion of shape-shifting should not suggest quick abandonment of your primary reactive strategy. To the contrary, ignoring, time-out, and pausing are not always immediately effective. Often these strategies only work when parents firmly commit, stay the course, and follow through. Even so—please read carefully here—"shift happens." So it's always a good idea to have a solid backup plan.

Homework for the Eighth Mile

Now that you understand *why* different reactive strategies are used for different behaviors, you can decide *when* to use each one. Take out your problem behavior inventory from the First Mile. Look down the list.

1. Consider your progress with proactive strategies used so far. Update your number rating for problem severity: 0 = not all, 1 = little, 2 = medium, 3 = big. Have you made progress? Are there some behaviors that you can take off the list? Any that you need to add?
2. Now go down the list and write "log," "lightning," or "rock" next to each problem behavior. If you prefer, write "ignore," "time-out," or "pause" to indicate which reactive strategy makes the most sense.
3. For ignoring and time-out, review technique and use as indicated.

Ninth Mile: Pausing for Empathy and Self-Reflection *(Rocks)*

• • •

"Don't just do something; stand there."

—The White Rabbit in Walt Disney's 1951 animated version of *Alice in Wonderland*

"You shall love your neighbor as yourself."

—Leviticus 19:17

And if there was a rock, Hawk could stop the boat. Floating, still, in front of the rock, they would pause to consider their reflections in the water. Hawk saw Hawk. Raph saw Raph. And then, Hawk and Raph saw themselves looking at each other.

• • •

Over the years, behaviorists and psychotherapists have remained locked in gratuitous battle. Behaviorists focus on what's outwardly measurable; psychotherapists on often-hidden inner emotions (Greenspan et al., 1998; Skinner, 1976). Purists from each camp accuse the other of neglecting essential dimensions of human development. Behaviorists criticize psychotherapists for too much talk, play, and process and too little science, accountability, and product. Psychotherapists criticize behaviorists for too little attention to thoughts, feelings, and the irrational and not enough individuality, humanity, and compassion.

In my view, the behaviorists and psychotherapists both have their points. But contrary to the purists, I feel that both perspectives can and should be integrated into a comprehensive whole. Behaviorists, psychotherapists, and even we "integrationists" are too often guilty of viewing children in isolation, not as part of larger family, cultural, and socioeconomic systems (Grinker, 2008; Kerr & Bowen, 1988; Lancy, 2015). As demonstrated by the Gander back in the First Mile, all these perspectives are essential to truly understanding and effectively helping each child. Unfortunately, detailed consideration of "systems thinking" is beyond the scope of this book. Even so, I have tried to stay sensitive to these broader viewpoints.

So far, we have focused primarily on outer behavior; that is, how to help children succeed and how to respond when they don't. Along these lines, miles two through six and mile eight covered proactive and reactive behavioral strategies. In miles two, seven, and this mile, I weave in some psychotherapeutic perspectives; more cognitive and emotional approaches. In terms of reactive strategies, ignoring (logs) and time-out (lightning) are about managing behavior. Pausing for empathy and self-reflection is more about inner thoughts and feelings—both yours and your child's. In my opinion, all these windows are worth a look through.

When to Pause for Empathy and Self-Reflection (Rock)

The younger the child, the more logs and lightning, so more situations will call for ignoring or time-out. As discussed in the Eighth Mile on logs and lightning, sometimes the best reactive strategy is separation; immediate, nonemotional, and nonverbal. Although there are times when distance may be necessary, there are many other times when children and parents need to pause and come together. Ignoring and time-out "tell" children what they *should not* to do. However, these distancing techniques don't help children learn what they *should* do. So let's look for rocks. Consider pausing for empathy and self-reflection whenever:

- Ignoring or time-out is inappropriate or counterproductive, especially as children get older.
- You and your child need mutual understanding, compassion, support, and connection.
- You and your child are feeling distressed or frustrated.

Why Pause?

The evolution of species depends on natural selection of certain survival reflexes (Dawkins, 2006). All animals—including humans—inherit a set of automatic responses to danger. When threatened, our primitive brains suddenly fire to "fight, flee, or freeze." When there is a threat to family, we react protectively and instinctively, without hesitation or forethought, even if it means sometimes endangering ourselves (Pfaff, 2015). When the danger is imminent, and we react to protect ourselves or our offspring, we don't stop to think things over. These protective reflexes or survival instincts are largely inherited, programmed into our DNA. But some reflexes are "learned on the job," conditioned by our own personal experience. Whether inborn or acquired, these responses are sudden, powerful, and often irrational. These primitive reflexes can sometimes save our lives and help us save the lives of those we love. Other times our irrational brains need our rational brains to say, "Whoa there. Let's pause and wait a second."

> *Sam, a boy with learning disabilities, came home from school sobbing. His teacher had asked him to read out loud in front of the class. He struggled. His classmates laughed. Sam felt devastated. When he came home from school that day, he saw his mother and broke down, sobbing. He told her all about it. How he felt so stupid. His mother was furious about this public humiliation. She reached for her phone. She would give that teacher a piece of her mind! And the principal too! She felt like screaming at them for their insensitivity. They had failed to support her vulnerable boy. Although her feelings were understandable, picking a fight would damage her relationship with the school team and compromise her ability to work with them in the future. Sam's mother took a deep breath, put the phone down, and steadied her shaking hand.*

What separates humans from other animals is our ability to pause. After all, if our irrational brains are so great, why would we have developed the ability to think at all? Thankfully, although we need our primitive reflexes, we also have the capacity to hesitate. Between an environmental stimulus and our conditioned response, we can take a moment, break the neurophysiologic circuit, and analyze. Taking a breather allows us to consider the source of our child's behavior and the source of our own reflexive reactions.

Empathy means pausing in response to your child's thoughts and feelings.

> *Sam's mother turned, dropped to both knees, and held him gently by his shoulders. She absorbed his pain and let her face reflect his sorrow. Softly and with genuine aching, she said, "Sam, that must have felt really bad." He melted into her arms.*

Self-reflection means pausing in response to your own thoughts and feelings.

> *Sam's mother thought about her own angry reaction to what happened at school. Over the first few months of school, the teacher had proved inexperienced, but her heart was in the right place, and she was very open to advice. The principal had not been very energetic about advocating for Sam. Even though this was Sam's third year at the school, his mother felt like she was starting from scratch every year. It didn't help that her partner was traveling and her own work was especially stressful. She was battle weary. Sam's mother called a friend who also had a child with learning disabilities. That helped her regain perspective. She gathered herself and decided: "Right now, I just need to get a good night's sleep. Tomorrow I'll reach out to the teacher and talk about what happened. If I'm going to help Sam, I'll need to work with the school team collaboratively, respectfully, and patiently."*

Why Empathy?

Empathy means actually experiencing another person's feelings, putting yourself in another person's shoes, and cultivating a personal understanding of what he or she is going through. It means facing another person's problems as if they are your own. For a parent, nothing is more important than pausing in this way to reflect on your child.

- ***Empathy helps keep parents and children out of power struggles:*** Remember the power struggle? Your child does not meet your expectations. You repeat yourself. Your child resists. With increasing intensity, back and forth you go. In the end, either you overpower your child or you just give up. We have discussed a variety of proactive and reactive strategies to stay out of power struggles. But what if proactive strategies don't work and it's inappropriate to ignore or use time-out? As a reactive strategy, empathy often works best. Whereas ignoring and time-out avoid power struggles by creating physical and emotional distance, empathy can deescalate difficult situations by bringing parents and children closer together.
- ***Empathy helps your child feel understood:*** Children need to understand their parents' expectations, but parents need to understand their children's expectations too. Parents should pause to seriously consider the world through their child's eyes. Make a genuine effort. Ask: "What must you be thinking? How must this feel for you?" When you truly understand your child's inner life and communicate that understanding to your child, he or she feels loved, supported, and validated. When you pause to respond empathically, your child also pauses to learn self-understanding and self-acceptance. Your empathic response is like holding up a mirror. When you share your personal understanding of your child, he or she learns to understand him or herself too.
- ***Empathy helps teach your child the language of emotion:*** Every time you pause to respond empathically, your child learns something about his or her own feelings. Seeing your face, eyes, and body language, your child sees a reflection of his or her inner self. Feeling your touch, your child experiences his or her "inside

out." Hearing your words, your child learns how to describe his or her own feelings. By demonstrating the nonverbal and verbal language of emotion, you teach your child to identify his or her own feelings and get in touch with his or her emotional self. Emotional or intrapersonal intelligence comes more naturally to some than others (Gardner & Laskin, 2011; Goleman, 2005). Children who tend to think and feel in black and white need to be taught all the shades of gray. As discussed previously, between 0 and 10, they need to learn 1 through 9. With no earth in between, if it doesn't feel like heaven, it must feel like hell. If your child's emotional vocabulary only includes "happy," "sad," "angry," and "scared," he or she will simplistically mislabel more complicated emotions. Children need help filling up a deep drawer of linguistic file folders. They need brain maps for a broad range of more subtle and nuanced emotions: disappointment, contentment, frustration, jealousy, apprehension, and many more. Some children have difficulty learning the language of emotion. They might even appear to lack the capacity for empathy. Still, just like we can teach children with dyslexia to read books, we can also teach children with social-emotional learning disabilities to read other people's thoughts and feelings. We just need to meet them at their level of emotional development. It might be hard and take a while, but that does not mean it's impossible. And who better to help your child develop their emotional intelligence than you? You will provide the modeling—over and over and over again. By showing your child empathy, you teach your child how to feel empathy for others.

- ***Empathy helps parents gain traction with their child for problem-solving together:*** It's hard to problem-solve with an upset child. First, you need to help your child get beyond his or her raw emotional reactivity to a place of calm. Children need to feel understood by their parents. They can then understand themselves. And then, this self-awareness leads to self-regulation. Empathy turns the irrationality switch off and the rationality switch on. Empathy makes people emotionally available to one another. Empathy opens the door for clear thinking and collaboration. Without empathy, there can be no true partnership.

How to Respond Empathically

In *Motivational Interviewing*, Miller and Rollnick (2012) provide one of my favorite metaphors for how to pause and respond with empathy: What to do if your car is skidding off an icy road?

- ***Taking your foot off the brake:*** When your child is emotionally "skidding off the road," your first reflex is to "slam on the brakes." You repeat, explain, or reprimand. You want to stop your child from melting down, shutting down, or breaking down. But he or she fails to respond. Not only that, but your child spins further out of control. He or she thinks or screams: "You don't understand!" The power struggle ensues. By slamming on the breaks, you lock the wheels, lose all traction and unintentionally amplify the skid. It is counterinstinctive to relinquish control of the car and let the wheels roll. But that's exactly what you need to do. You need to allow your child's emotional wheels to turn at their own speed. The unnatural thing is exactly the right thing. Instead of reflexively hitting the brakes, you need to pause and ask: "If I were in my child's shoes, how would I feel? Wouldn't I want my feelings to be acknowledged instead of discounted? Validated instead of brushed aside?" Pausing to answer these simple questions is the essential first step in the empathic response.
- ***Turning the wheels in the direction of the skid***: When things are not going well, parents often shift right into problem-solving mode. After all, the solution is so painfully obvious, and you so

desperately want to help your child. You just want to tell your child: "If only you would think this, feel this, do this! It would be so easy to set you straight and keep you on the road." But your emotionally flooded child can't listen to your good advice. And the more you try to help, the more your child resists. It's like trying to turn your skidding car back onto that icy road. The natural thing is to turn the steering wheel in the opposite direction of the skid and force the car back onto the road. But if you do, the wheels will be perpendicular to the momentum of the car. They will not be able to spin with the car, and you will lose all traction, the skid gets worse. Again, the right thing to do is counterintuitive. Instead of turning the wheels back onto the road, you have to turn the wheels in the direction of the skid—off the road! What? Unnatural, but yes. The only way to regain control is if you align the wheels with the momentum of the car. Then, and only then, the wheels can roll *with* the car. Then, and only then, can you regain traction. If your child is "skidding off the road," the empathic response turns your attention in the direction of your child's feelings. Your words and your nonverbal language move with your child's emotions, not against them. By pausing to respond empathically, you regain parent-child traction.

- ***Letting the car slow down:*** With your foot off the brake and your wheels turned into the skid, you give the car whatever time it needs to slow down and get back under control. Even as the car continues its wayward slide, do not panic. Do not hit the brake or turn the wheel prematurely. Keep the tires aligned with the car, and wait for it to slow down—on its own. When you pause to respond with empathy, the length of the pause is determined by your child's response. Be patient and stay the course. Take whatever time he or she needs. Wait until your child sees his or her feelings reflected in your eyes, hears his or her feelings in your words, and softens his or her face and body with the realization that you are in this thing together.

- ***Gradually turning the car back onto the road:*** Once your car has slowed and you've regained traction, then you can gently turn the wheels back onto the road. You can turn the wheel back in the right direction only after the skid has stopped. Be careful that you and your child make this pivot together. Resist the temptation to launch into a full discussion. Gently frame the problem. Maybe suggest a goal. Sympathetically, softly, and slowly, you might say, "Hmmm. It looks like you want to do this, but I need to do that. I guess we've got a bit of a problem here. But ya know, I bet if we put our heads together, we can solve this problem. Should we talk about it now or wait until later?" If your child seems ready and accepts the invitation to problem-solve, great. If not, for now that's OK too. When a problem is fresh or pressing, it is harder to stay calm. Maybe it's better to wait until everyone can think clearly and communicate productively. Later can be better. Go back to the Seventh Mile for some problem-solving when you and your child are really ready. And sometimes, when you pause and respond with empathy, it turns out that problem-solving isn't even necessary after all. Not every problem needs to be solved. Sometimes you can just let it pass. Other times, given the opportunity, your child can figure things out on his or her own. All he or she really needed to "get back on the road" was a bridge of love and understanding. Think about the last time you were frustrated or upset. Did you really want someone to discuss possible solutions? Maybe all you really wanted was someone to just listen and be there for you.

Remember to individualize how you use empathy. Just like time-in, different children "feel felt" in different ways. Consider your child's developmental and behavioral profile. What's the best way for you to respond empathically to *your* child? If empathy hasn't worked well in the past, maybe you just need to modify your approach.

VERBAL EMPATHIC RESPONSES

For some children, it's all about finding the right words. For example:

- "I guess you really don't feel like doing this right now."
- "That sure is frustrating!"
- "It seems like you don't want to stop what you're doing."
- "It sounds like you're pretty angry."
- "That looks hard to do."
- "Bummer."
- "You were really expecting that to go differently."
- "I'd feel a little nervous about that too."
- "That sure was scary."

NONVERBAL EMPATHIC RESPONSES

For many children, words don't work as well. It often doesn't matter so much what you say but how you say it. Try using a softer voice, slower rate of speech, and more loving tone. Sometimes you don't have to say a word. Do not underestimate the power of nonverbal communication, such as:

- Coming close (but not too close)
- Body language
- Facial expression
- Touch/hug
- Nonverbal vocalizations (such as a sigh)
- Just staying 100 percent present and truly listening

It may be difficult to empathize when your child is expressing negative or complicated emotions; especially ones that make you feel upset, confused, anxious, or defensive. Children will sometimes express self-hatred (including suicidal ideas); anger (directed at you or others, including homicidal ideas); or sexual, gender identity, or other thoughts and feelings that might catch you by surprise. Facing these loaded situations, you might feel a greater impulse to correct, reassure, or reprimand. But the empathic parent reflects, validates, and connects with their child—*no matter what.* Empathy does not necessarily represent endorsement; just understanding and compassion.

It was Sally's birthday party. Her friends all brought presents. Her sister Sadie felt intensely jealous. Sadie broke down crying and screaming: "Sally's getting all the presents!"

Sadie's father was about to reprimand her for being selfish, but then he paused. He thought about explaining how she would get presents when it was her birthday, but then he paused again. He took a moment and just looked into her eyes. He came over, held her, and softly said, "Yeah, it really seems unfair doesn't it?"

Between sobs, Sadie wailed: "It's so—not—fair*!"*

Again, her father almost shifted into a speech on learning to accept life's injustices, but he caught himself, held her closer, and said: "This really stinks for you, doesn't it?"

One last little sob, and then she looked up into her father's eyes and said, "Yeah, this stinks."

Sally opened her presents. Sadie and her dad just sat there and watched, together.

• • •

Robbie's school friends had been teasing him about his long hair. He finally got up the courage to get it cut. His mom and older brother Nathan took him to the barbershop. Excited about a new image, Robbie asked the barber for a buzz cut. Robbie loved it.

"Wait until my friends see this!" he exclaimed.

Nathan immediately burst Robbie's bubble, saying, "Now you look even dumber. Gay to butch, you dweeb!"

Robbie's smile turned to anguish. Horrified and confused, his mother wanted to scream at Nathan for being so mean and comfort Robbie for being so hurt. But she couldn't scream and comfort at the same time. So she paused. Turning her back to Nathan, she said to Robbie, "You were so excited about your haircut, and then Nathan said such a mean thing."

Robbie exploded, "Yeah and he's the meanest brother in the whole world. I want him to be dead. Right now."

Robbie's mother dropped to one knee so that they were face to face. "I understand how angry you must feel."

Robbie shouted, "You don't *understand! Nathan's right. It does look dumb. After Nathan gets dead, I wanna be dead too! And then I wanna kill you for bringing me for this stupid haircut!"*

Robbie's mother took a deep breath. With genuine compassion and an even softer tone, she said, "This haircut really turned out to be a disaster for you, Robbie. I guess this feels like the worst day in your whole life."

His shoulders drooped. After a moment, he turned to walk out to the car. They all got in and rode home in silence. But while she drove, Robbie's mom reached back and touched his leg. He did not move her hand away.

(Nathan lost electronics privileges for a week and got them back only after he apologized to Robbie. Robbie's mother e-mailed his teacher and got permission for him to wear his favorite baseball cap

to school. Robbie's friends ended up telling him that his buzz cut was supercool.)

Why Doesn't Empathy Always Work?

Common Pitfalls

- *No "buts":* Naturally, when children are in distress and "skidding off the road," parents just want to make it all better. Parents commonly might give one quick hit of empathy and then shift prematurely into teaching or problem-solving mode. For example: "I understand how you're feeling, *but* this is how you should feel." Or, "I see you want to do that, *but* you need to do this." There's not enough traction for "buts" yet. Far and away, this is the most common misapplication of the empathic response. Stay with it. Wait for traction. Hold off on quick "buts." Sometimes you don't need any "buts" at all. Consider not moving on to problem-solving and just letting empathy be enough.
- *Do not be afraid to empathize with negative feelings or inappropriate wishes:* If saying "but" too quickly is the most common empathy error, then parent anxiety is the most common underlying issue. If your child expresses negative feelings or inappropriate desires, you might worry about giving too much validation. In some situations more than others—and with some parents more than others—it may be very difficult to resist "slamming on the brakes or jerking the wheel." However, with empathy you recognize the source of your child's feelings without endorsing any specific thoughts or calls to action. Empathy is agnostic and neutral. Robbie's mother, as described previously, empathized with his homicidal and suicidal ideas. Then, and only then, she was in a better position to help him deal with

his distress and desperation. Empathy grants in fantasy what would never be condoned in reality. Empathy accepts that children cannot be held responsible for their thoughts even though they should be held responsible for their behavior. Empathy accepts that there is a limit to what you can do to fix your child's every problem. Even so, with empathy, you never need to leave your child alone in distress.

Roy: *I want you to buy me those Legos, right now!*
Dad: *Those are very cool, aren't they? (Empathic response.)*
Roy: *Yeah, and let's get 'em and take 'em home and play.*
Dad: *Wouldn't that be great! Wow. If you could have every Lego in the whole world, what would you want to build? (Granting in fantasy what he will not grant in reality.)*

This goes back and forth until Roy and his dad feel well aligned in the Lego fantasy. But Roy will not move on. Then, and only then, comes the gentle pivot to reality and collaborative problem-solving.

Dad: *Ya know, Roy, we've got a little problem. But I bet if we put on our thinking caps, we can figure it out together.*

Roy is not very interested in collaborative problem-solving. Immediately sensing that he is not going to get his Legos, he stomps his foot. Under his breath, anger mounting, he says, "You never let me get anything. I hate you!" Roy's dad pauses and says, "You really wanted me to get you those Legos today. I understand why you're mad at me."

Roy's dad realizes that his invitation to problem-solve has been declined. He backs off and sticks with plain empathy for now. Tomorrow they'll be able to have a more productive discussion about what to do.

- *Rocks shape-shifting into logs or lightning:* Sometimes a parent responds empathically but it just doesn't work.

  Roy has a full-blown tantrum. A rock has shape-shifted—maybe into an ignorable log? Roy's father walks away, turns his back, and waits for him just outside the door. He hopes that withdrawal of attention will extinguish the tantrum. Maybe Roy will let out just a few more yelps of protest before following his dad out of the store.

  But no, Roy is fully steamed. Grabbing the Lego box, he makes a mad dash for the door. Roy has now converted a potential log into definite lightning. Roy's dad, anticipating this shape-shifting, steps into the door to block Roy's path. Immediately, nonverbally, and nonemotionally, he positions himself directly behind Roy, quickly encircles Roy in his arms, and drops to the floor in a big bear hug. Roy tantrums. Roy's father just waits, calmly, without saying a word.

  Other shoppers pass by. They see a Lego box on the ground, a father in control, a young child having a tantrum. Sympathetically and respectfully, they nod.

- *Mistaking logs and lightning for rocks:* Everybody has bad days. Sometimes a child is not so responsive to empathy or a parent is less than perfect with his or her technique. Just because empathy doesn't work all the time doesn't mean that you should give up on using it as a first-line reactive strategy. Just be ready for some shape-shifting. On the other hand, if there is a regular pattern of empathy backfiring, maybe it wasn't a rock in the first place. Maybe you were really dealing with a log or lightning and should have used ignoring or time-out. Rock, log, or lightning? When in doubt, default to empathy. But if—despite good technique—empathy usually fails, then don't keep using it.

Roy's father began to see a pattern. In other situations, like anxious moments, empathy worked great. But most of the time, when Roy didn't get what he wanted, empathy just seemed to make him want it more. Roy's father figured that empathy was reinforcing Roy's demands. Empathy was backfiring. So at least in these situations, Roy's father decided to go with immediate distraction and redirection; that is, ignoring the requests. For now anyhow, a log, not a rock.

Why Self-Reflection?

You may embrace the idea of empathy for your child. However, no one would blame you for wondering, "When do I get some empathy for me?" If you have ever felt this way, you should not feel selfish or guilty. Parents need and deserve understanding just as much as children do. And if you can't keep your own head above water, how can you possibly keep your child afloat? Back in the Second Mile, we talked about how time-in for children requires time-in (self-care) for parents. Here in the Ninth Mile, the same principle holds true. Empathy for your child requires you to get some empathy for yourself. This can come in the form of self-reflection. You might ask, "Hey, wait a minute. You mean I have to give myself my own empathy?" Hopefully, you'll get some empathy from other people too, but so it is. To a large degree, our children can understand themselves only if we can understand ourselves.

Although there are many similarities between the second and ninth miles, there are some important differences too.

- In the Second Mile, time-in for children and self-care for parents are both *proactive strategies* for giving positive attention. With time-in and self-care, there are no external expectations and, therefore, no disappointments. The world is bent to accommodate the individual. There is calm, relaxation, and joy. Problems melt away. We do time-in and self-care to create islands of peace and rejuvenation for children and parents.

- In this Ninth Mile, empathy for children and self-reflection for parents are *reactive strategies* for validating and understanding feelings. Empathy and self-reflection are called for when expectations are not met and frustration ensues. The individual feels bent—sometimes broken—to accommodate the world. There is tension, stress, and anxiety. Problems dominate. We pause for empathy and self-reflection to survive stormy waters.

The reasons for empathy are similar to the reasons for self-reflection. However, instead of pausing to hold a mirror up for your child, you pause in front of the mirror and take a nonjudgmental look at yourself.

- ***Self-reflection helps you stay out of internal power struggles:*** Parents often find themselves sucked into self-conflict. Your idealized self has expectations. Your real self falls short. Your perfect self-issues commands: "You can do better. Don't be a bad parent!" Your imperfect self-protests, resists, or shuts down: "I can't do better. I am a bad parent." With increasing internal intensity, back and forth you go, your internal selves locked in battle: "I must. I can't." In the end, your idealized self might force your real self into compliance. But then you feel exhausted, defeated, and resentful. Or you just give up and feel guilty. Either way, you don't forgive yourself for your ambivalence, powerlessness, and imagined incompetence. We have discussed a variety of proactive and reactive strategies for parents to stay out of power struggles with children. But how can you stay out of these power struggles with yourself? Begin with self-reflection. Resentment and guilt estrange you from yourself; self-reflection helps you feel genuine, authentic, and true.

Tammy was having a rough day. Her boss was being a jerk. Her husband was deep and heavy into his own projects. And the kids were being especially difficult. Why did they always have to be at their worst when she was feeling most stressed? They just kept picking fights with each other. Each fight seemed worse than the last. Her mother offered to come over and help, but having her around just made things worse. Tammy's mother didn't have to say a word. The look on her face was more than enough. Tammy felt desperate and alone; like no one understood, and there was nothing she could do to make things better. She just wanted to scream. Instead, Tammy took a deep breath and paused.

- ***Self-reflection helps self-understanding:*** Pause to consider your self-expectations. When you are struggling or fall short, stop and ask: "What am I thinking? What am I feeling?" When you truly understand your own inner life and take time to reflect on that understanding, then you can love yourself, support yourself, and validate yourself. You don't need anybody else to do that for you. When you pause in self-reflection, you give yourself the gift of self-acceptance. You see yourself objectively without judgment or disappointment. Self-reflection means stepping outside of yourself, looking back at yourself, and simply noticing your own thoughts and feelings.

Tammy noticed her heart thumping in her chest, her facial muscles tensing, and that burning feeling in her stomach. She started to think about why her kids couldn't just behave and give her a break; why her mother couldn't just stop scowling and just take one of the kids to the park. But then Tammy turned and reflected on herself. Tammy caught herself wanting to be the perfect mom. She thought about how her own mother's presence served as a reminder of the impossible standard to which she aspired. She thought about her current situation and how some things were just out of her control. She thought, "There I go again. I'm feeling way too stressed." Then, after a deep breath: "But who the hell wouldn't?"

- ***Self-reflection helps you learn the language of self-acceptance:*** Every time you pause for self-reflection, you learn something new about yourself. Externalizing your thoughts and feelings means describing and labeling what would otherwise be hidden and subconscious. This allows you to get in touch with different aspects of your emotional self. Self-reflection can then lead you to calmly notice your distorted thoughts; such as, all-or-none, minimizing, catastrophizing, and blame shifting. Pausing for self-reflection buys you time to substitute shades of gray for black and white. Say to yourself: "There I go again. Blowing things up even worse than they are." You might need to work on all of this. It might take time, and you might need help. But who knows you better than you know yourself? You just need to practice regularly and develop your own language of self-awareness. With time, you will become fluent with your own self-vocabulary and self-labels. You will learn to turn overwhelming confusion and despair into something more understandable and ordinary. Sometimes you'll even laugh at yourself: "Funny how my thoughts and feelings can have a mind of their own."

Tammy thought, "After all, this is nothing new. I've fallen into this emotional trap before. I know that I've idealized my own childhood. But my mother couldn't have been that perfect. And I don't have to be so perfect anyhow. I don't need to hold myself to some ridiculous standard. I can be plenty good enough. I know that I've got a predisposition to anxiety. I know that this is a stressor. I need to stop moaning, "Why does stuff always happen to me?" and just start accepting, "Sometimes stuff just happens. Such is life."

- ***Self-reflection helps you stay calm and rational for problem-solving:*** Unless you work toward a reasonable level of self-understanding, you will continue to suffer with anxiety and self-doubt. Self-reflection calms. Self-reflection turns the irrationality switch off and the rationality switch on. Self-reflection makes you available to yourself. Self-reflection opens the door for clear thinking and problem-solving.

  Tammy realized that this was not a great time to problem-solve. But she decided that she would sit down at the kitchen table later that night, when the kids were asleep and her mother had gone home. Then she'd be able to think straight and come up with a survival plan for the next few days.

How to Self-Reflect

Externalize your inner thoughts and feelings. If it helps, write them down. Examine them. Calmly consider:

- What am I dealing with in this moment?
  - Today? This week? This year? At this phase of my life?
  - What am I thinking?
  - What am I feeling?
- What am I carrying with me from my own past?
  - From my own childhood family system?
  - From my community?
  - From my culture?
  - From my environment?
  - From my experience?
  - From my genes?
- What judgments am I making about myself? What distorted or irrational thoughts am I having?

When you pause, you give yourself the opportunity to simply observe. You control your inner life. It does not have to control you. You can notice your own psyche just the way you can notice your own breath. It doesn't matter if you call this mindfulness, Buddhism, radical acceptance, or just "cutting through the BS." All that matters is turning subjective experience into objective self-awareness.

> *Gregg had four operations for cervical spine disease. Each time the pain was different. But each time, he got better at separating himself from his pain. He learned to pretend that the pain was outside of his body. Then he would study it with sympathetic detachment—as if it belonged to somebody else. It was interesting how the pain could sometimes be a 4 and sometimes a 9; sometimes electrical and sometimes numbing; sometimes in the shoulder; other times in the bicep or radiating down into the hand. Why this variation? What nerves were involved? What brain regions? How did this pain compare to previous pains; his own and the pain of others? Was this anything like the pain his father had experienced when he was a young man injured in war or when he was an old man battling Lou Gehrig's disease? Wasn't it fascinating how different types of pain could stir different thoughts and different emotions? How the same pain might be experienced in different ways by different people depending on their upbringing, their family, their culture, their own history of pain? Instead of feeling like an object of oppression and injustice, Gregg learned to embrace his pain as a rich and personal subject of endless fascination (Cousins, 2005).*

When Self-Reflection Fails

Just as empathy for your child doesn't always work, empathy for yourself is never 100 percent effective. When self-reflection fails, ask yourself why. Did you break any of these rules of self-reflection?

- ***No "buts":*** When self-reflecting, don't cut your needs short or turn prematurely to problem-solving. Don't shift too fast into fix-it mode. Just acknowledge your situation, your thoughts, and your feelings. Self-acceptance takes time.
- ***Do not be afraid of negative feelings or inappropriate wishes:*** You are entitled to some negative thoughts and bad days. Do not feel guilty or inadequate. It's normal to have ups and downs. It's normal to have all kinds of emotions and urges. They are just thoughts and feelings. You don't have to let them determine what happens to you or how you choose to live your life. You can be free.
- ***Internal rocks shape-shifting into—or mistaken for—internal logs or lightning:*** There's sometimes just too much going on for self-reflection. For the moment, you might just have to push aside your own thoughts and feelings: ignore, distract, and redirect yourself until the negativity passes. Other times you might try to pause but your own feelings escalate to a dangerous and unignorable level. Then it's wise to withdraw to a safe place. If necessary, call for help.

Homework for the Ninth Mile

1. *Practice pausing for empathy.* When it is inappropriate to ignore or use time-out, or if you are just unsure which reactive strategy to use, try empathy. Help your child feel understood. Validate his or her feelings. Help your child learn the language of emotion. Resist the temptation to say "but." Do not shift prematurely into teaching or problem-solving mode.
2. *Practice pausing for self-reflection.* Do not battle yourself. Avoid self-criticism. Identify, validate, and accept your own internal thoughts and feelings. Stay calm. Practice self-awareness.

Tenth Mile: Weaknesses, Strengths, and Independence *(Patches, Sails and Raph Takes the Wheel)*

• • •

Franklin's illness…gave him strength and courage he had not had before. He had to think out the fundamentals of living and learn the greatest of all lessons—infinite patience and never-ending persistence.

—Eleanor Roosevelt, Franklin Delano Roosevelt Memorial, Washington, DC

One could do worse than be a swinger of birches.

—Robert Frost, *The Poetry of Robert Frost* (1969)

Mile by mile, in sputters and spurts, they continued their journey. Hawk taught Raph how to handle the boat. On bad days, they hit some rocks and the boat leaked. They used tambalacoque shells to bail the water.

They used poop to patch the holes. Raph hated bailing and patching. Hawk did too, but they had no choice.

On good days, when there was a strong wind at their backs, they hoisted sail and spread their wings. Hawk's wings were so big. Raph's wings were so little.

Raph knew, *I can't fly like other birds.*
But when they caught the wind just right,
Raph felt like their boat could fly!

• • •

As we hit the Tenth Mile mark, it's important to look back and appreciate the distance traveled. By now you should have a much better understanding of your child's challenging behavior. I hope that you have experienced some success individualizing and combining different behavioral strategies. But what about the challenges that remain? Although we are reaching the end of our *Journey* together, this river is more than ten miles long. What if you are doing the best you can, but you and your child are still struggling? You're using all your strategies for engagement, understanding, and motivation, but your child is still not able to meet reasonable expectations. You wish that you could feel more confident about the miles ahead. Don't give up. Maybe you just need more time and practice. But maybe there's another reason.

Bailing and Patching

Many children have significant developmental differences or true disabilities and need more than just good behavior management. To make progress, they require specialized accommodations ("bailing water") and interventions ("patching leaks"). In Your Gander Instruction Manual Part A: The Gander Explained, I suggest specific accommodations for each facet of your child's profile. Take a good look. In this Tenth Mile, we will focus on interventions. While you may need to do some accommodating ("bailing") and some intervening ("patching") for your child's weaknesses, you should pay at least as much attention to identifying and harnessing your child's strengths. You need to teach your child how to "know which way the wind is blowing and catch it with every sail and feather you've got." For this tenth and last mile in our Journey together, we consider two goals: (1) helping your child in areas of persistent difficulty; *and* (2) nurturing your child's natural interests and abilities.

Let's begin by discussing some general principles and do a little philosophizing. Then we'll review some specific strategies.

Realistic Expectations

In dealing with your child's relative skill deficits, here's a list of general dos and don'ts. Effective intervention is all about matching your expectations to your child's abilities and potential.

- ***Don't expect too much:*** Some children have legitimate weaknesses or disabilities that go underappreciated. Even subtle skill deficits can cause significant impairment. Make sure that specific tasks are not too difficult. Remember to match your expectations to your child's developmental—not chronological—age. On the other hand, what seems like a disability may be the result of unreasonable expectations. Many adults have lost perspective on normal development and the meaning of childhood. In today's performance-driven culture, there is a real danger of pushing children too hard (Elkind, 2006).
- ***Don't expect too little:*** When a child struggles, parents might blame one another for "pushing too hard" or "not accepting" the child the way he or she is. Parents, teachers, therapists, or doctors might point fingers at one another for expecting too much. But sometimes we expect too little. Consequently, some children are overaccommodated and overprotected. Subconsciously, parents are more likely to lower their expectations when a child is considered "at-risk" or "vulnerable." This is common when there's a history of real trauma, medical problems, or disability (Green

& Solnit, 1964). But we do not want to interfere with a child's development by underestimating his or her potential or letting our own anxiety lead to self-fulfilling pessimism. We want all children to achieve their true potential. We want all children to learn responsibility. We want all children to feel good about their accomplishments. We want all children to have their best chance at successful relationships. We want all children to make some meaningful contribution to their larger community. We are not doing our children any favors if we give up on them too easily. Especially for children with "issues," what could be more important than helping them learn and grow despite life's challenges?

- ***Do assessment* before *intervention:*** It is crucial to know your child's current functional level. What is he or she able to do now? Where is your child's development relative to other children? What represents their next rung on the developmental ladder? By understanding normal childhood pathways and sequences, goals can be set; not too high and not too low—just one step up from the current level of competence. For some skills, such as toilet training, you can easily determine current abilities. Either your child can poop on the pot or not. However, for academic, language, social, emotional, or other complicated functions, it may be harder to tell what's normal. You may need to get standardized testing or professional consultation.
- ***Do not think "can versus can't"; do think "easy versus difficult":*** Ability is usually not a matter of black versus white or can versus can't. You need to know your child's skills profile in all its shades of gray. Then you and your child can understand why some tasks might be *relatively* easy and others might be *relatively* hard. Thinking in these terms, weaknesses represent explanations, not excuses; degrees of challenge and necessary levels of support, not absolute limitations.

- ***Do not confuse inconsistency with inability:*** Just because a child is able to do some things some of the time does not mean that he or she can do all things all the time.
    - *All things:* Many children have very uneven developmental profiles. Your child is probably at least a bit inconsistent across different types of tasks. In some domains, some children need to be treated as if they are younger than their years. In other domains, the same children might be able to perform at or above age expectations. For example, some children test in the "gifted" range on IQ testing but also have serious learning disabilities (Weinfeld, Jeweler, Barnes-Robinson, & Shevitz, 2013). It's unusual for any child to function at age level across all tasks.
    - *All the time:* Most children are inconsistent over time. Some days they might be able to "bring their A game"; other days not. Children are often misunderstood, judged, or blamed for being inconsistent: "You could do that yesterday! Why can't you do it today? What's your problem?" If these children could speak for themselves, they would say: "Inconsistency is my problem. It's not that I can't ever. It's just that I can't always. I may not be consistently disabled, but I am disabled by inconsistency" (Levine, 2004). Helping a child with performance inconsistency is just as important as helping a child with consistent inability. Expect your child to be somewhat inconsistent over the hours, days, and weeks.
- ***Do break it down:*** Multistep commands are hard to understand and hard to carry out. Some children can do one piece many times, but not many pieces at one time. Your child's performance may be compromised when "job chunks" are too complex, too big, too numerous, or too prolonged. This often leads to unnecessary frustration and loss of motivation. Parts

of an assignment should be simple enough, small enough, few enough, and short enough for your child to succeed at each step.

- ***Don't underestimate the importance of patience and hard work:*** Some children just need more time and more practice. Many children receive the right kind of help, but not enough. They fail only because the intervention was insufficiently intensive, frequent, or sustained. Parents and children both tend to want results that are instant and easy. Who doesn't want a quick fix? But let's be realistic. If your child gets frustrated too easily, be reassuring. Learning and success require mistakes and failures. Some children just need more instruction and more drilling, especially in areas of weakness. Good old-fashioned coaching and practice make all the difference. In the long run, grit and determination matter. If you want to reach the finish line, you've got to stay the course.
- ***Do consider response to intervention:*** According to Nietzsche, health is not freedom from illness; rather, it is the ability to overcome it (Kaufmann, 2013). In other words, everybody's got "something." Doctors customarily make a diagnosis before treating. But what if treatment, time, and shifting circumstances modify a child's degree of impairment? A nontraditional approach to developmental pediatrics (promoted here) defers diagnosis of disorder until *after* functional assessment, treatment, and time. After all, children change, often substantially and unpredictably. Feuerstein and Rand (1998) distinguishes between fixed "traits" and transitory "states." Emphasizing the importance of assessment over time, he defines "disorder" as low "modifiability" of impairment despite sufficient intervention. Conversely, he defines "health" as high "modifiability" of impairment. Like Nietzsche, according to

this way of thinking, health depends more on resilience than luck. It is important to remember that destiny is not wholly determined by either biology or circumstance, especially in our current era of debate over nature versus nurture and genes versus environment. The capacity for change is at least as important as the stuff we're born of or the circumstances we're born into.

- ***Do promote self-awareness and self-responsibility:*** When possible, parents should obtain their child's informed consent. However, if your child is not able to appreciate the reasons for accommodations or interventions, you will have to act on his or her behalf. You can explain later; that is, as soon as your child is old enough to understand. Your child must ultimately take ownership. He or she has to understand his or her own problems and take part in formulating his or her own solutions. You should make every effort to help your child become his or her own best advocate. Parents and children should choose strategies that create a clear path to self-reliance. Although all children need considerable support in the early going, an overly dependent relationship can easily become self-perpetuating for children with developmental differences. Deliberately and gradually, prompts and reinforcers should be spaced and faded. Realistically but steadily, you should raise expectations for self-care, independence, and autonomy. Only true competence and real-life success lead to genuine optimism and a positive self-image. Parents who learn to believe in their children have children who learn to believe in themselves.
- ***Do not just focus on weaknesses; do nurture strengths:*** Children need time to do the things they love and that they are good at. Otherwise they spend all their time feeling

> like they are broken and need to be fixed. "What are your child's natural abilities?" As Gardner (2011) would say, "There are many different kinds of smart." Although we all have strengths and weaknesses, children and parents tend to get frustrated and make pessimistic generalizations when skills develop unevenly. Just because you have a hard time in one area does not mean that you are "stupid." Special interests and talents should be nurtured and strengthened. Positive self-image and success usually come from specializing in areas of strength; that is, finding "islands of competence," not just fixing weaknesses (Brooks & Goldstein, 2002).

Parents and professionals should keep these principles in mind when considering accommodations and interventions for children. Parents and professionals would also do well to keep these principles in mind when considering our own growth and development.

When Things Are Too Hard: Accommodations and Interventions

There are two ways to deal with a leaky boat. On the river, you can bail water. Up on the shore, you can patch the holes. Likewise, there are two general types of developmental strategies: *accommodations* and *interventions*. Effective developmental plans often employ both types of strategies, striking a just-right balance between letting your child be who he or she *is* while also challenging your child to become who he or she *can be*.

Let's take a deeper look at some key differences between accommodations and interventions.

Acceptance versus Development

- *Accommodations:* Accommodations require parents to hear a child say: "Accept me as I am!" Just because a child is expected to do something does not mean that he or she *can*. When necessary, accommodations bypass weaknesses. At home, in school, and in social situations, accommodations promote success through sensitivity to the child's developmental and behavioral profile. Accommodation sometimes means adapting a very different idea of success. When parents accommodate, you modify your expectations but not your child.
- *Interventions:* Interventions require parents to hear your child say: "Don't accept me as I am!" Interventions fix weaknesses and restore function. The desire to intervene stems from a belief in the capacity of your child to grow and develop. Interventions may be necessary if your child is significantly impaired. Interventions are built on the hope that current difficulties need not block future success. The need for interventions reflects a heightened awareness of the awaiting world. When parents intervene, you modify your child to minimize lowering expectations.

Dependence versus Independence

- *Accommodations:* Immature children or children with impairments must depend on others. Although your child might be taught to request certain accommodations, it's usually up to parents, teachers, or others to help with implementation. As they get older, children can learn to accommodate their own weaknesses. However, there is nothing wrong with getting and giving some necessary help along the way.

- *Interventions:* Although most children depend on others to overcome their problems, help is best when it can lead to greater degrees of independence. The ultimate goal is self-help. Interventions should point your child in that direction.

Public versus Private

- *Accommodations:* Bypass strategies should be used in public situations to minimize impairment, and thereby avoid unnecessary anxiety, frustration, and humiliation. Public attention to areas of weakness just adds to a child's sense of inadequacy and embarrassment. Until your child achieves a sufficient degree of competence, consider ways to help that avoid stigmatization.
- *Interventions:* Interventions should be initiated in private. Over time, sensitive one-on-one skill building can allow your child to function in front of others with greater pride and confidence. In the meantime, do the hard work in a relatively protected environment.

Inconsistency versus Consistency

- *Accommodations:* Just because a child is *sometimes* able to do something does not mean that he or she is *consistently* able to do it. Accommodations allow for a certain amount of performance inconsistency. It's hard to always do your best. Accommodation means cutting your child some slack; not always expecting him or her to bring his or her "A game."
- *Interventions:* Mastery means steady and predictable demonstration of competence. Anybody can hit a good golf shot once, but only elite players (on their best days) can hit it well every single

time. Interventions target improved performance consistency. With time and practice, your child can achieve greater degrees of competence, fluency, and automaticity.

Alternatives versus Persistence

- *Accommodations:* Whenever possible, tasks should tap a child's strengths rather than tax his or her weaknesses. Accommodation sometimes requires excusing your child from poorly suited activities or situations. Accommodation sometimes means finding alternatives that better fit your child's behavioral style and skills.
- *Interventions:* If one strategy does not work immediately, parents and professionals should not give up. Maybe the strategy just needs some tuning. Your intervention might be the right kind, but you need to apply it with more intensity, fidelity, and persistence. Your child's failure to respond might be due to partial application; not the wrong treatment. It's like giving the right medicine but the wrong dose, or stopping treatment too soon. Change is never easy. Your child needs you to stick with one proven technique and do it well. Don't hop from one half-tried remedy to another. Durable results take hard work and time.

504 Plan versus Individualized Education Plan (IEP)

- *Accommodations:* For children with minor challenges, informal communication between parents and teachers can lead to adequate educational accommodations. But for children who need more, parents can request an education management team (EMT) meeting. The EMT meeting can result in either a 504 plan for accommodations or an individualized education plan (IEP) for interventions. Some common 504 accommodations include preferential seating, extra time, and reduced work load. These accommodations can be implemented by a regular classroom teacher without costing the school extra time, money, or other resources.

- *Interventions:* The EMT meeting can lead to an IEP. To qualify for this kind of special education, the IEP team has to make one of thirteen diagnoses:
  1. Autism
  2. Blindness
  3. Deafness
  4. Emotional disturbance
  5. Hearing impairment
  6. Intellectual disability
  7. Multiple disabilities
  8. Orthopedic impairment
  9. Other health impaired (such as ADHD or other medical problems that interfere with availability for learning)
  10. Specific learning disability (e.g., disorder of reading (dyslexia), disorder of writing (dysgraphia), difficulty with math calculations (dysgraphia), etc.)
  11. Speech or language impairment
  12. Traumatic brain injury
  13. Visual impairment

  The team then drafts an IEP that includes specific remedial services and therapies. IEP interventions can be partially implemented by a regular classroom teacher, but they usually require special educators, therapists, equipment, classrooms, or even schools, usually costing the school system extra time, money, and other resources. Pediatricians and parents should become familiar with the range of special services and school programs available in their communities. As discussed further below, special advocates can be very helpful. (Weinfeld & Davis, 2008).

Empathy and Common Sense versus Expertise and Science

- *Accommodations:* Some types of help are based on empathy, not expertise. When your child struggles, just ask: "Why? What is it about my child that makes this task difficult? How does this feel for him or her?" Simple compassion then compels you to act. By just understanding the source of your child's problem, you know what to do.
- *Interventions:* Other types of help require expert assessment and advice. For effective remediation of skill deficits, you have to answer a more complicated set of questions: "Where is your child developmentally? What is your goal? How can you help your child get there? Who can best provide the answers to these questions and this kind of help?" For most parents, choosing the best intervention can be difficult if not overwhelming. There are so many therapies out there; each with its advocates and critics. Parents are bombarded with conflicting advice from the Internet, other parents, and various professionals. When it comes to these complexities, common sense should not be ignored, but it most certainly cannot be trusted. The long history of medicine and the brief history of developmental pediatrics are filled with tales of therapeutic misadventure and quackery. Some "treatments" are promoted by the well-intentioned but ill-informed. Other "cures" are advertised by profit-driven charlatans. Anxious, underinformed, and sometimes desperate parents cannot be blamed for latching onto unproven remedies. Here's where science comes to the rescue. Scientific method is the only reliable way to separate evidence-based interventions from quackery.

The rest of this Tenth Mile is all about how to pursue the right interventions for your child.

Identify the Biggest Remaining Factors

If you had one magic wand (or maybe two): At this point in your *Journey*, it's time to consider remaining obstacles. For optimal development, the behavioral strategies described in miles gone by may be necessary but insufficient. Think back to the Gander and ask yourself: "If I only had one magic wand, which facet of my child's profile would I want to wave it over?" In other words, if you could improve just one thing about your child, what would it be? What's the biggest deal? Inflexibility? Impulsivity? Language weaknesses? Family stress? Something else? You might be able to identify one primary source of difficulty and think, "If only *that* were better, then *everything* would be better." Or your child's remaining challenges might be more complicated, in which case you would say: "Thanks, but I really need more than one magic wand!" And if I could, I'd give you extra magic wands.

But it's reality time. In varying degrees, everyone faces limited resources. Even though there's nothing more important than your child's development, there's only so much time, money, and energy that anybody has to spend. Rather than trying to do everything, I recommend getting the most bang for the "intervention buck." Do a few things well instead of a lot of things poorly. Identify your child's primary sources of impairment and spend your limited resources there. Don't waste energy on issues that are secondary or minor. Even if you had unlimited resources, you wouldn't want your child to become some kind of therapeutic pincushion. Just because an intervention is possible does not mean it's necessary or effective. And besides, children should not be forced to spend all their time working on areas of weakness. There's only so much poking and prodding any kid can take. For your child and you, there's got to be some time left over for fun.

You need to set priorities, weigh options, and make some tough decisions. For problems that have proven relatively unresponsive to behavioral strategies, what are the biggest issues standing in the way? What are your child's core factors? Which developmental differences are most at the center of your child's difficulties? Which have the greatest negative impact? What aspects of your child's profile cause the largest amount of drag? What facets should be assigned greater weight?

Look down your child's Gander. Assign each facet of your child's profile a relative weight. This time, using the scale that follows, choose a number that represents the current degree of impairment caused across all problem situations and problem behaviors; that is, all items on the Behavioral Topography Survey. For children with two involved parents, ratings should be done by both. You can also ask for ratings from teachers, therapists, case managers, or others who know your child very well. Certainly, if your child is old enough, you should ask him or her too! This exercise can be a good opportunity for teaching self-understanding. Ratings will inevitably vary from one person to another. However, there's usually some consensus about which developmental differences continue to have the greatest impact.

Across observers, settings, and tasks, which facets of your child's Gander profile seem to be "the biggest deal"?

Relative Impact Scale

Rate each facet: *0, insignificant (no big deal); 1, causes a minor degree of impairment (little deal); 2, causes a moderate degree of impairment (medium deal); 3, causes a severe degree of impairment (bid deal)*

Gander facet	**Relative impact 0–3**
Temperament	
Motor activity level	
Impulsivity	
Attention span	
Initial reaction	
Adaptability	
Intensity of reaction	
Usual mood	
Regularity/predictability	
Sensory	
Hearing speech	
Hearing noise	
Vision	
Taste	
Smell	
Light touch	
Deep touch	
Movement/body position in space	
Internal body awareness/physical symptoms	
Skill	
Fine motor	
Handwriting	
Gross motor	
Speaking	
Listening	
Writing	
Reading	
Understanding spatial relations	
Visual arts	
Music	
Math	
Time awareness	
Planning, organization, and implementation	
Social skills	
Life Stresses	
Physical health, environment, school placement	

At this point, some of you may find that your problem situations, problem behaviors, and impact ratings are all low enough that you don't need any special help. But for those of you with ongoing challenges, the Gander facets with the highest impact ratings should be allocated more intervention resources. Those are the baskets you want to put your eggs in. Those are your primary intervention targets.

Who Ya Gonna Call?

Once you have identified your child's most important sources of persistent impairment, it's important to get some expert advice. You never know what can change until you try. And you may never know how to try until you get some professional help. In some situations, this might just mean reading a good book. In other situations, science-based support can come relatively cheap and easy. But for more serious problems, it makes sense to consult an expert. Who ya gonna call? For each item on the Gander, here's a list of specialists:

- For motor activity level, impulsivity, attention span:
  - Medication: pediatrician, child psychiatrist, developmental-behavioral pediatrician
  - Behavior therapy: behavior analyst, psychologist, social worker
- For initial reaction, adaptability, intensity of reaction, usual mood, regularity/predictability:
  - Cognitive-behavioral therapy: psychologist, social worker, behavior analyst
  - Medication: child psychiatrist, developmental-behavioral pediatrician
- For sensory differences:
  - Occupational therapist, psychologist, behavior analyst
- For fine motor, handwriting:
  - Occupational therapist
- For gross motor:
  - Physical therapist, sports therapist, occupational therapist
- For language: speaking, listening, writing, reading:
  - Speech-language therapist, teacher, tutor
- For understanding spatial relations, visual arts:

    - Art teacher/therapist
- For music:
    - Music teacher/therapist
- For math:
    - Math teacher/tutor
- For time awareness, planning, organization, and implementation:
    - Speech-language therapist, executive skills coach, teacher/tutor
- For social skills:
    - Individual, group, or parent-centered therapy: psychologist, speech-language therapist, social worker, developmental consultant
- For physical health, environmental/life-stresses, school placement:
    - Social worker, primary care or specialist physician, psychologist, marriage counselor, special education consultant

For care coordination: Especially if you're not sure what to do or who to call, you may need a case manager. This person is often *the* missing ingredient when progress depends on setting priorities, coordinating care, and providing ongoing assessment. A case manager can be your pediatrician, school counselor, or one of the specialists listed previously. The case manager is ideally someone with broad developmental expertise and deep familiarity with local resources. Obviously, he or she needs to know your child well and earn your trust. An increasing number of communities have "navigators" who assume this role.

The Science of Choosing Specific Interventions

In God we trust. All others (must) bring data!

—William Edwards Deming (Walton & Deming, 1988)

Extraordinary claims require extraordinary evidence.

—POPULARIZED BY CARL SAGAN

Good doctors do not entirely trust their own judgment, they trust good science. I strongly recommend that you do the same. Some possible interventions have a better evidence base than others. Some have been proven; others disproven. Interventions that have been well-studied may have been found safe and effective, unsafe and ineffective, safe but ineffective, or unsafe but effective. Others just haven't been studied enough to reach any conclusions at all. How can you tell good science from bad science? What should you do if some interventions seem reasonable but lack sufficient research? Consider the following general guidelines.

- ***Seek out objective experts:*** You can't believe everything you hear on TV or read on the Internet. You receive all kinds of advice from friends, family, coworkers, and total strangers. They really do want to help, but what worked for one child may not work for yours. And sometimes that child would have improved anyhow. You are vulnerable. You would do anything to help your child, but don't be naïve. There are some folks out there who cloak themselves in pseudoscience but lack sufficient training. Some make recommendations motivated by profit and self-promotion. Good science distinguishes coincidence from probability; correlation from causation. Trust recommendations from reputable research institutions or professional organizations that have no conflict of interest. Studies should be published in reputable scientific journals; critically reviewed by other experts in the field. Look to major academic and university research centers. To name a few, trust the American Academy of Pediatrics (aap.org), the American Academy of Child and Adolescent Psychiatry (aacap.org), the National Institutes of Health (nih.gov and nimh.gov), the Centers for Disease Control and Prevention (cdc.org), and the Society for Developmental-Behavioral Pediatrics (sdbp.org).

- ***Do not trust just one source or one study:*** Look for interventions that have been repeatedly proven effective. This always means comparing a large number of children in a treatment group against a large number of children in a placebo or nontreatment group. Observers should be blinded to who got the treatment and who didn't. That's the only way to know if improvement was a direct result of the intervention and not due to coincidence or bias. The best interventions show very significant differences between control groups and treatment groups—so-called large effect size. But one good study is never enough. Scientific proof depends on replicability and consensus. Even if the study seems good, stay skeptical. Withhold judgment until different researchers at different centers do the same study and get the same results. Before suspending doubt, look for expert meta-analyses (studies of many studies) and consensus statements from trusted scientific organizations.
- ***Don't speculate, experiment:*** When good research is available, it should guide your initial selection of interventions. You still need to see if it is safe and effective for your child. Just because a treatment has been proven effective for many does not mean that it works for everybody. When good research is not available and there are no proven interventions, you might be tempted to try some options that *seem* safe and promising. Depending on your child's needs, that might be appropriate. Stay hopeful, but skeptical too. Whether the treatment is standard or not, you should conduct a carefully controlled trial for yourself. Here's how.

The Science of Conducting a Treatment Trial

Intervention strategies should be selected according to the best available research and then should always implemented on a trial basis. It is impossible to draw conclusions about the effectiveness of specific strategies if trials are not carefully controlled. The best trials are usually designed and performed in consultation with professionals. Yet even clinicians with sterling reputations must hold themselves accountable and earn your trust. Any responsible professionals should be able to tell you what they are targeting, how they are going to measure it, how they plan to get from the current baseline to a specific goal, and roughly how long it will take. If you or your consultant cannot answer those questions, you should not proceed with the trial. This sometimes means taking the time to find measurable outcomes. Other times this means finding a different therapy or a different therapist.

Let's go over the Treatment Trial Form that follows. Then we'll work through some examples. Feel free to customize this form to fit your child's target symptoms, the chosen intervention, observation intervals, and the possible side effects.

TREATMENT TRIAL FORM for: ______________________________

Child's name: ______________________ Grade: ___________ Year: _______

Person completing this form: ____________ Relation to child: _________________

Usual observation time: *mornings/ afternoons/ evenings/ weekdays/ weekends* (circle)

Observations will be recorded every*: day/ week/ month* (circle)

Dear Parents, Teachers, and Child:
Thank you very much for your help. It is so important to conduct this trial in a careful and controlled fashion. Please complete the table below. If you were not able to make observations for a period, leave that column blank. In addition to these numbers, your written comments are very helpful. On the back, please record the date and provide general impressions, including the following: Were there any problems with the intervention? Were there any benefits? Give details. If you have any questions or concerns, please call. After each set of observations, please copy/e-mail/fax and send to:
Thank you.

During the observation period, how big were these problems?
0 = no problem, 1 = little problem, 2 = medium problem, 3 = big problem

Goal: **Intervention:**	**Baseline**									
DATE ***Targets***										
Possible Side Effects										

How to use the treatment trial form

1. ***Choose a goal:*** What needs to change? Resist the temptation to work on more than one problem at a time. Set priorities. What

is your child's most important remaining challenge? What is it about your child's profile that represents "the biggest deal?" What is your child's greatest and most persistent source of impairment? Write in your overall intervention goal on the trial form.

2. ***Choose an intervention strategy:*** As discussed previously, good science depends on controlled and reproducible experimentation. Avoid speculation, bias, and fad. Objectively weigh relative risks and benefits. Using your best judgment, consulting experts and the best available scientific information, choose your intervention and write it on the form.
3. ***Establish baseline measures for targets and possible side effects:*** After choosing a goal, decide on specific targets and outcome measures. How will you know if your intervention is working? To objectively evaluate positive and negative changes, you need to know where you started. For the chosen intervention, you and your consultant should list possible benefits and risks. On the trial form, record the date, and then rate targets *and* possible side effects at baseline:
   - 0 for no problem
   - 1 for little problem
   - 2 for medium problem
   - 3 for big problem

   Note: Just because something is listed as a *possible* side effect does not necessarily mean it wasn't a problem *before* the trial or that it might not get *better* during the trial. Also, if you don't have any 2s or 3s for targets at baseline, you probably don't need to do the intervention!
4. ***Establish observation intervals:*** How long would it take for this strategy to start working? How long would it take to see an optimal response? Some interventions take more time. If so, we need to be patient, stay the course, and give the intervention a fair chance. Other interventions work quickly or not at all. In these cases, we should not wait so long to reassess that we miss early signs of change, either troubling

or promising. With the help of an experienced expert, decide how often to reassess your child's response to the intervention; daily, biweekly, weekly, or monthly. On the Treatment Trial Form, write in observation dates accordingly.

5. ***Observe:*** If an intervention works, it should help your child's everyday functioning. There should be observable positive results outside the walls of an expert's office. Meaningful assessment of real-life results usually depends on pooling observations across different people, settings, and tasks. Sometimes, to eliminate bias, you may deliberately "blind" observers to the type of intervention. Other times it's helpful to let everyone know what's going on. Whenever possible, your child should participate in the trial and feel included in his or her own care. Your child's observations are valuable. Some things you can tell better than your child. But other things your child can tell better than you. Your child's participation in his or her treatment trial also represents a wonderful opportunity to teach self-monitoring, self-regulation, and self-advocacy.
6. ***Evaluate and reevaluate:*** With each new set of observations, compare baseline and follow-up ratings. Write in any unanticipated effects, either positive or negative. Where do we seem to be heading with this strategy? Overall, we will consider the intervention a success if the 2s and 3s for targets on the top half of the rating scale come down to 0s and 1s; and the baseline numbers for possible side effects on the bottom half do not go up.
   a. *Promising:* If numerical ratings of targets are tracking steadily downward or all turn to 0s and 1s, while ratings of potential side effects have not gone up at all, then stay the course. Looking good!
   b. *Disappointing or even harmful:* If numerical ratings of targets have not gone down and ratings of possible side effects have gone up, then modify or stop. Not what we hoped for.
   c. *Inconclusive:* If ratings of targets and possible side effects remain unchanged (essentially at baseline levels), then it

might make sense to give it more time, intensify, modify, or abandon. Consult your expert and sort it out. It's sometimes hard to know for sure. To clarify, you can deliberately start (A) and stop (B) the intervention; then start (A) and stop (B) again. Other times you can compare one strategy (A) against a different strategy (B); back (A)-and-forth (B). These "ABAB" design trials can be very useful. Sometimes this is the only way to clear up confusion about cause-effect connection, evaluate relative effectiveness of one intervention versus another, and see if a previously effective intervention is still making a difference (a discontinuation trial).

Confused? Let's get practical and take a look at four different treatment trials:

1. Medication trial for ADHD
2. Occupational therapy trial for poor handwriting
3. Gluten-free/casein-free (GF-CF) diet for irritability
4. *Parent Child Journey* program for behavior management

Medication Trial for ADHD

Ironically, of all pediatric developmental interventions, stimulant medication for ADHD is supported by the largest number of good studies, yet it remains one of the most controversial treatments. Medication management is a safe, effective, and crucial intervention for properly diagnosed ADHD; that is, hyperactivity, impulsivity, and/or distractibility causing significant impairment over time and across tasks, settings, and observers (Barkley, 2014). A comprehensive review of the research literature is beyond the scope of this book (American Academy of Pediatrics, 2011). But the science is in (the MTA Cooperative Group, 1999). Here, I will settle for footnoting a few of the many scientific sources and quoting two leading researchers (Barkley, 2005).

According to Dr. John Weery: "In any other medical or psychiatric condition where the evidence for drug efficacy is this substantial and for drug side effects is this benign, the failure of a physician to consider medication treatment for the disorder would be considered tantamount to malpractice" (Barkley, 2005).

According to Barkley (2005): "The idea that human self-control is largely self-determined and largely instilled by one's parents during childhood should be discarded on history's conceptual scrap heap. Until such time as more effective treatments having even fewer side effects have been scientifically identified, the use of stimulant medication as part of a larger treatment package for the management of ADHD should be a first-line and mainstay treatment, without apology."

According to his father, Phillip had always been "a live one." As a toddler, he was fun but "high maintenance." He'd been "counseled out" of two different nursery schools for being a "little tornado." In kindergarten, the teacher had to keep him right next to her all the time. Even then, he called out constantly. He got too physical with other kids and liked to "breakdance" on the floor. Through the fall of Phillip's first-grade year, the teacher expressed concern about his availability for learning. One day Phillip came home and asked his mom, "Am I stupid? That's what Tommy said."

Phillip's parents called his pediatrician, Dr. Mehta. He had them and his teacher do some screening questionnaires. Dr. Mehta spoke with the teacher on the phone. He asked Phillip's parents to send a video of him playing with other kids. He blocked out an hour at the end of a day to talk with them in detail. Then he blocked out twenty minutes another day to watch Phillip play, write, read, and do some puzzles. He also asked Phillip some questions. Dr. Mehta met with Phillip's parents again and explained, "Phillip's ADHD is pretty obvious." They agreed. He reviewed the science and recommended a carefully controlled trial of stimulant medication. They decided to consult a subspecialist if the trial didn't go well but start the medication trial with Dr. Mehta. Dr. Mehta told Phillip: "Ya know how sometimes it's hard for you to sit still and pay attention? How sometimes it's hard to stop and think? Well, I've got some medicine that might make all that easier for you. Whaddaya say we give it a try?"

Phillip said, "OK."

Dr. Mehta asked Phillip's parents and teacher to do baseline ratings off medication, then repeat their ratings twice each week. He made a simpler rating scale for Phillip with just a few items: "stop and think," "distracted," and "sit still." For each item, he had Phillip circle a smiley face, neutral face, or frowny face to indicate no problem, little problem, or big problem. Phillip's parents faxed their scales along with Phillip's and the teacher's every Tuesday and Friday and then spoke with Dr. Mehta for five minutes as scheduled.

Phillip started with a very low dose of long-acting methylphenidate. At 2.5, 5.0, and 7.5 mg, nothing much happened, good or bad. But then at 10.0 mg, most of the 2s and 3s came down to 0s and 1s. Phillip's frowny face turned smiley. And there were no side effects. He was still missing details and forgetting stuff, but as the doctor explained, that might have had more to do with Phillip's learning profile than his ADHD per se. Still, they decided to try 12.5 mg just to see. At that higher dose, there was no additional improvement and some side effects appeared. Phillip lost some of his appetite. More upsetting to his parents, Phillip lost some of his sparkling personality. He got a little irritable and edgy. He did not seem as interested in playing with his friends. Dr. Mehta reassured Phillip's parents that this would all return to normal if they just went back to the 10 mg dose and settled for "a triple, not a home-run." Just as he said, the 10 mg seemed plenty good enough. Phillip was back to himself—minus the severe ADHD symptoms.

Here's what his treatment trial form looked like.

TREATMENT TRIAL FORM for: ADHD Medication

Child's name: Phillip Doe Grade: 1st Year: 2016

Person completing this form: Mrs. Smith Relation to child: teacher

Usual observation time: *mornings/ afternoons/ evenings/ weekdays/ weekends* (circle)

Observations will be recorded every: *twice each week*

Dear Parents, Teachers, and Child:
Thank you very much for your help. It is so important to conduct this trial in a careful and controlled fashion. Please complete the table below. If you were not able to make observations for a period, leave that column blank. In addition to these numbers, your written comments are very helpful. On the back, please record the date and provide general impressions, including the following: Were there any problems with the intervention? Were there any benefits? Give details. If you have any questions or concerns, please call. After each set of observations, please copy/e-mail/fax and send to:

Dr. Mehta: 222-222-2222

Thank you.

During the observation period, how big were these problems?
0 = no problem, 1 = little problem, 2 = medium problem, 3 = big problem

Goal: reduce ADHD symptoms Intervention: Methylphenidate-ER (mg)	Baseline 0	2.5	5.0	7.5	10	12.5	10
DATE	***5/2***	***5/5***	***5/8***	***5/10***	***5/15***	***5/19***	***5/22***
Targets							
Restless, squirmy, fidgety, on-the go	3	3	2	2	1	0	1
Demands must be met immediately	2	3	2	2	1	1	1
Distractibility/attention problem	2	2	2	3	1	0	1
Problems with peer relations	2	2	2	2	1	1	1
Misses important details	3	2	2	3	2	2	1
Excitable, impulsive	3	3	2	2	1	0	1
Fails to finish things	2	3	3	2	1	1	1
Problems controlling behavior	2	2	3	2	1	0	1
Easily frustrated	1	2	1	2	0	1	1
Difficulty learning	2	2	2	2	1	1	1
Disorganized/time mismanagement	1	1	1	1	1	1	1
Forgetful, loses things	2	2	2	2	2	2	2
Possible Side Effects							
Poor appetite	1	1	1	1	1	2	1
Trouble falling/staying asleep	-	-	-	-	-	-	-
Irritability/sadness	0	0	0	0	1	3	1
Social withdrawal	0	0	0	0	0	2	0
Tics/nervous habits	1	1	1	1	1	1	1
Headaches/stomachaches/dizziness	0	0	0	0	0	0	0
Drowsiness	0	0	0	0	0	0	0
Anxiety/nightmares	2	2	2	2	1	2	0
Stares off/daydreams	1	1	1	1	0	0	0

Two weeks later, Dr. Mehta had Phillip come back with his parents. Phillip's mom said, "You forgot to put two things on your chart, Doc."

Dr. Mehta asked, "What?"

Smiling, Phillip's mom said, "Number one: Does your boy think he's pretty smart after all?"

Phillip's dad added, "Number two: Are your boy's parents happy again?"

With the help of his stop-and-think medicine, Phillip finished off the school year doing great. After talking with Dr. Mehta, Philip's parents decided to keep him on the medicine through the summer. Clearly it helped Phillip just as much outside of school. For the first time, other kids wanted to play with him. And he wanted to have real conversations with his parents.

In the fall, Phillip had a great new teacher. On medication, he was doing so well that his parents wondered if he still needed to take it. They called Dr. Mehta, who suggested having the teacher do baseline ratings on medication, then follow-up ratings during a trial week off. After the second day off medication, the teacher faxed the form and called to talk with Phillip's parents. All the 0s and 1s had turned back into 2s and 3s. Phillip and his parents repeated the experiment on the weekends and found the same thing. Phillip told his mom and dad, "I want my medicine again." They agreed.

Phillip's case is not unusual, but, of course, things do not always go this well. Success varies with each child. If you're not so lucky with a first medication, don't give up. Carefully trying others will often prove well worth your patience. No matter what happens, the medication trial form helps with data collection, communication, and decision making. Always do medication trials in very close communication with an expert physician.

Occupational Therapy Trial for Poor Handwriting

Let's shift gears and take a look at using the treatment trial form for a different kind of intervention.

Joe's parents were concerned about his handwriting. They couldn't read it. His teacher couldn't read it, and Joe couldn't read it either. Plus, he hated writing. He held his pencil all wrong. His hand hurt after just a few lines. Whenever Joe had to write anything, he made excuses, shut down, or melted down. The school recommended an occupational therapy (OT) consultation.

From October through November, the occupational therapist pulled Joe out of class and worked with him for thirty minutes every week. He learned how to hold the pencil better, but his handwriting did not improve, and he still shut down. Plus, he felt very self-conscious about being pulled from class. The teacher reported that he did not know what was going on when he returned from OT time. So through December, Joe's parents had him take a break from OT. They lined up private OT at home. Joe did not mind this so much. His friends didn't know, and he didn't miss class. The private therapist was really fun, and she helped him with his homework. He didn't tantrum so much. But still, his handwriting didn't improve, and it was costing Joe's parents a lot of money. They kept track of all this on a treatment trial form.

TREATMENT TRIAL FORM for: handwriting OT

Child's name: Joe Jones Grade: 3rd Year: 2016

Person completing this form: Mrs. Smith Relation to child: teacher

Usual observation time: *mornings/ afternoons/ evenings/ weekdays/ weekends* (circle)

Observations will be recorded every: *day/ week/ month* (circle)

Dear Parents, Teachers, and Child:
Thank you very much for your help. It is so important to conduct this trial in a careful and controlled fashion. Please complete the table below. If you were not able to make observations for a period, leave that column blank. In addition to these numbers, your written comments are very helpful. On the back, please record the date and provide general impressions, including the following: Were there any problems with the intervention? Were there any benefits? Give details. If you have any questions or concerns, please call. After each set of observations, please copy/e-mail/fax and send to:

Joe's parents

Thank you.

During the observation period, how big were these problems?
0=no problem, 1= little problem, 2=medium problem, 3=big problem

Goal: better writing **Intervention: OT**	**Baseline**	School	school	break	home	Home
DATE ***Targets***	***10/3***	***11/1***	***12/4***	***1/7***	***2/2***	***3/5***
Legibility	**3**	**3**	**3**	**3**	**2**	**2**
Amount written	3	3	3	3	2	2
Avoidance of writing tasks	3	3	3	3	2	2
Tantrums about writing	3	3	3	3	2	1
Possible Side Effects						
Child stress	2	3	3	2	2	1
Stigma	1	3	3	2	1	1
Missed class instruction	0	1	2	0	0	0
Cost	0	0	0	0	3	3

Joe's parents knew that OT helped other kids, but it just didn't seem to make much difference for Joe. They shifted from fixing to accommodating. At a school meeting, the team agreed to reduce Joe's written workload, allow dictation, and get him going with keyboarding. These bypass strategies worked better.

Gluten-Free/Casein-Free (GF-CF) Diet Trial for Irritability

Jamie was a girl with autism and severe tantrums. Jamie's parents read online that some children with autism have mood problems because of a "gut-brain" connection. They asked their pediatrician, Dr. Sanchez, about the GF-CF diet. She wasn't so sure about this. Dr. Sanchez found some studies that confirmed her skepticism (Hyman et al., 2016). Respectfully, she shared her research, but said, "If you want to try it anyhow, just be scientific."

They asked, "What do you mean?"

Dr. Sanchez helped them set up a treatment trial. She explained that food elimination trials were best done with an ABAB design; specifically, twelve weeks on the diet, twelve weeks off, twelve weeks on, twelve weeks off. That way, they could be more certain whether changes were just coincidental or the direct result of the diet. Jamie was already a picky eater. Why eliminate two major food groups unless they were sure it was going to make a big difference? After recording baseline observations, they changed Jamie's diet every two weeks: on, off, on, off. They continued recording. They had Jamie's teacher do the same thing. At the end of the trial, parent and teacher ratings were very much the same.

TREATMENT TRIAL FORM for: diet and mood

Child's name: Jamie age: 2 and ½

Person completing this form: mom

Observations will be recorded every: *12 weeks*

During the observation period, how big were these problems?
0=no problem, 1= little problem, 2=medium problem, 3=big problem

Goal: better mood **Intervention:** GF-CF diet	Baseline OFF	ON	OFF	ON	OFF
DATE	***4/1***	***7/1***	***10/1***	***1/1***	***4/1***
Targets					
Irritability	**3**	**2**	**3**	**3**	**3**
Meltdowns	3	1	2	3	3
Emotional inflexibility	2	1	3	3	3
Trouble with transitions	3	3	3	3	3
Aggression	2	2	2	2	2
Possible Side Effects					
Resistance to diet	0	2	0	3	0
Poor nutrition	1	2	1	3	1
Trouble eating at friends	0	2	0	2	0
Cost	1	2	1	2	1

At first, they thought the diet might actually be working. Some of the numbers came down. But they weren't sure that Jamie's improved mood was from the diet. After all, her older brother was on spring vacation. He was relieved to be off school. His parents didn't have to help him with homework. The weather was great, and the kids played outside together all day long. Going back on the diet just happened to coincide with the end of spring vacation and a rainy week. Jamie's mood turned sour again. But what was causing what? Then in May, the truth became clear. Whether on or off the diet, Jamie's numbers stayed high. Meanwhile, it became harder and harder to stick to the diet. Jamie's parents figured that this diet experiment was worth a try but not worth continuing.

Parent Child Journey Training Trial for Behavior Management

Let's not have any double standards. What about the effectiveness of the interventions recommended in this program? Although the *Parent Child Journey* has some unique features, it is based on a solid body of research. Over the years, there have been hundreds of studies documenting the effectiveness of the strategies presented here. When these techniques are used as part of an integrated parent training program, study after study demonstrates significant improvement in child behavior outcomes (Furlong et al., 2012; Wyatt Kaminski, Valle, Filene, & Boyle, 2008).

In more than thirty years of parent group training, using variations of the *Parent Child Journey* program, I have collected baseline and follow-up data from participants. At the beginning and the end of the ten sessions, parents have completed variations of the Behavioral Topography Survey; that is, the problem situations and behavior topographical analysis. I have also asked parents to describe their own feelings about the course. Parents were encouraged to be honest and objective in their assessment of course benefits and side effects.

My data (unpublished) has been encouraging. Although I do not have longer-term follow-up data, on average and consistent with the research literature, my pre- and post-course parent ratings consistently show significant positive change:

- At least 75 percent and up to 95 percent reported 10 to 25 percent improvement (significant but small effect size)
- At least 25 percent and up to 50 percent reported 25 to 50 percent improvement (moderate effect size)
- At least 10 percent and up to 25 percent reported better than 50 percent improvement (large effect size)

Based on a large body of research and my own outcome measures, was it reasonable for you to try the *Parent Child Journey*? Yes. Does this mean that it works for everybody? No. But how has it worked for you so far? To a large degree, your results depend on how well you did your homework. Until you consistently implement these strategies and fine-tune your approach, your trial is not done. Let's assume that you did a pretty good job. If you used *circles* on the precourse Behavioral Topography Survey, you could use *triangles* to indicate your postcourse ratings. Did your 2s and 3s come down to 1s and 2s? Did your 1s and 2s come down to 0s and 1s? In this way, you can use your Behavioral Topography Survey as a treatment trial rating form for this course. Like in the example of Felipe and Nancy that follows, you could use the Behavioral Topography Survey numbers and customize a treatment trial form to highlight the specific behaviors that led you to the *Parent Child Journey* in the first place.

> *Felipe and Nancy took a* Parent Child Journey *course to help with their daughter Maria's behavior. Together they made a treatment trial form to sum up their experience with parent training. They started the ten-session course in September and finished in December. Felipe and Nancy rated Maria's most problematic behaviors at baseline, then monthly until the course was over. Here's what they recorded.*

TREATMENT TRIAL FORM for: parent behavior management training

Child's name: Maria Rodriguez Grade: preschool Year: 2016

Person completing this form: Felipe and Nancy Relation to child: parents

Usual observation time: *mornings/afternoons/evenings/weekdays/weekends* (circle)

Observations will be recorded every: *day/week/month* (circle)

Dear Parents, Teachers, and Child:
Thank you very much for your help. It is so important to conduct this trial in a careful and controlled fashion. Please complete the table below. If you were not able to make observations for a period, leave that column blank. In addition to these numbers, your written comments are very helpful. On the back, please record the date and provide general impressions, including the following: Were there any problems with the intervention? Were there any benefits? Give details. If you have any questions or concerns, please call. After each set of observations, please copy/e-mail/fax and send to:

Dr. Shapiro

Thank you.

During the observation period, how big were these problems? 0 = no problem, 1 = little problem, 2 = medium problem, 3 = big problem

Goal: better behavior **Intervention:** ***Parent Child Journey*** **parent group** **10 sessions**	**(Pre)** **baseline**	Fourth Mile	Eighth Mile	**(Post)** Tenth Mile plus
DATE ***Targets***	***9/1***	***10/1***	***11/1***	***12/1***
Getting ready in the morning	3	2	2	1
Mealtime	2	2	1	1
Unstructured free time	3	3	1	0
Getting ready for bed	3	3	2	2
Temper tantrums	2	2	0	0
Defiance	2	2	1	1
Parent frustration	3	2	1	0
Parent isolation	2	1	1	1
Possible Side Effects				
Parent stress	0	1	1	1
Time spent	0	1	1	1
Finding babysitter	0	2	1	0
Conflict with wife	3	1	0	0

By the end of the program, Felipe and Nancy were both pleased with the results. Maria's 2s and 3s had turned into mostly 0s and 1s. It was a little stressful rushing from work and finding a babysitter, but they both came to most sessions. And at least one of them came to every

session. Most importantly, every mile, they talked about the strategies and did their homework. For the first time in their marriage, they felt like they were really working as a team. Before the course, Maria's behavior had stressed their relationship. Funny how her tantrums ended up bringing them closer together. Meeting other parents and hearing them talk, they did not feel so alone. They even became close friends with one of the other couples who had a "similarly different" child.

Nurturing Strengths and Interests

Boat maintenance never really ends. There's always more bailing and patching to do. But attending to leaks does not have to mean ignoring the wind at our backs. Likewise, raising a challenging child is a long-term project. Your child will continue to need your help. Over the years, parents and professionals may focus too much on a child's weaknesses and not enough on his or her strengths. When considering allocation of time, money, and energy, we should not forget to spend at least as much on natural abilities and interests. Strengths-based interventions are crucial for positive self-image, social connection, and success. So let's try to balance this boat and raise some "sails."

Your child's long-term success may depend more on "strengthening strengths" than "fixing weaknesses." But much also depends on broadening your idea of what success means. College is right for many but not for all. Children sometimes end up working in the family business; other times not. Success does not necessarily mean realizing dreams and being "the best." For most, success means pursuing opportunities and "doing well enough."

Some in the disability rights movement have criticized the so-called "Myth of the Super-Crip;" that is, the idea that, "If you just work hard enough, you can do anything" (Shapiro, 1994). "Super crips" have climbed Mount Everest, won Olympic medals, gained acceptance to

Harvard, and won academic prizes, all despite significant disabilities. These tales can be inspirational, but they can also be demoralizing. After all, disabled or not, most of us could never come close to these accomplishments. To suggest that grit and perseverance can close all achievement gaps is unrealistic and potentially harmful. Even the strongest winds and the biggest sails can't really make boats fly. However, if you and your child set realistic goals, then he or she may still feel like soaring when the possible is achieved.

The most important measure of a successful childhood is not getting into the "best college." Ultimately and more practically, success is really about getting and keeping a good enough job. Sure, strengths and interests should be pursued for the sake of positive self-image, social connection, and pleasure. All are important. But your child's strengths profile may also guide vocational education and career choice. School requires children to demonstrate proficiency across a broad range of academic domains. But most of us are not good in all school subjects. And most people end up in jobs that depend more on real-life experience than traditional academic skill sets. More children, especially those with significant developmental weaknesses, should be encouraged to specialize early in life, pursue interests that are intrinsically motivating, and develop legitimate expertise in areas of strength. For every hour your children spend crunching through homework, maybe they should spend at least one hour pursuing their true passions and natural abilities. Encourage your child to choose his or her own journey.

Homework for the Tenth Mile

1. Assign each facet of the Gander a number that reflects its potential for ongoing negative impact. Can these areas of need be successfully accommodated? Which facets of your child's profile require intervention most? Consult an expert. Review the science. Consider all possible benefits and side effects. Set up a well-controlled treatment trial.
2. Assign each facet of the Gander a number that reflects its potential for positive impact. Be sure to give your child regular opportunities to enhance these natural skills and pursue these passions.

EPI-"LOG": A DIFFERENT ENDING

• • •

The way up and the way down are one and the same.

—HERACLITUS (2001)

HISTORY OF RAPHUS CUCULLATUS

It must be so.

—RICHARD DAWKINS, *RIVER OUT OF EDEN: A DARWINIAN VIEW OF LIFE* (1996)

One day, Hawk flew away and never came back. Raph let go of the wheel and sat down in the boat. Alone. Raph let the boat drift all the way back down the river. Raph watched the shoreline pass by. After a while, Raph noticed that everywhere they'd stopped, little tambalacoque trees were beginning to grow. The fruit they'd eaten. The seeds they'd pooped. The pebbles they'd kicked to drive those seeds into the ground. The farther Raph drifted downriver, the taller the trees. Each tambalacoque tree was stronger and more majestic than the last. Then there were a few with little buds. And finally, Raph saw a few tambalacoque trees bearing large, ripe fruit.

Raph called out, "I want tambalacoque!" Magically, one tambalacoque fruit appeared in the water, bobbing and floating right up to the boat. Raph caught the sweet fruit in its beak. Raph took a bite-and smiled.

• • •

In the Indian Ocean, off the southeast coast of Africa, is a huge island called Madagascar. Just a bit farther east is a tiny island called Mauritius. There, in the woods near the water, lived a bird named *Raphus cucullatus*; or for short, as affectionately nicknamed in this book, Raph. This bird was descended from a proud old family of pigeons and doves. But in many ways, Raph was a bird of a different feather.

Raph was a big bird, standing more than three feet tall and weighing more than thirty pounds. Raph had brown-gray feathers all over its body, a little extra tuft of feathers for a tail, but no feathers at all on its head. In fact, Raph's last name, *cucullatus*, means "wearing a hood." Raph's beak was very large: black, yellow, and red, with a huge bulb for smelling. Like a turkey, Raph kept rocks in its gizzard for grinding up swallowed food. Raph's wings were too weak to fly. But with big yellow feet and strong, sturdy legs, Raph could walk around just fine. And there was plenty of ground food, mostly nuts and fruits.

Raph's favorite fruit was the tambalacoque, a round, juicy kind of peach with a woody pit containing its seeds. Raph enjoyed picking up tambalacoque fruit with its beak and grinding up the pit with stones in its gizzard.

On the little island of Mauritius, Raph had plenty of friends and no enemies. With nothing to fear, there was no need to fly. Raph only needed to lay one egg at a time to ensure its family's survival.

Even if Raph was a different kind of bird, Mauritius suited Raph just fine. And in one very special way, Raph suited the island of Mauritius.

Not only did Raph get big eating tambalacoque fruit, the tambalacoque tree flourished thanks to Raph. Each time Raph ate tambalacoque fruit, seeds germinated in Raph's intestines. With each poop, Raph disseminated tambalacoque seeds. The more tambalacoque fruit Raph ate, the more tambalacoque seeds were planted. A win-win, bird-tree relationship! Talk about recycling! Propagation through defecation!

For thousands of years, there were no human beings on the island of Mauritius. But then, starting in the 1500s, Portuguese explorers made occasional visits. The Raphinae family's first sustained encounters with people were not until about 1600, when Dutch sailors came to Mauritius. They had never seen birds like Raph. These birds didn't know flight or fear. They were defenseless and naive. The Dutch easily killed them, ate them, and destroyed their habitat. The Dutch boats also brought cats, rats, pigs, and monkeys. These nonnative animals ate the Raphinae family's eggs. Extinction came quickly.

This strange bird is now known as the "dodo." It's not clear how such a derogatory name originated. The most generous explanation is that "dodo" might have been an approximation of the bird's call, a two-note pigeon-like sound, "doo-doo." More likely, and still not so bad, "dodo" might have been a term related to the Dutch word *Dodaars*, which means either "fat-arse" or "knot-arse," referring to the tuft of feathers on its hind end. But because these flightless and fearless birds were so easily caught, it's likely that "dodo" came from the Dutch word *dodoor* for "sluggard" or the Portuguese word "*doudo*" (currently *doido*), meaning "fool" or "crazy." Despite this uncertainty about origins, everybody today knows to "go the way of the dodo" means to be "dead as a dodo" because you clearly must have been "stupid as a dodo."

The last living bird from the Raphinae family was seen in 1662. But the name "dodo"—and a very important message—lives on.

History of the Tambalacoque Tree

"Never let a crisis go to waste."

—Rahm Emmanuel

Sideroxylon grandiflorum, known as the tambalacoque tree, is endemic to the island of Mauritius. It is a majestic tree with many strong roots and sprawling, thick branches that provide plenty of shade. Each tree normally lives for hundreds of years.

As you have already read, the Raphinae family needed the tambalacoque tree for food, and the tree needed the bird to be its "Johnny Appleseed." Up through its extinction in the seventeenth century, Raphinae ate the tambalacoque fruit and spread the seeds. Because of this mutually beneficial relationship, the tambalacoque became known as the "dodo tree." But if so linked in life, what would keep the "dodo" and "dodo tree" from being likewise linked in death? Was the tambalacoque tree too dependent on the Raphinae?

Over the centuries, since the last of the Raphinae died, there has been a steady decline in the number of tambalacoque trees. But this sad story has a hopeful epilogue. Ironically, the rapid extinction of the Raphinae helped inspire the wildlife conservation movement. *Raphus* became a powerful early "poster bird" for protection of other endangered species. Locally, alarmed by the dodo bird's fate, Mauritians devoted themselves to saving its namesake tree. Globally, recognition of the bird and tree's mutual decline served as a cautionary tale about the interconnection of all life. To whatever degree Raph's extinction endangered the tambalacoque, their relationship shed light on the importance of protecting individual species for the sake of entire ecosystems.

The seventeenth century was a terrible time to be a flightless bird. There were no conservationists around to save the Raphinae. But their extinction made the twenty-first century a more encouraging time for the tambalacoque tree. Legions now rally to protect the tambalacoque tree and the diversity of all natural life. One can only wonder: What if Raph was alive today? Would it be listed as an endangered species? Would hunting be illegal? Would people defend its habitat? Moreover, would it still be called a dodo bird?

Neurodiversity Lives

Decade by decade, more children are being identified with all types of developmental disabilities. Many complicated factors account for this rise. Much of the increase is because of broader diagnostic categories, better identification, and heightened sensitivity. Children with special needs have always been around. But they have been hidden from view in basements, institutions, and prisons, or otherwise marginalized by blame, shame, and derogatory names. Relatively "flightless" but completely innocent, they are not "dodos." They are our children. They are us. And we are all in the same boat together. With limited resources, our crisis—our challenge—is how to provide services, education, and jobs for the growing number of children and adults with special needs.

Despite this crisis—perhaps because of it—the twenty-first century has become a much more hopeful time to have a child with developmental differences. These children are finally getting recognition and help. The Americans with Disabilities Act prohibits discrimination against individuals with disabilities. The Individuals with Disabilities Education Act guarantees early intervention, special education, and related services to infants, children, and adolescents with disabilities. The disability rights and inclusion movements grow stronger every year. A powerful army of parents, providers, educators, and researchers have spearheaded a truly revolutionary change in sensitivity, expertise, and advocacy. Brain science and developmental practice continue to advance at an extraordinary pace. There is a growing awareness of the need to keep neurodiversity alive. We are only as great as our compassion for one another, not despite but *because of* our wonderful differences.

A Different Approach

In my own Greater Washington, DC, community, we have excellent public and private schools, world-class clinical and research centers, and strong networks of devoted professionals and parents. When I speak with colleagues around the country and the world, I am reminded of how very fortunate we are in this economically advantaged region. But even here, there is a crisis in the affordability and availability of care for children with developmental differences.

Quite by accident, through "a series of spontaneous mutations and natural selection," a different kind of developmental care seems to be evolving in this and other little corners of the world. Thirty years ago, I began offering behavior-management training for small groups of parents in my primary-care pediatrics practice. There were usually ten to twelve folks sitting in a circle, sharing and learning together. But then came four cervical spine operations for me. Luckily, I was able to adapt by narrowing my focus to developmental-behavioral pediatrics. Suddenly, this shift to an underdoctored specialty turned me into a scarce commodity. Like all physicians in developmental-behavioral pediatrics, my waiting list for new patients grew longer and longer.

Things took a turn when my colleague Dr. Sarah Wayland secured a grant for me to offer this group training program at a very low price in an underserved area. Instead of the usual intimate group of a dozen or so, more than eighty parents came. These parents would not have been able to afford weekly training sessions otherwise. They sat for ninety-minute sessions on folding metal chairs in a community center all-purpose room. Much to my amazement, there was strength in numbers. These parents made one another feel less alone in their struggles. They motivated one another to learn and change. There was positive energy. The large group format worked surprisingly well.

Since then, I have offered this program to groups of fifty to eighty parents on a regular basis. Dr. Wayland has continued to run groups too. We have met at various venues around town—always on a pay-what-you-can basis. The fates of participants have become intertwined. In a beautiful display of "obligate mutuality," parents have paid a range of registration fees, some below the recommended range and some above, all supporting one another. This fascinating experiment in cross-germination continues to bear fruit to this day. To the best of my knowledge, this very large group/ pay-what-you-can format represents a unique response to the crisis in availability and affordability of developmental-behavioral services. I encourage other professionals to give this model a try.

Thanks to the input of parent group participants, the content of this program has morphed from one version into another. This first published edition of *Parent Child Journey* is just the latest reincarnation. No doubt it will keep on evolving. *Parent Child Journey* depends on your feedback and suggestions. Thanks for letting me know what worked for you and what didn't. Like Raph and the tambalacoque fruit, if you sniffed out this Journey, swallowed it whole, and liked its taste, please feel free to disseminate. Enjoy your sweet children. Believe in your ability to plant and nourish seeds for generations to come.

RETURN MIGRATION: REPRISE OF THE TALE OF HAWK AND RAPH

• • •

Hawk soared high over the river. Down below, he saw a little boat with a funny-looking bird. It was drifting downstream, toward Great Falls. Hawk flew down and perched on the boat. Hawk screeched, "You're going to kill yourself staying in that tiny tub! Fly away, you stupid bird!"

But the strange bird just stood there in its boat and said, "I would if I could."

Hawk couldn't believe it. Incredulously, he asked, "What kind of bird doesn't even know how to fly?"

The odd bird answered, "*Raphus cucullatus*, of course. You can call me Raph." Then Raph added, "I want tambalacoque."

Well, Hawk had never heard of a *Raphus cucullatus* bird—or tambalacoque! All Hawk knew was that Raph was soon to be a goner. The sound of Great Falls was getting louder and louder. Hawk grabbed Raph in his talons and flapped his wings-hard. Hawk didn't get twenty feet before realizing that Raph was just too heavy, so Hawk dropped Raph back on the boat and thought, *Not much more I can do here.*

Hawk started to fly away. But Raph called out, "I want tambalacoque."

Hawk muttered, "What am I getting myself into?"

Hawk sighed, swooped back down, and perched on the back of the boat. Hawk's talons dug deep into the stern. Hawk's wings flapped hard. The little boat moved up the river, far away from the falls. Raph was safe, but Hawk was exhausted. No way could Hawk push Raph's boat all the way up the river. What to do?

Just then, for no good reason, Raph said, "I want to go back down the river."

Hawk said, "Remember Great Falls. Raph, you need to go up the river!"

Raph said, "No, I don't. I don't care about Great Falls!"

Hawk yelled, "You have to do as I say!"

Again, Raph yelled back, "No, I don't!"

Back and forth they fought. The little boat rocked from side to side. Before they knew it, they'd thrown each other overboard. Underwater, they struggled to breathe-but they kept on fighting.

Finally, the fight ended. Maybe Hawk won the fight. Or maybe Hawk just gave up. Who can remember, and what did it matter? Raph and Hawk drifted backward in the cold water. The boat drifted beside them. The sound of Great Falls again grew louder. Somehow, Hawk and Raph dragged themselves back onto the boat. Hawk flapped and pushed the boat ashore, safe once more. Staying at different ends of the boat, not saying a word, they caught their breath. Just then, a round fruit fell out of a tree and into the boat.

Raph cried, "Tambalacoque!" and he ate it with one joyful gulp.

Hawk smiled and thought, *So that's what tambalacoque is.* At that moment, Hawk knew they were in this boat together.

As they fell asleep, exhausted, Hawk wondered, *What kind of bird is this anyhow?*

In the morning, Hawk and Raph started up the river. The current was strong. It wasn't long before they ran into trouble. There were logs. There was lightning. There were rocks. It wasn't easy traveling.

After a while, Hawk decided that they should take a break and just let the boat drift ashore. They pulled up on the bank. Raph was relieved to get back on land. Hawk was glad to perch up in a tree. First Raph pooped. Then Raph kicked a pebble into the water and watched it skip across the surface. Raph glanced up to see if Hawk was watching. Hawk smiled. Raph kicked another pebble. It skipped even farther. Raph looked up again. Hawk flew down and tried kicking a pebble like Raph did. They had fun kicking pebbles together.

Raph said, "I didn't know hawks kicked pebbles."

Hawk said, "I didn't know hawks kicked pebbles either."

They both laughed. Then Hawk flew off high into the sky. Hawk had been stuck on the boat with Raph awhile. It felt good to be airborne again. After a good fly, Hawk collected a few more tambalacoque fruit and came back to Raph.

Hawk squawked at Raph, "Time to get back on the boat."

But Raph didn't seem to hear. Raph was too busy kicking pebbles.

Hawk squawked again. Nothing. So Hawk tickled Raph's tail tuft.

Raph looked up: "What?" Hawk squawked to come.

Hawk pointed to the boat. Raph looked confused. Finally, Hawk just got on the boat.

"Oh," cooed Raph. "Why didn't you say so?"

But Raph was never eager to leave the shore and get back on the boat. Raph always wanted to kick "just one more" pebble. Hawk tried different ways to get Raph back onboard. Sometimes Raph came if Hawk sang and danced in the air.

Sometimes Hawk squawked and sang, but Raph still wouldn't stop playing on the shore. So Hawk just flew to the boat and waited.

Raph kept on playing. But suddenly, Raph looked up and thought, *Where's Hawk?* For a moment, Raph was scared. Raph ran fast back to the boat. There was Hawk, patiently perched.

Sometimes Raph just wouldn't get back on the boat at all-unless, of course, Hawk promised Raph a tambalacoque fruit.

And then there were times when nothing seemed to work. Hawk wanted to get going, but Raph could be a stubborn bird.

Hawk would say, "Let's go."

Raph would say, "I want to stay on shore and kick more pebbles."

So they talked and worked out a compromise; like, five more pebble kicks, and then Raph gets to help steer. OK? OK. And so they'd go, back up the river. Together.

Hawk had never been a navigator, but the more they traveled, the better he became. If there were logs, they could just cruise the boat right over the tops of them. If there was lightning, Hawk carried Raph off the river onto a safe island.

And if there was a rock, Hawk could stop the boat. Floating, still, in front of the rock, they would pause to consider their reflections in the water. Hawk saw Hawk. Raph saw Raph. And then, Hawk and Raph saw themselves looking at each other.

Mile by mile, in sputters and spurts, they continued their journey. Hawk taught Raph how to handle the boat. On bad days, they hit some rocks and the boat leaked. They used tambalacoque shells to bail the water. They used poop to patch the holes. Raph hated bailing and patching. Hawk did too, but they had no choice.

On good days, when there was a strong wind at their backs, they hoisted sail and spread their wings. Hawk's wings were so big. Raph's wings were so little.

Raph knew, *I can't fly like other birds*. But when they caught the wind just right, Raph felt like their boat could fly!

One day, Hawk flew away and never came back. Raph let go of the wheel and sat down in the boat. Alone. Raph let the boat drift all the way back down the river. Raph watched the shoreline pass by. After a while, Raph noticed that everywhere they'd stopped, little tambalacoque trees were beginning to grow. The fruit they'd eaten. The seeds they'd pooped. The pebbles they'd kicked to drive those seeds into the ground. The farther Raph drifted downriver, the taller the trees. Each tambalacoque tree was stronger and more majestic than the last. Then there were a few with little buds. And finally, Raph saw a few tambalacoque trees bearing large, ripe fruit.

Raph called out, "I want tambalacoque!" Magically, one tambalacoque fruit appeared in the water, bobbing and floating right up to the boat. Raph caught the sweet fruit in its beak. Raph took a bite-and smiled.

YOUR GANDER INSTRUCTION MANUAL

• • •

Your four-part Gander Instruction Manual is designed to help you better understand and remember your child's developmental profile. The Gander rating scale and Map were both presented in the First Mile of the Journey. Both are reproduced here for easy reference with a few extra twists. Staying true to the idea of different learning styles and the importance of multimodal instruction, the Gander is represented in four different ways:

- Part A: The Gander Explained
- Part B: Know Your Boat
- Part C: Know Your Song
- Part D: Know Your Map

Refer back to the First Mile of *Parent Child Journey* for more complete explanation. I recommend that you start by doing the Gander on one child. Later, you can also use the Gander on yourself, other children, and other adults. You can just do the Gander, or you can also do the boat, song, or map. Whatever works for you!

So here's the Gander, followed by each of the four parts of "Your Gander Instruction Manual."

The Gander

Child's name: ______________________________ Age: __________

Rater's name: ______________________________ Date: __________

Please circle the most appropriate number.

Behavioral Style/Temperament

Motor Activity Level:

3	2	1	0	1	2	3
High activity			Average			Low activity

Impulsivity

3	2	1	0	1	2	3
Acts before thinking			Average			Thinks before acting

Attention Span

3	2	1	0	1	2	3
Short			Average			Long

Initial Reaction

3	2	1	0	1	2	3
Slow to warm up			Average			Quick to warm up

Adaptability

3	2	1	0	1	2	3
Very inflexible			Average			Very flexible

Intensity of Reaction

3	2	1	0	1	2	3
Dramatic			Average			Reserved

Usual Mood

3	2	1	0	1	2	3
Unpleasant, serious, tense			Neutral			Pleasant, joyful, relaxed

Regularity/Predictability

3	2	1	0	1	2	3
Low regularity, unpredictable		Average	High regularity, predictable			

Sensory Profile

Hearing Speech

3	2	1	0	1	2	3
Tunes in people talking			Average			Tunes out people talking

Hearing Noise

3	2	1	0	1	2	3
Oversensitive			*Sounds and noises*			Undersensitive

Vision

3	2	1	0	1	2	3
Quick to notice			*Visual stimuli*			Slow to notice

Taste

3	2	1	0	1	2	3
Oversensitive			*Changes in foods, hidden tastes*			Undersensitive

Smell

3	2	1	0	1	2	3
Oversensitive			*Odors*			Undersensitive

Light Touch

3	2	1	0	1	2	3
Oversensitive			*Sensitive to light touch, tickling, clothing texture*			Undersensitive

Deep Touch

3	2	1	0	1	2	3
Avoids, dislikes			*Physically close contact*			Seeks, likes

Movement/Body Position in Space

3	2	1	0	1	2	3
Avoids			*Moving, spinning through space (swing, seesaw, rides, heights)*			Likes

Internal Body Awareness/Physical Symptoms

3	2	1	0	1	2	3
Overreports			*Symptoms of illness, not feeling well*			Underreports

Skills Profile

Fine Motor

3 2 1 0 1 2 3

Difficulty, avoids *Manipulating small objects* Ease, enjoys

Handwriting

3 2 1 0 1 2 3

Difficulty, avoids *Writing with crayons, pencils, markers* Ease, enjoys

Gross Motor

3 2 1 0 1 2 3

Difficulty, avoids *Running, jumping, climbing, playing sports/athletics, dancing* Ease, enjoys

Speaking

3 2 1 0 1 2 3

Difficulty *Putting thoughts into words* Ease

Listening

3 2 1 0 1 2 3

Difficulty *Understanding spoken communication* Ease

Writing

3 2 1 0 1 2 3

Difficulty *Putting thoughts onto paper* Ease

Reading

3 2 1 0 1 2 3

Delayed *Reading skills* Advanced

Understanding Spatial Relations

3 2 1 0 1 2 3

Poor *Understanding puzzles, shapes, block design, maps* Excellent

Visual Arts

3 2 1 0 1 2 3

Poor *Drawing, crafts, painting* Excellent

Music

3 2 1 0 1 2 3

Poor *Musical ability* Excellent

Math

3 2 1 0 1 2 3

Delayed *Math ability* Advanced

Time Awareness

3	2	1	0	1	2	3
Difficulty, inaccuracy			*Estimating, pacing*			Ease, accuracy

Planning, Organization, and Implementation

3	2	1	0	1	2	3
Difficulty			*Planning ahead/strategizing/sequencing/preparing*			Ease

Social Skills

3	2	1	0	1	2	3
With difficulty, rejected			*Makes friends*			Easily, popular

Physical Health, Family, Environmental, and other Life Stresses

Problems with Physical Health

3	2	1	0	1	2	3
Severe			Average			None

Family, Environmental or Life Stresses

3	2	1	0	1	2	3
Severe			Average			None

Other Family, Environmental, or Life Stresses (experienced by child)

Circle best answer according to **current** ***impact:***
0 = no problem; 1 = little; 2 = medium; 3 = big problem

FAMILY STRESSES

0	*1*	*2*	*3*	Death of parent
0	*1*	*2*	*3*	Death of other family member
0	*1*	*2*	*3*	Death of pet
0	*1*	*2*	*3*	Substance abusing parent(s)
0	*1*	*2*	*3*	Physical or sexual abuse of family member
0	*1*	*2*	*3*	Mental or behavioral disorder of parent or sibling
0	*1*	*2*	*3*	Disability of parent or sibling
0	*1*	*2*	*3*	Physical illness of parent or sibling
0	*1*	*2*	*3*	Addition of a sibling
0	*1*	*2*	*3*	Physical separation from primary caregiver
0	*1*	*2*	*3*	Change in primary caregiver
0	*1*	*2*	*3*	Caregiver does not speak language of community
0	*1*	*2*	*3*	Marital discord
0	*1*	*2*	*3*	Separation/divorce
0	*1*	*2*	*3*	Parent dating
0	*1*	*2*	*3*	Remarriage
0	*1*	*2*	*3*	Blended family
0	*1*	*2*	*3*	Domestic violence
0	*1*	*2*	*3*	Parent or family member with crime problem
0	*1*	*2*	*3*	Parent underemployed
0	*1*	*2*	*3*	Parent working long hours outside the home
0	*1*	*2*	*3*	Lack of support from extended family

CHILD'S PERSONAL STRESSES

0	*1*	*2*	*3*	Physical changes (e.g., weight, acne, puberty, etc.)
0	*1*	*2*	*3*	Sexual/gender identity issues
0	*1*	*2*	*3*	Physical or sexual abuse
0	*1*	*2*	*3*	Neglect
0	*1*	*2*	*3*	Foster care/institutional care
0	*1*	*2*	*3*	Adoption
0	*1*	*2*	*3*	Witness to violence
0	*1*	*2*	*3*	Chronic, long-term, or undiagnosed illness
0	*1*	*2*	*3*	Disability (diagnosed or undiagnosed): ___________
0	*1*	*2*	*3*	Not enough free time

PEER RELATIONSHIP STRESSES

0	*1*	*2*	*3*	Discord with peers (e.g., bullying, exclusion, etc.)
0	*1*	*2*	*3*	Not enough peers with shared interests
0	*1*	*2*	*3*	Loss of a good friend
0	*1*	*2*	*3*	Friends who are struggling
0	*1*	*2*	*3*	Social media stress

COMMUNITY STRESSES

0	*1*	*2*	*3*	Adjustment to a new and different culture
0	*1*	*2*	*3*	Social discrimination or isolation of family
0	*1*	*2*	*3*	Religious or spiritual problem

EDUCATIONAL STRESSES

0	*1*	*2*	*3*	Inadequate school facilities
0	*1*	*2*	*3*	New school and/or new teacher (circle)
0	*1*	*2*	*3*	Unexpected change of teacher or classroom (circle)
0	*1*	*2*	*3*	Does not get along with teacher(s)
0	*1*	*2*	*3*	Does not get along with classmates
0	*1*	*2*	*3*	Poor academic performance
0	*1*	*2*	*3*	Homework problems
0	*1*	*2*	*3*	Undiagnosed/unrecognized/unsupported disability

INADEQUATE RESOURCES

0	*1*	*2*	*3*	Food insecurity/lack of adequate nutrition
0	*1*	*2*	*3*	Homelessness or uncertain housing
0	*1*	*2*	*3*	Financial instability
0	*1*	*2*	*3*	Lack of adequate health care

ENVIRONMENTAL STRESSES

0	*1*	*2*	*3*	Unsafe neighborhood
0	*1*	*2*	*3*	Dealing with relatives
0	*1*	*2*	*3*	Exposure to upsetting news stories
0	*1*	*2*	*3*	Natural disaster

OTHER STRESSES

0	*1*	*2*	*3*	______________________
0	*1*	*2*	*3*	______________________
0	*1*	*2*	*3*	______________________
0	*1*	*2*	*3*	______________________

YOUR GANDER INSTRUCTION MANUAL

• • •

THROUGHOUT THE *PARENT CHILD JOURNEY* program, parent and child are represented as two birds, Raph and Hawk. The story of their river adventures weaves in and out of the ten-session parent training manual. In this appendix, I offer Your Gander Instruction Manual as a supplementary experiment in progress. Part A: The Gander Explained, stands on its own and should be of immediate use to the interested reader. In a straightforward way, it provides more detailed discussion of the Gander's different facets. Much less straightforward, Your Gander Instruction Manual also includes part B, a boat pictograph; part C, a birdsong; and part D, a river map. These odd modes of presentation are not for everybody. But I hope that some of you find this instruction manual experiment helpful or, at the very least, strange fun.

Your Gander Instruction Manual Part A: The Gander Explained

What it means: Some aspects of the Gander might seem complicated and confusing. Here, I will try to explain each facet of the Gander profile in clear and simple language. The number system is intended to help parents avoid black-and-white generalizations and see their children more accurately in shades of gray. Parents should give a number rating of 0 or 1 if your child is pretty close to average and this facet of his or her profile is not a big deal. Number ratings of 2 or 3 should be assigned if this facet of the profile might be a more significant factor; possibly are probably contributing to ease or difficulty in certain situations. It is important to remember that your child's profile might change over time. The Gander is just a here-and-now description and was designed to be practical.

Goodness of fit: Everybody has differences in behavioral style (Carey, 2004). Everybody has different strengths and weaknesses (Gardner, 2006). There is no such thing as a "good" or "bad" profile. However, a child's profile can make some situations relatively "easy" and render others more "difficult." As you describe your child's profile, you should consider "goodness of fit"; that is, how each facet of your child's profile explains why some situations and tasks are naturally easier, while others are more challenging. For each facet of your child's profile, I will discuss situational advantages ("good for") and disadvantages ("problem if"). Also, after having a Gander at your child, you can take a Gander at yourself. Looking at one problem situation after another, consider "goodness of parent-child fit" between your profile and your child's profile. For each facet of your child's profile, I will discuss the following:

- ***Good for:*** I will give examples of common situations or tasks for which each facet of your child's profile might be protective; that is, a strength or an advantage.

- ***Problem if:*** I will also give examples of common situations or tasks for which each facet of your child's profile might be a risk; that is, a weakness or a disadvantage.
- ***Parent-child fit:*** Children do not grow up in glass bubbles. Relationships matter. It is important to consider the potential overlap of different child and adult profiles. Throughout this program, you will think about how your own profile fits with your child's. This perspective will explain why some parent-child interactions go more easily than others. We will not be analyzing every important relationship in your child's life. But it is important to note how many different types of relationships lend themselves to this kind of analysis: parent-parent fit, parent-grandparent fit, parent-teacher fit, professional-patient fit, sibling-child fit, and so on. The point is, it's not just about the kid! Adults and other children have their own differences and challenges too. When you start overlapping a lot of Ganders, it gets very interesting but very complicated. We should keep these family and community complexities in mind, especially how the dynamic interplay of individual differences and relationship triangles can change over time. All that being said, here, we will keep things simple and focus primarily on parent-child relationships.

Accommodations: As discussed in the Tenth Mile, there are two different kinds of strategies: accommodations and interventions. Most children with developmental differences need a combination of both. Accommodations are built on an acceptance of the child's developmental differences; interventions are about changing the child. Accommodations require some degree of dependence on adults; interventions are about increasing the child's independence. Accommodations are often used in public; interventions tend to be more private. Accommodations usually involve bypassing difficulties or finding alternative strategies; interventions are about working hard to fix skill deficits. Accommodations are usually based on empathy and common sense; interventions require expertise and science. In the Tenth Mile, we reviewed "leaks in the boat" and necessary interventions or "patches" for different facets of your child's profile. Here we will cover "bailing" strategies; that is, accommodations. Simply understanding the source of your child's behavior should automatically lead to some common sense and relatively simple solutions. In this section, I will provide some practical strategies for accommodating each facet of your child's profile. For example, if your child has high motor activity level, don't make him or her sit forever; allow for regular movement breaks. As we go through the Gander, I will focus on accommodations that you can start using on your own right away.

Strengthen strengths: As emphasized throughout this discussion, it's just as important to nurture talents and interests as it is to accommodate weaknesses. The Gander should highlight abilities, not just weaknesses. In the sections covering your child's skills profile, I will offer a few comments on how to foster growth in areas of strength.

Side notes: In these side notes, I will offer some additional thoughts on developmental differences. I hope that readers will find these tangential comments interesting and helpful.

Discussion of Behavioral Style/Temperament

We will begin with eight facets of "temperament" or behavioral style:

1. motor activity level
2. impulsivity
3. attention
4. initial reaction
5. adaptability
6. intensity of reaction
7. mood
8. regularity

Starting in the 1940s, Chess and Thomas (1989) used similar categories to describe infants and categorize them as "easy," "difficult," and "slow to warm up." In one of the longest and most fascinating studies ever done, these infants were followed throughout childhood and into adult life. This pioneering work dispelled the old idea that babies are born a blank slate on which parents write the child's destiny. We now know that everybody is born different. Brazelton (2011) developed the Neonatal Behavioral Assessment Scale as a tool to describe such inborn differences even in the first days of life. This is not to say that personality is prenatally carved in stone. Rather, we all have certain genetic predispositions. It's nature *and* nurture—not just one or the other. We are the products of our genes *and* our environment—both in dynamic interplay (Ridley, 2003).

So on the Gander, let's work through your child's behavioral style together. Check off the ratings directly on the Gander. If it suits you, feel free to draw a boat part, sing a song verse, or graph a map point. More on all that later in parts B, C, and D of Your Gander Instruction Manual.

Motor activity

What it means: Some children are hyperactive and act as if driven by a motor. They are constantly moving, restless, and fidgety. Others are underactive and act as if they have no fuel in their tanks. They prefer to stay in one place, sedentary and still.

Goodness of fit:

- *Good for:* **High motor activity** is obviously good for activities that require extra physical energy, such as athletics, dance, and theater. Being a "mover" is also advantageous in unstructured settings where extra energy creates opportunities for enjoyable activity; for example, the playground or backyard. These children might be better at entertaining themselves because they energetically check things out. And they can be more fun for some similarly active children. On the other hand, naturally **low motor activity** can be good for activities that require long periods of sitting still. These children tend to have an easier time meeting expectations in school or quiet social situations.

- *Problem if:* **High motor activity** can be a problem if school, home, or social settings require sitting or being still for longer periods. Children with **low motor activity** can have a problem if they need to get moving to perform certain tasks. It might be hard for them to keep up or fit in when high physical energy is required.
- *Parent-child fit:* Parents who have high motor activity may find it easier—in fact, enjoyable—to keep up with a child with high motor activity. On the other hand, adults who naturally move at a slower pace may find such high energy difficult, if not exhausting or exasperating. Parents who are more sedentary find similar children to be relatively easy. Parents who prefer more active lifestyles can become frustrated when their children cannot keep up. It is important for such "motorically mismatched" parents to remember that low motor activity level does not represent laziness any more than high activity level represents disobedience. Both are just natural tendencies.

ACCOMMODATIONS:

- Strategies to accommodate a child's **high motor activity** include limiting the amount of time that the child has to be still. For these bouncy children, parents should plan and encourage physical activity breaks. Sometimes vigorous physical activity can be combined with otherwise sedentary tasks, such as shooting baskets or playing Ping-Pong while talking or memorizing. There is an educational movement built on the importance of "kinesthetic" or movement-based learning (Dennison & Dennison, 1992). Hands-on experiences, role-playing, and dance allow these active children to use their bodies and make learning more fun. For example, carpentry, cooking, and sports activities can be used to teach measurement, math, and statistics (Smith, 2004).

- Strategies to accommodate **low motor activity** are designed to facilitate participation without causing frustration. Unlike high motor children who need activity breaks, these low motor children need *inactivity* breaks.
  - For very young children, brief stretches of walking can be alternated with relatively longer periods of being carried or pushed in the stroller. Parents might have to use transportation rather than insisting on long hikes.
  - On the athletic field, underactive children on the soccer field can play goalie or defense rather than forward or midfield. Baseball is a relatively slow-moving sport; especially if you play catcher or first base. Underactive children can enjoy just relaxing in the swimming pool.
  - Some of these slower moving children have a hard time performing certain daily chores, such as cleaning up or getting themselves dressed. Parents might have to provide more assistance to help them get going. Tasks can be broken down into smaller chunks. These children just might need to be allowed a little more time.

Side notes: In some ways, our modern "screen culture" reinforces sedentary habits. In other ways, our "fast-paced culture" often has too little tolerance for people who simply move at a slower pace. Many people are concerned that this has led to the "medicalization" or "pathologizing" of normal developmental differences.

Astute readers will notice that the first three items on the Gander—activity level, impulsivity, and attention span—are in fact three core features of ADHD. True, if there is an impairing degree of hyperactivity, impulsivity, and distractibility—across settings and over time—then a diagnosis of ADHD should be considered (Barkley, 2013b). Subsequently, a trial of medication might be recommended (Wilens & Hammerness, 2016). However, medication is never the whole answer. Rather, it is part of a comprehensive management strategy including behavior management, educational care, and other psychosocial interventions (Garber, 1997).

Not all inattention is from ADHD. And not all ADHD-type symptoms are impairing enough to warrant such a diagnosis. There is a place on the planet for people who are somewhat hyperactive, impulsive, and distractible but do not have a true disorder—just a normal degree of human variation. On the other hand, just because a child is below threshold for a formal diagnosis does not mean that his or her normal developmental differences might not cause some challenging behaviors. The flip side of an ADHD-like profile can be just as problematic. Some children struggle because of low activity level, too much inhibition, and hyperfocusing. In this program, I encourage you to just "call it the way you see it" and not get too hung up on formal diagnostic categories.

Impulsivity

What it means: Children with **high impulsivity** act as if they have "no brakes." They have difficulty stopping and thinking before acting. These children live "in the moment," without considering past experience or future consequences. Children with **low impulsivity** act as if they "never take their foot off the brakes." They stop and think too much without acting. These children live too much in the past and the future, and perhaps not enough in the present.

GOODNESS OF FIT:

- *Good for:* **High impulsivity** can be good for spontaneity, creativity, fun, and excitement. **Low impulsivity** is good for staying safe and out of trouble. A little extra caution usually means fewer mistakes. These children usually win when playing "Simon Says," exercising restraint if Simon doesn't say.
- *Problem if:* **High impulsivity** can be a problem if situations require a certain degree of self-control. It is normal for babies and toddlers to expect immediate gratification, but as children grow up, they must learn to exercise greater degrees of restraint. These children usually lose when playing "Simon Says," failing to inhibit when Simon doesn't say. On the other hand, **low impulsivity**, or too much inhibition, can be a problem if it interferes with the development of intimacy, trust, and healthy experimentation. These children can be too hesitant, guarded, or anxious. Fewer errors of commission can mean more errors of omission. People grow and learn by experiencing new things and making mistakes. Children who are always thinking, *What's going to happen?* have difficulty enjoying life in the present.
- *Parent-child fit:* Parents with relatively **high impulsivity** may be less likely to stop and think ahead on behalf of their children. However, relatively uninhibited parents may find it easier to relax, "connect with," and enjoy their children in the "here and now." Parents with **low impulsivity**, who are more restrained, anxious, or even hypermoral, might be quicker to praise prudence and provide necessary guidance. On the other hand, they could be more prone to reinforce the anxieties of a like-minded child or micromanage and become frustrated with an impulsive child.

Accommodations:

- Strategies to accommodate **high impulsivity** require adults to "accept, loosen up, and chill." Young children do not consistently consider the consequences of their actions. The development of behavioral brakes is a long-term project. Until their children develop better self-control, adults can try—within reason—to "let kids be kids." After all, childhood should be a time of innocence and relative freedom from worry. Children should be allowed to make some mistakes without always having to learn a lesson or endure serious hardship. Children do not need to grow up *too* fast, without any kind of emotional cocoon. When high impulsivity might put a child at serious risk, then the physical environment should be modified, and responsible adults should tighten their supervision. When safety cannot be ensured without undue negative feedback, then the activity should simply be avoided or prohibited. The child can be distracted or redirected to safer alternatives. For problematic impulsivity, adults may need to bring the future into the present by providing more feedback and more consequences, more often.
- Strategies to accommodate **low impulsivity** include allowing these overly thoughtful children extra time. If prolonged reflection ultimately leads to action, they need not be rushed. Preview, gradual exposure, and time to acclimate can make it easier for these children to transition and face the unfamiliar. There is significant overlap between accommodations for low impulsivity and negative initial reaction.

Side notes: ADHD may be diagnosed when high impulsivity is significantly impairing, across settings, across people, and over time. Despite concerns about overdiagnosis and overtreatment, ADHD is a serious condition with serious consequences. In childhood, the gradual development of "behavioral brakes" allows for improved function in the family, with friends, and at school. In adulthood, better self-control can mean a higher chance of success in the larger community and the workplace. Early problems with "behavioral disinhibition" increase the risk of school failure, social difficulties, and family stress. As children with poor self-control get older, they might suffer from negative self-image, accidental injury or death, substance abuse, sexual promiscuity, and other unhealthy behaviors. Marketing strategists capitalize on consumer impulsivity, especially when purchases are just a tap or click away. People who celebrate and glorify impulsivity sometimes tragically confuse uninhibited self-expression with true artistic creativity. A sufficient degree of impulse control may actually represent the foundation of morality itself, that uniquely human ability to pause and free oneself from conditioned reflexes, to sometimes live in the present as if the future depends on it (Barkley, 2005).

On the other end of the self-control spectrum, low impulsivity can be just as significantly impairing. Excessive inhibition might indicate an anxiety disorder. Too much hesitation and self-restraint can cause distress or even paralysis. These children need help learning how to ease up on the brakes and "let it roll." They need to live more in the moment and not worry so much about the past or the future. They need to take more risks and not worry so much about consequences (Zucker, 2017).

It is interesting to note that medication used to treat ADHD can cause too much inhibition. Medication used to treat anxiety disorders can cause too much impulsivity. That's why, when ADHD and anxiety coexist, treatment of one can lead to worsening of the other (Shapiro, 2016).

But these thoughts are offered only as interesting considerations. As with all facets of the Gander, just because high degrees of impairment can suggest specific diagnoses in some children does not mean that most children with less impairing developmental differences require professional attention.

Attention span

What it means: Children with a **short attention span** might notice everything all around. They shift rapidly, flitting from one thing to another. They have difficulty focusing on any one thing for long. They are easily distracted (Hallowell & Ratey, 1995). Children with **long attention span** focus on one thing for a long time; sometimes to the exclusion of everything else. They tend to become engrossed in one activity or thought. They may hyperfocus or perseverate. They do not easily shift their focus. As discussed in the side notes that follow, but worth emphasizing here, most children do not have *either* short *or* long attention spans. Rather, attention spans can vary across different tasks and settings. It is common, for example, to have a shorter attention span for nonpreferred activities or tasks that tap into weaknesses. Most people have a longer attention span for preferred activities or tasks that tap into strengths. So when completing the Gander, make a generalization about your child's attention span if you can, but feel free to specify task and setting-specific differences too.

Goodness of fit:

- *Good for:* A **short attention span** or distractible nature can be good for letting bygones be bygones. Sometimes it is a gift to be able to just move on and let unpleasant thoughts or feelings quickly fade into the past. It is easier for parents to redirect these children away from undesirable activities. Distractibility and "soothability" often go hand in hand. Some children with short attention spans are good "noticers." They can be more attuned to interesting background details; more fun or sensitive in certain social situations; more appreciative of myriad stimuli in art, music, or nature. **Long attention span** or perseverative tendencies can be good for activities or tasks that require prolonged focus. These children may be able to work well even in environments that would be distracting to others. Children who can "stick with it" might reach surprisingly high levels of achievement and expertise. Success can flow from sustained engagement and concentration.

- *Problem if:* Obviously, a **short attention span** can be a problem if it interferes with learning, responding to others, and performing necessary tasks. Insufficient persistence and perseverance make it difficult to work efficiently, complete jobs well, and achieve one's true potential. High levels of persistence or **long attention span** can be a problem if a child tends to become too self-absorbed, oblivious to what is going on, missing environmental or social cues. These children may be misunderstood. They may be accused of ignoring or being rude. They may have trouble shifting from one activity to another. It may be difficult to distract or redirect them away from undesirable feelings or activities (Attwood, 2008).
- *Parent-child fit:* Parents with short attention spans may find it difficult to pick up on their children's cues or follow through during important parent-child interactions. On the other hand, these parents may find it easier to let go of some things that really don't matter. Parents with long attention spans may have trouble just moving on, yet feel well-suited for working through difficult problems.

Accommodations:

- Strategies to accommodate children with **short attention span** require a high level of adult acceptance, creativity, and energy.

- Children should not be reprimanded or embarrassed if their minds tend to wander.
- Selectively, parents can lessen some attention requirements and demands. These children should be expected to sustain focus only for as long as they are capable. They may need frequent breaks while doing long or multistep tasks. By allowing short and frequent breaks, the child may return to the task more successfully. Parents can break down tasks into small, simple chunks. Instructions should not be complicated or long-winded.
- Environmental distractions should be minimized. Use multisensory presentation or your child's preferred sensory pathways, such as visual versus pure auditory. Block, eliminate, or tone down undesirable stimuli. At the same time, highlight, amplify, or draw near to the preferred center of focus. For example, in the classroom, distractible children generally do better when seated front and center, away from the outside window or hallway door (Silverman, Iseman, & Jeweler, 2009).
- Some children find that a regular change of sensory input helps them maintain attention, such as changing rooms or seats or using different color transparencies to read through. Novel approaches to routine tasks are likely to make them more interesting.
- To keep their minds from wandering, these children may need more one-on-one time, more reminders, and more feedback. Sometimes they might just need some help getting started. "I'll do one, and then you do one...good! Now I'll do one, and you do two."
- Secret signals (such as touching the shoulder or tapping the desk) can be used to let a child know when his or her attention seems to be fading.
- Schedule more challenging tasks for times when a child is likely to be more alert and less distractible.

    - Use special interests and preferred activities to offset the child's tendency to lose focus. This might mean that you couple learning with computers, movies, or video games.
- Strategies to accommodate **long attention span** generally mean allowing these children to stay with an activity for longer periods. They should not begin an activity that will take them longer than the time available unless they understand that they will have to stop it before completion. Timers, clocks, schedules, and warnings may be necessary. Sometimes it is appropriate to prompt and encourage a child to move at a more rapid pace, even imposing time limits when necessary. These children do better if they can see transitions coming well in advance. If persistence is so high that a child becomes too self-absorbed and unsocial, then parents might have to be more deliberate and creative about engagement. Limit the amount of time spent on TV, computers, video games, and other isolating activities. For some very perseverative children, there is such a thing as too much time spent reading or doing homework. Try to strike a healthy balance between activities that are done solo and others that require more social interaction.

Side notes: Inattention is a common and important problem of childhood. Unfortunately, and all too often, well-meaning adults boil this complicated facet of development down to an overly simplistic question: does the child have ADHD or not? But inattention is far more intricate than that (Levine, 2003).

There are at least four types of inattention:

1. *Distractible type:* As described previously, many children have difficulty with inattention because their attention spans are just too short.

2. *Perseverative type*: Also as described previously, some children hyperfocus and pay attention to one thing to the exclusion of others. They are not inattentive. They are just not focusing on the "right thing." It's just hard for them to flexibly shift away from what they prefer and attend to what's required.
3. *Task or setting-specific type:* All children have difficulty attending to difficult tasks. As described throughout the Gander, a pattern of strengths and weaknesses in other facets of your child's developmental profile could cause this kind of inattention *secondary* to challenges with specific demands, settings, or expectations. For example, a child with reading or writing difficulties will naturally have more trouble sustaining focus for that type of work.
4. *Stressed-type:* Many children have difficulty with attention regulation secondary to underlying problems with mood regulation or environmental stress. It is very difficult for anyone to focus when anxious, stressed, or "down in the dumps." Sometimes mood difficulties have nothing to do with the task at hand, but they still cause powerful distraction. Other times anticipation of difficulties—real or merely perceived—triggers anxiety or avoidance.

Some children with inattention have just one of these four factors in play. Others, especially children on the autism spectrum, may have a *"mixed-pattern" of attention dysregulation* involving all four types, stirred together in varying degrees; that is, distractibility, perseveration, task-specific difficulties plus anxiety or other mood disorder.

To complicate things further, most children do not have across-the-board problems or total inability to pay attention. Rather, they have a problem with inconsistent attention. There are two patterns of attention inconsistency.

1. *Predictably inattentive:* This pattern of attention inconsistency is not random. These children are "consistently inconsistent." How well the child is able to focus and sustain attention often depends—in a predictable way—on the task or situation at hand. Other aspects of the child's profile factor in, especially his or her Gander sensory profile and skills profile. For example, it is not unusual for a child to display a short attention span when people are talking (relative weakness) but a long attention span for visual-motor activities (relative strength).
2. *Unpredictably inattentive:* Some other children are "inconsistently inconsistent." They have no predictable pattern. Sometimes they bring their "A game." Other times they just don't. These children are often blamed for their success. Parents and teachers might assume that just because they can pay attention some of the time, they have the capacity to pay attention all the time. Such inconsistency all too often leads adults, peers, or the child him- or herself to use pejorative labels and denigrating comments, such as "lazy," "poorly motivated," or "doesn't care" (Levine, 2004). But if these children could speak for themselves, they would say, "I don't have a problem being able to pay attention some of the time. I just can't do it all the time. I don't have a total attention deficit. My problem is attention inconsistency. If I could pay attention all the time, I would."

Initial reaction

What it means: Initial reaction is about adjusting to new situations. Children with **negative initial reaction** are generally "slow to warm up." When encountering new situations, these children tend to take a first step backward, as if saying, "I'm not so sure about this." Children with **positive initial reaction** are "quick to warm up." These children are usually eager to experience new things. They tend to take a first step forward, as if saying, "Hey, check it out!"

Goodness of Fit:

- *Good for:* **Negative initial reaction** can be good for avoiding unsafe or undesirable situations. A little bit of natural caution can help keep these children from getting sucked too easily into trouble. Parents can imagine many situations, from early childhood through adult life—social, sexual, recreational—in which a bit of natural hesitation would be protective. A tendency toward **positive initial reaction** is obviously good for making unfamiliar transitions. Social interaction can come more naturally when a child is intrinsically trusting and open. For these children, variety is the spice of life. A willingness to experience new things can enhance growth and development.
- *Problem if:* **Negative initial reaction** or instinctive withdrawal can be a problem if children avoid activities that are safe, possible growth experiences and fun. Ordinary, desirable or necessary transitions might be way too difficult. Change can be harder than it needs to be. Children who are slow-to-warm-up may have a hard time quickly adjusting to new school situations, teachers and students. On the other hand, **positive initial reaction** or relative lack of caution can be a problem if the situation is risky or dangerous. Novelty and excitement can draw such children into unhealthy or dangerous relationships and behaviors. For these children, the lines between innocence, naïveté, and victimization can be all too thin.
- *Parent-child fit:* **Negative initial reaction** *or* slow to warm up parents can demonstrate a healthy degree of prudence in some situations but too much caution in others. Slow to warm up parents are likely to feel some tension or anxiety if they have a quick to warm up child. Parents who tend to have a **positive initial reaction** might not model sufficient caution. If their child is relatively careful, then quick to warm up parents might become impatient or frustrated.

ACCOMMODATIONS:

- Strategies to accommodate **negative initial reaction** include adjusting initial expectations and demands or limiting unnecessary and unsettling exposures. A certain amount of familiarity is essential for emotional stability. These children should not be required to tolerate too many new experiences and transitions. When avoidance of novelty is not practical or desirable, parents should understand that the child's first reaction might not represent their true potential interest. Parents should go by what they think will happen after their child is over that first hump of resistance. They should not be too discouraged by their child's initial reluctance. In these cases, it is OK to push these children to "just try it" and "give it a chance" before deciding. Children can be reminded about previous times when they did not want to try something but ended up enjoying or profiting from the experience. There is an interesting overlap between initial reaction and adaptability. For children who are *initially* slow to warm up and remain inflexible over time, gradual exposure can be helpful, like acclimating gently to cold water by putting one toe in the pool at a time. On the other hand, for children who are initially slow to warm up but then generally adapt well, gradual exposure just prolongs the torture! These children do better if they just jump right into the deep end, get through the transition phase more quickly and let their adaptability strengths kick into gear. These generalizations about temperament can help parents predict whether their child will do best with an approach that is gradual, prolonged, incremental, and step-by-step or an approach that is more "cold turkey," "get it over with all at once," and quicker. These considerations come in handy when managing a variety of common problems with novelty and change, such as dropping off on the first day of nursery school, kindergarten, or even college; or managing problems with sleep initiation, picky eating, or social success.

- Strategies to accommodate **positive initial reaction** include extra supervision and explicit rules, especially when safety is an issue. Environments must be more tightly controlled when the child's first reaction cannot be trusted. Parents should understand if these novelty-seeking children are drawn to certain activities and then quickly change their minds. Excessive curiosity just requires more explicit teaching rather than admonishment or punishment. Some novelty seeking and risk taking should not only be tolerated but encouraged.

Side note: In completing the Gander, parents often ask, "Where do I put anxiety?" After all, anxiety disorders affect at least 10 percent of all children; the most common of the developmental disabilities. And negative initial reaction might not capture all anxiety. So why isn't there an additional Gander item called "anxiety"?

Most developmental differences of childhood cannot be plunked neatly into one diagnostic box. When we're talking about anxiety, there are usually many variations, many subtypes and many factors at play (Rapee et al., 2008; Zucker, 2017). This heterogeneity is just as true across other diagnoses; such as so-called oppositional defiant disorder, autism, ADHD, learning differences, and sensory differences. The Gander splits apart and captures complexities of your child's profile that traditional diagnostic categories lump and lose (Cuthbert & Insel, 2013).

To demonstrate the point, let's break the anxiety box down into more meaningful Gander facets. Anxiety can stem from a temperament marked by various degrees of negative initial reaction, low adaptability, and low impulsivity. Anxiety can come and go with general fluctuations in mood. Some children can be worried sick today and totally chill tomorrow. Beyond behavioral style, anxiety is often task- and setting-specific. For example, one child's insect phobia may be another child's social anxiety. Anxiety can be secondary to specific sensory stimuli, ranging from haircuts to swimming pools. Anxiety can be tied to specific learning difficulties, such as reading, writing, math, or study skill deficits. Environmental stresses may be relevant, for example, when there is a birth of a sibling, marital discord, trauma, or a move to a new home. Anxiety may be secondary to medical problems, such as allergies, asthma, or constipation. There are so many different types of anxiety: generalized, specific phobias, obsessive-compulsive disorder, post-traumatic stress, social, performance, and more. And anxiety manifests in so many different ways: headaches, stomachaches, aggression, withdrawal, avoidance, sleep disturbance and more. Anxiety changes over the years; shifting, for example, from separation anxiety in preschool, to burglars in early childhood, then performance anxiety in high school. The relative importance of underlying factors changes as children travel through different developmental phases. Good assessment should result in an accurate description of all these factors and manifestations. The Gander facilitates this kind of multidimensional assessment. Successful management of anxiety depends on understanding this complexity.

Adaptability

What it means: When situations prove challenging or unpleasant, children with **high adaptability** easily make adjustments. They are flexible and naturally "go with the flow." Children with **low adaptability** do fine along their chosen path but do not feel comfortable shifting course. They tend to be inflexible and strong-willed (Greenspan & Salmon, 1996).

Goodness of fit:

- *Good for:* **High adaptability** or natural flexibility is good for getting along with others. These children are more accepting of differences. They are OK with compromise. They tolerate physical and emotional discomfort. When things prove difficult, they adjust. They look for different ways to solve problems. When solutions prove elusive, they are open to suggestion. But **low adaptability** has its advantages too. Inflexibility can be good for maintaining healthy habits. Once desirable routines and morals are internalized, these children naturally protect themselves in unsafe environments. They are less likely to follow negative examples or bend to the influence of others. Some of the most inflexible children grow up to be some of the world's greatest leaders.

- *Problem if:* **High adaptability** or flexibility can be a problem if the child uncritically accepts undesirable influences. Some of these children are too ready to fit in. They might follow when they should lead. **Low adaptability** can be a problem if adjustments must be made. Some situations require children to transition smoothly and accept change. These children can have trouble with "microtransitions," such as the morning routine at home or activity shifts at school. They can also struggle with "macrotransitions," such as beginning a new school year, losing a friend, or a parent starting a new job. Relatively inflexible children may cause others to feel stressed, frustrated, sad, or angry. Children who are slow to make adjustments might exclude themselves from important activities, opportunities, or relationships.
- *Parent-child fit:* High adaptability parents have an easier time accepting life's inevitable surprises, challenges, curveballs, and setbacks. Sometimes being too flexible is a disadvantage when parents need to take a strong stand despite pressure or uncertainty. When parents and children are both inflexible, they do well in the absence of conflict. However, trouble can be amplified and prolonged when two inflexible parties need to adjust or compromise.

ACCOMMODATIONS:

- Strategies to accommodate children with **high adaptability** are generally not necessary, as these children are so ready to accommodate others. However, parents might have to exercise greater vigilance monitoring such a child's environment for undesirable activities, ideas, and friends. Fortunately, these children should be able to adapt just as well to healthier alternatives.
- Strategies to accommodate children with **low adaptability** require parents to provide extra preview and warm-up time in new or unexpected situations. These children will do best if given plenty of advance warning regarding necessary adjustments. Whenever possible, they should first receive coaching and practice then brief and frequent exposure. Desensitizing exposures can gradually increase in duration, intensity, and unpredictability, giving the child as much time as necessary to acclimate. In general, these children do better with this kind of preview, rehearsal, practice, and incremental warm up. "Sink or swim" approaches usually backfire causing low adaptability children to sink. Unnecessary or potentially overwhelming change should be kept at a minimum. If feasible, when one change has to be made, other changes should be postponed.

Side notes: Adaptability can be inborn and hardwired; a cradle-to-grave character trait. However, just because people may be born with certain predispositions does not mean that such tendencies are carved in stone. With time, changing circumstances, hard work, and help from others, there is not a single facet of your child's developmental profile that cannot change. In fact, all facets usually do change; even if only to a certain degree. Ironically, Nelson Mandela's greatness was in large part due to his extraordinary inflexibility in the face of injustice, both before and during his prison years. However, his ability to build a new coalition government in South Africa—with the same leaders of apartheid who jailed him for nearly three decades on Robin Island—was due to his equally extraordinary adaptability (Mandela, 1995).

Inflexibility is often secondary to other aspects of your child's developmental profile. For example, children with long or perseverative attention spans, high self-inhibition, and negative initial reaction may come across as being inflexible when all they really need is a little extra time to shift focus, relax, and acclimate. As we will see in discussing more facets of your child's profile, individuals with either over- or under-responsive sensory systems can have secondary problems responding flexibly to environmental stimuli. And any skill deficit can masquerade as inflexibility. It's hard to adapt when something is difficult.

For example, low adaptability is a very common problem in children who have weak language skills. Inflexibility can be a direct consequence—perhaps the most obvious symptom—of difficulty understanding or expressing complicated language. Some children have excellent language skills on standardized testing. However, when stressed or emotionally flooded, they struggle to process or organize language on demand. Other children simply don't have the words. Either way, a child who only thinks in black and white will have difficulty seeing all the in-between shades of gray. For these children, there are no numbers 1 *through* 9, only 0 *or* 10. There is no yellow light; only red or green. There are no alternative plans B through Z; only plan A. There is no compromise; just your way *versus* my way. There is no earthly variation; only heaven *or* hell. If life isn't perfect, it might not seem worth living.

It is not unusual for these linguistically limited children to express their frustration in alarming ways. If a parent does not yield to such a child's inflexible demands, the child might say, "I'm going to kill you!" If the child is not able to perform up to their own expectations, they might threaten to kill themselves. Such children are not truly homicidal or suicidal; nor, deep down, as poorly adaptable as they seem. They are simply defaulting to "black-or-white/all-or-none" language and behavior for lack of skill generating more nuanced and adaptive alternatives. Without the language to think and express "many shades of gray," a child's conceptual, emotional, and behavioral menu can be very limited. In this way, language (or other) skills deficits can masquerade as unmodifiable inflexibility. But these children may not be so inflexible as they seem. They just need more words. With help, they can learn the language of emotional intelligence—or correct other skill deficits—*underlying* their inflexibility. Not easy, but possible.

Intensity of reaction

What it means: Children with **high intensity of reaction** tend to be loud and demonstrative. Whether their feelings are positive or negative, those feelings are "all out there" and obvious. Children with **low intensity of reaction** tend to keep their feelings to themselves. They "fly under the radar" and "hold their cards close to their chest." These children may be harder to read.

Goodness of fit:

- *Good for:* **High intensity of reaction** is good for drawing attention to legitimate needs. Sometimes the squeaky wheel truly does need to be greased. These children are unlikely to have their needs ignored. They let others know how they feel. Such openness and transparency may be necessary for mature communication and deep relationships. A tendency to display one's emotions can also be a positive source of entertainment and joy for others. Their contagious laughter and effervescent spirit can make such children the life of any party (Kurcinka, 2015). But children with **low intensity of reaction** have potential upsides as well. More reserved and restrained children can be less obtrusive. These children can be easier to live with. Such children (and adults) might be admired as "strong, quiet types" (Cain, 2013).

- *Problem if:* **High intensity of reaction** can be a problem if a child too often "cries wolf." Parents (and pediatricians) may not be sure how seriously to take frequent and dramatic complaints. Others may perceive a child's demonstrative style as loud, obnoxious, irritating, or insensitive. On the other hand, children with generally **low intensity of reaction**, who tend to keep their feelings under wraps, can have their physical distress or inner emotional life go unnoticed and unattended. Such underreporting can make it difficult for adults to respond and provide validation. Sensitive parents learn not to take everything at face value and gently dig a little deeper. Experienced pediatricians learn very quickly which infants and children "cannot be trusted" to display important symptoms of illness (Schmitt, 2005).
- *Parent-child fit:* If a parent and child both have "high voltage" tendencies, there is wonderful potential for shared joy and excitement. Interpersonal connection can be deeper when people are naturally open with one another. However, successive volleys of high-intensity negative reaction and higher-intensity counterreaction can quickly escalate and spin out of control. A pattern of perpetual conflict can result from such similar but incompatible behavioral styles. High intensity parent-child dyads might have a hard time finding the source of the fire through all the smoke. They might fight then forget what they were fighting about. Parents who have low sensory thresholds might have a harder time with such high-intensity children. These parents might cling to old-fashioned views, such as "good children should be seen and not heard," or "good children should not speak unless spoken to." On the other hand, parents who are less sensitive and have a lower intensity or

reaction are less likely to fuel these emotional spirals. Although they are relatively unlikely to get sucked into power struggles, such quiet parents may be more difficult for their children (and spouses) to read. This can be a problem for children who might need a more animated and amped-up style of engagement and communication. Parents who have very high sensory thresholds or inattentiveness should be particularly cautious about overlooking these children.

ACCOMMODATIONS:

- Strategies to accommodate children with **high intensity of reaction** require parents to mind the difference between style and substance. The child's manner of communication may not accurately reflect the magnitude of the issue. So these parents should not overreact, either positively or negatively, to their child's drama. Such children tend to provoke parents to feel helplessness or rage, leading to avoidance or counterintensity. This is not to say that the high-intensity child's feelings should be discounted or ignored. It is just the depth or volume of display that might be out of proportion. Before rushing to judgment or action, parents should objectively evaluate the substance of the issue. If necessary, they should gather data from other sources. They should deliberately pause, evaluate the true nature of the issue, and avoid getting sucked into the child's high drama. Parents should not give in for the sake of peace. Neither should they fight back for the sake of justice. They should respond with equilibrium and wisdom. For example: "I can tell how upset you are. And I think I understand why. Let's wait until we can both be calm and work through this problem together." Nobody can effectively problem-solve when smoke is coming out of his or her ears. That goes for both children and parents.

Giving these children socially acceptable outlets for their high intensity is important. The bedroom, basement, and backyard are usually better suited for venting than the family room, dining room, or public places. Punching bags and pillows can be handy. If it helps, parents can provide places, times, and activities that allow these children to blow off some steam. There is a limit to how much we should encourage children to "let it all out." To a certain degree, children (and parents) should learn to "just move on" (Hanh, 2002).

- **Strategies to accommodate** children with **low intensity of reaction** involve maintaining a high level of suspicion. Minor complaints and subtle symptoms should be taken seriously. Adult antennae need to be way up. These children might be experiencing more distress than they show. The depth of feeling may not be adequately displayed. More demonstrative siblings or peers might deprive these quiet ones of their due attention. Parents and teachers should be sure to distribute their time thoughtfully. Parents who place a high value on expressiveness may just need to accept and enjoy such a child's more reserved manner.

Side notes: Across all facets of your child's profile, "goodness of fit" does not depend only on the behavioral style of parents and others, but also on setting, context, and culture. This is especially true regarding intensity of reaction. Children with high intensity of reaction can fit more naturally at the swimming pool, playground, and other settings where it's fun and appropriate to "let it all out." High intensity of reaction is more often the cultural norm in Mediterranean, Latin, and U.S. East coast communities. Children with low intensity of reaction might not seem to fit as naturally in these environments and cultures. More subdued children might seem to do better in school, religious services, and other activities where quiet behavior is expected. Low intensity of reaction may be the more common cultural expectation in some Asian, Eastern

European, Scandinavian, and US Midwestern and Southern communities. In some cultures, what might be considered a problematic—even pathological—degree of extroversion or introversion might seem relatively normal or even admirable in other cultures. Thus, there can be a problem if the child's natural intensity of reaction—high or low—is inappropriate for a specific setting or falls outside of his or her family or community's cultural norms.

Each facet of your child's profile exists in dynamic interplay with every other facet. Previously, we considered the interplay between initial reaction and adaptability. Here, let's examine the overlap between intensity of reaction, social skill, and adaptability. In the discussion of social skills that follows, we will consider how easy or difficult it is for some children to read social context and modify their intensity of reaction (along with other aspects of their behavioral style) accordingly. Socially attuned adjustments in intensity of reaction can be simple, such as shifts between "inside voice" and "outside voice." Other context-driven adjustments in intensity of reaction can be more complex and nuanced (Duke, Martin, & Nowicki, 1996). For example, there are very different greetings across cultures. In some communities, people expect a quiet bow and downcast eyes. In others, it is normal to give prolonged and exuberant hugs with double kisses on each cheek! For some children more than others, this kind of "context reading" and "social shifting" can be difficult. The consequences can be humorous—or serious.

Mood

What it means: Some children tend to "see the glass half-full." Children with a generally **positive mood** just seem to carry a smile on their faces, even when the chips are down. They are usually relaxed, optimistic, and happy. Other children with generally **negative mood** tend to "see the glass half-empty." Even when things are going well, these children just seem to be serious, sad or—most commonly—irritable.

GOODNESS OF FIT:

- *Good for:* A generally **positive mood** and cheerful predisposition are obviously good for the child and for others. Who doesn't enjoy feeling happy and being around happy people? On the other hand, **negative mood** can be a reflection of seriousness of purpose. Some great champions of social justice and humanity carried a sad or even angry predisposition. Their deep sensitivity and passion stirred them to act, serve, create, and inspire. A smiley face is not necessary for a good life. For example, in some families and cultures, far more importance is attached to meaningful work and good deeds (Seligman, 2004).
- *Problem if:* A **positive mood** or perpetually sunny demeanor might be a problem if it is socially inappropriate. If someone's mood seems disconnected from sad or serious events, it might come across as insensitive. To others, this perpetual sunniness can be socially off-putting or irritating. Of course, **negative mood** or melancholia can be a problem if it causes too much distress, not just for the child, but for others too. Pessimistic individuals are not often fun to be around. Of greatest concern, negative mood can be truly impairing, socially and developmentally. Some people can be disabled by their darker emotions. Keep in mind that the most common symptom of depression in childhood is irritability, not sadness (Koplewicz, 2003).
- *Parent-child fit:* Parents who carry a positive mood have obvious advantages. However, they may have some difficulty understanding their child with a more serious nature. Adults who are naturally or culturally conditioned to place high value on a rosy predisposition may have a hard time accepting thornier definitions of the "good life." Parents with a negative mood may find that their pessimistic outlook is contagious, either amplifying a similarly predisposed child's helpless feelings or confusing a child who would otherwise tend toward the positive.

ACCOMMODATIONS:

- Strategies to accommodate **positive mood** are generally not necessary. The only real concern (as with high adaptability) might be gullibility. There are some situations that a child should not feel good about. Parents may need to monitor, supervise, and restrict if such overly optimistic and innocent children might come to harm. Parents may need to help these children examine some social and moral issues more explicitly, objectively, and critically. For these children, "if it feels good, do it" might result in them doing just about anything.
- Strategies to accommodate **negative mood** should begin with loving acceptance of the child's behavioral style. Adults should not take such a child's negative mood personally or pessimistically. For some (not all) very healthy individuals, it's just the way they are. Do not react with counternegativity, frustration, blame, or guilt. Do not feel compelled to be a cheerleader. These children should not be coached to "just put on a happy face!" Such a child may just show his or her interest and enjoyment differently, such as through their level of attentiveness and engagement rather than the number of smiles and laughs. Parents of children with negative moods should be no less available and attentive.

Side notes: Mood is a complicated facet of your child's profile and stems from a combination of factors: genetic, environmental, and experiential. As discussed elsewhere in the *Parent Child Journey*, Seligman (2006), the father of positive psychology, traced depression in many to an unhealthy habit of negative self-talk or pessimistic explanatory style. He studied dogs, life insurance salespeople, and Olympic hopefuls. When faced with adversity or failure, he found that pessimists tend to take things too *personally*. They jump to conclusions about the *permanence* of a bad situation. They tend to generalize their failure in one situation to a *pervasively* helpless/hopeless attitude about their chances of achieving any kind of success. The three Ps of this pessimistic response to failure—that setbacks seem *personal*, *permanent*, and *pervasive*—represent the "mud" of self-fulfilling prophecy into which too many children (and parents) fall and get stuck. On the other hand, Seligman found that children and adults with a positive mood are better grounded in hopeful self-talk. When these optimists faced failure, they just called it bad luck, nothing personal; a setback, not permanent; just one failure, not necessarily a barrier to future success.

Also worth repeating here asd elsewhere, Dweck (2007) wrote about two different kinds of mind-sets. People with a "fixed" mind-set view abilities, intelligence, and talents as if "carved in stone." They feel that "we are who we are—and that's that." Their goal: just try to look smart, not dumb; always succeed, don't fail. On the other hand, people with a "growth" mind-set tend to think that talents and abilities can be developed through effort, good teaching, and persistence. It's not that everyone is the same or that anyone can be an Einstein. But everyone can grow, learn, change, and achieve more success. Similar to Seligman's optimists, children and parents with Dweck's "growth" mind-set see mistakes and failures as opportunities to learn more, work harder, and do better.

So if your child is predisposed to a negative mood or even clinical depression, don't have a pessimistic or fixed mind-set about that. In the Seventh Mile of *Parent Child Journey*, we dive further into this important subject. In a highly individualized way, you can help your child define problems in specific and solvable terms, then practice effective problem-solving—with hope and optimism (Brooks & Goldstein, 2002).

Regularity/predictability

What it means: Children with **high regularity and predictability** act as if an internal clock governs their body functions, behavior, and mood.

Their parents know exactly what to expect. They know when these children will wake up, go to sleep, go to the bathroom, feel hungry, and play. Parents of regular children may even be able to tell when they will be happy or sad. With these children, there are very few surprises.

Children with **low regularity and predictability** seem different every day. Their parents learn to "expect the unexpected." These children are "consistently inconsistent" regarding mood, wake-sleep cycles, and daily activities. They do not easily internalize daily routines. They might shift through monthly, weekly, or even daily cycles of change. Sometimes their emotional "skin" can seem "thick"; other times it seems "thin." Parents of these children never know "which kid" they're going to get.

GOODNESS OF FIT:

- *Good for:* **High regularity and predictability** are good for scheduling. Life is usually easier when everyone knows what to expect—and when. Plans can be made with little chance of surprise or disruption. A certain amount of biological rhythmicity can lead to the development of healthy habits, efficiency, and peace. Such steadiness can also make it easier to fit in and get along with others. These predictable children engender feelings of reliability and trustworthiness. **Low regularity and predictability** can be good for getting along with others who are also relatively unscheduled. These children might be more tolerant of disruptions to routine. Some people argue that mood instability can be good—even a necessary ingredient—for artistic inspiration. Myths abound and research seems to confirm a connection between "the unquiet mind" and creative genius (Jamison, 1996). Some people speculate that civilization would have been deprived of artistic masterpieces if, for example, Van Gogh and Beethoven had been less volatile.

- *Problem if:* **High regularity and predictability** may be a problem in the face of unexpected change or if such a child's preferences cannot be accommodated. Other people's schedules will not always fit the child's. On the other hand, **low regularity and predictability** can be a problem if certain routines must be imposed. There is a difference between irregularity and flexibility. Just because a child is unpredictable does not mean that he or she will tolerate unpredictability in others. However, it does mean that parents will have to tolerate unpredictability in the child. The behavior of these children can be very upsetting and difficult. The irregular child might feel confused or out of control. Parents, family, and teachers might overreact and let their own moods ride up and down with the child's. Although irregular shifts in the child's mood might not accurately reflect his or her true desires, family and social relationships can become strained when this instability and unpredictability is misunderstood.
- *Parent-child fit:* Very regular parents may have difficulty with very unpredictable children. High-regularity parents and children may have an easier time with one another when their schedules are in sync but feel tension when marching to the beat of different drummers. Parents who are irregular may have difficulty with a child who is more schedule-bound. Disorganized or spontaneous adults, who like every day to be different, will obviously have a harder time changing their own behavioral style to accommodate a naturally regimented child. More adaptable/low intensity of reaction parents will have an easier time with unpredictable children. Parents with high mood stability more naturally give their children a sense of security. Parents who have difficulty maintaining emotional equilibrium may struggle to meet normal child-rearing challenges.

ACCOMMODATIONS:

- Strategies for accommodating **high regularity** usually require some degree of adjustment to the child's natural schedule. If times for eating, sleeping, toileting, studying, and playing can be set by the child and accommodated by the adults, then life is simple. The more routine, the better. Highly regular children should be given a lot of warning and choices if their usual schedule has to be disrupted. Parents might choose to excuse these children from some disruptions to avoid unnecessary stress. If adults cannot anticipate changes in routine far enough ahead, then they can respond sympathetically and try to preserve as much of the child's preferred schedule as possible. If certain activities cannot occur at the usual time, maybe they can at least happen in the same way.
- Strategies to accommodate **low regularity** should be considered for children who cannot easily meet certain scheduling requirements. If the child is "predictably unpredictable," then parents might just have to learn to go with the flow—or at least have a plan B for every plan A. Insisting on an overly rigid schedule will backfire. Compromise is necessary. For example, an acceptable range for bedtimes or eating times might work better than one mandatory time. A distinction can be drawn between *set bedtime* (with quiet independent activities) and *flexible sleep time* (left more up to the child in accommodation of his or her fluctuating biorhythms). If some meals have to be relatively fixed, other mealtimes could be allowed to float. Strategies to accommodate low mood stability include understanding that such mood swings are truly nobody's fault. These children simply can't control their moods like other children. Parents should look for patterns to better anticipate triggers and cycles, but this is not always possible. The unpredictability of these swings might simply require a high degree of acceptance. Drawing, music, writing, dance, and

other creative outlets may help these children channel their rising and falling moods. Learning to put their feelings into words can help these children gauge their current moods and make appropriate adjustments. Ideally, parents and children can see down cycles coming and make timely shifts to less demanding and stressful activities (Harvey & Penzo, 2009). During times of relative emotional stability, children can be encouraged to pursue activities and interactions that might be difficult to handle at other times.

Side notes: Your child's irregularity and unpredictability may not be as random as it seems. Let's consider two "patterns of patternlessness":

- *Secondary irregularity:* For some children, there are underlying triggers. What's not immediately obvious might be extremely important. When you take a step back and carefully analyze the ups and downs, many of these overly sensitive children are reacting to hidden problems. Their unpredictability represents just the visible tip of an underwater iceberg. In these cases, irregularity is often secondary to negative initial reaction, inflexibility, sensory over-responsiveness, skill deficits, and/or other environmental stresses. Without going on a wild diagnostic goose chase, a pediatrician should be consulted to rule out hidden medical problems. Extreme irregularity may seem random if relatively minor triggers are considered separately. But it's the combination of factors that can pass a cumulative tipping point. Understandably, parents—and professionals—often struggle to identify such subtle but significant triggers, but it's worth trying. If you can put your finger on the main source (or sources), you can render your child's "unpredictability" more predictable.
- *Primary irregularity:* For other children, there really aren't any identifiable triggers. These children are truly and unpredictably

> unpredictable. Whether we are talking about irregular bowel, bladder, sleep, eating, mood, or behavior, parents of these irregular children never know what they are going to get: Kid A, Kid B, Kid C, or even D! Still, parents of children with this kind of untethered "shape-shifting" can often describe general rhythmic patterns. Some children cycle from one mode to another hour by hour; others day by day, week by week, month by month, season by season, or longer. If shifts are very extreme, binary, and prolonged, then there is a higher chance of true psychiatric illness, namely, bipolar disorder. However, as discussed further below, most of these children have a different kind of mood disorder with a better prognosis than bipolar (Leibenluft, 2011). And the overwhelming majority of children with poor mood regulation just have challenging temperaments—not a serious mental health problem. There is good news about high irregularity: Usually, Mother Nature is on our side. Over the years, as brains mature, most of these children settle into better self-regulation and more predictable patterns.

Here, it seems appropriate to make a few comments about the interplay between culture and temperament; not just regarding regularity and predictability, but about human variation in general.

For good and bad, the medicalization of developmental differences is here to stay. Following the publication of some poorly controlled studies and sensational books, it seemed like every child with behavioral irregularity or mood instability was being diagnosed with bipolar illness (Papolos, 2007; Wozniak et al., 1995). Some of these children had significant problems with irritability and explosiveness, but not the kind of prolonged cyclical episodes seen in true manic-depressive disorder. Other children received a diagnosis of bipolar when they were really just having medication side effects. Parents were told that their children had serious lifelong psychiatric illness. Potent medications were prescribed. Let me emphasize: bipolar illness is real and requires accurate diagnosis and comprehensive treatment, usually including potent medication (McClellan, Kowatch, Findling, & the Rand Work Group on Quality Issues, 2007). However, I have seen many children with low regularity—and other challenging temperaments—whose differences in behavioral style simply needed to be understood, not diagnosed; accommodated, not fixed; accepted, not mourned.

Cultural factors may be having a strong negative impact on the development of internal regulation. Over the last century, modern lighting and air conditioning have eliminated natural distinctions between day and night. Increasingly, indoor existence has blurred the change of seasons. More recently, the ubiquity of electronic screens, large and small, has had a profound impact on family communication, relationships, and activities. Extraordinary performance pressures, at school and work, have cut into family meals and other important rituals. Parents feel more pressure to have perfect children. Children put more pressure on themselves. In so many ways, the world feels less safe and secure. These seismic cultural shifts have had a profound impact on the development of behavioral regularity. Maybe our society, not your children, needs more diagnosing and more fixing. In today's chaotic world, isn't it even more important to have established routines, daily touchstones, family traditions, and community events? To foster emotional resilience, maybe we should stop accommodating cultural instability and start repairing these crucial foundations. If you're not already having regular family dinners, that might be a good place to start (David, Uhrenholdt, Baker, Foer, & Karp, 2010).

This concludes our discussion of temperament. Now for a discussion of various sensory profiles.

Discussion of Sensory Profile

The Gander prompts you to describe eight facets of your child's sensory profile:

1. Hearing speech
2. Hearing noise
3. Vision
4. Taste
5. Smell
6. Light touch
7. Deep touch
8. Movement/body position in space
9. Internal body awareness/physical symptoms

In this section of the Gander, you will be making generalizations about your child's sensory reactivity; that is, whether your child has relatively high or low responsiveness to a variety of sensory stimuli. Sensory differences are important, affecting all aspects of mood, behavior, socialization, and learning. Throughout life, sensory differences can influence personal preferences regarding eating, toileting, recreation, and sexuality. Understanding your child's sensory profile will help you custom-design effective strategies for engagement and communication. Through detailed understanding of your child's sensory profile, you will be able to move beyond general recommendations to "use multisensory techniques" to more specific and individualized sensory strategies (Kranowitz & Miller, 2006).

Sensory strategies always work best if integrated with an understanding of the whole child. The sensory brain is super–cross-wired with every other part of the nervous system. Consequently, your child's sensory differences exist in dynamic interplay with all other facets of your child's profile. Over- and under-reactivity, in any sensory domain, can affect motor activity level, impulsivity, attention, initial reaction, flexibility, intensity of reaction, mood, and regularity, plus the whole range of skill strengths and weaknesses. Likewise, all these other facets of your child's profile have a profound impact on sensory processing. To give just one example, children with high sensory reactivity tend toward negative initial reaction. If they were not so hypersensitive, they would be less anxious. Conversely, and just as true, children with negative initial reaction will tend toward high sensory reactivity. If they were less anxious, they would be less reactive to sensory stimuli. Keeping this interplay in mind, it may be easier to change a child's sensory reactivity by targeting other aspects of his or her developmental profile.

Directly changing a child's sensory system can be difficult (American Academy of Pediatrics, 2012). A variety of sensory therapies are touted to rewire the sensory system. Proponents of these interventions claim that they can help both oversensitive and undersensitive children toward a more favorable middle ground. Obviously, all children should be routinely screened and treated for hearing and vision deficits. But what about the myriad approaches available for other problems with sensory reactivity? They include auditory training, eye muscle exercises, and oral therapies; brushing, pressure, spinning, and biofeedback; and other occupational/sensory integration therapies. These interventions can help some children, especially when coupled with behavioral strategies targeting specific and measurable goals. However, the scientific evidence base for stand-alone sensory therapies is disappointing. The emphasis throughout most of the *Parent Child Journey* will be on appreciating, understanding, and accommodating sensory difference, not intervening to rewire your child's sensory profile per se.

For the Gander, eight facets of the sensory system have been chosen somewhat arbitrarily. In many sections, I will comment on how each sensory facet could be subdivided even further. For example, touch has been divided into "deep" and "light," but I could have added other types: "vibratory," "temperature," "stereognosis" (the ability to recognize objects through touch alone), and "pain" (of many different types), to name just a few. Furthermore, I could have added a number of other sensory facets. For practical purposes, I have tried to simplify. Parents are encouraged to lump if possible, but split if necessary. Try to make meaningful generalizations, but feel free to subdivide or add categories if it helps paint a fuller and more accurate picture of your child. Despite these caveats, I hope the sensory categories suggested in the Gander prove useful to most.

While completing this section of the Gander, keep in mind that most children are not hypersensitive, average, or undersensitive across the board. It is more common for children to have "mixed" and/or "inconsistent" sensory profiles. By "mixed," I mean that children can be hypersensitive to some types of stimuli and undersensitive to others. For example, many children are very sensitive to visual stimuli and light touch but under-responsive to speech and deep touch. Furthermore, by "inconsistent," I mean that sensory reactivity can change with mood, fatigue, or other underlying reasons. Most children are more reactive if a sensory stimulus catches them by surprise, but less reactive if they know what's coming. On the other hand, some children might be under-responsive unless they have their sensory "antennae" up with their sensory "receiver" switched to the right channel, ready for transmission. Also, sensory profiles change over time. Many problems with sensory reactivity get better with age. So your child's Gander sensory profile might be complicated, but try your best to make some meaningful generalizations.

Hearing speech and hearing noise

What it means: Children with high sensitivity to auditory stimuli seem naturally tuned in and over-responsive. Children with low sensitivity to auditory stimuli seem tuned out and under-responsive. Hearing means sensitivity to any kind of auditory signal. Different parts of the brain process different types of sounds: tone, pitch, frequency, harmonics, and so forth. Here, for practical purposes, we will distinguish between just two general types of auditory stimuli: speech (words said) and noise (everything else). It is very common for some children to have a "mixed pattern"; that is, either high sensitivity to speech *and* low sensitivity to noise or high sensitivity to noise *and* low sensitivity to speech.

Also, in describing your child's sensory profile, we are just talking about registration (from ears to the back of the brain), not processing (which involves regions closer to the front of the brain). Just because your child *hears it* does not mean that he or she *gets it.* For some children, the sound of others talking is only so much noise. We will move beyond simple registration of auditory stimuli to the more complicated processes of understanding in the skills section that follows—specifically, under language, musical, and social abilities.

Every child should have regular hearing screening for hearing deficits.

GOODNESS OF FIT:

- *Good for:* **High sensitivity to speech** is good for registering spoken communication at home, with friends, and in the classroom. Even in this Age of the Internet, human beings still communicate primarily by talking with one another. **High sensitivity to noise** is good for noticing important environmental cues. For example, heightened auditory registration may be lifesaving if a car is coming just around the corner. It can be socially advantageous to notice tone of voice. An open channel for beautiful sounds in nature or music can bring pleasure. **Low sensitivity to speech or noise** can be good for filtering out conversations or other background "static" that could be distracting or irritating. Children with low auditory sensitivity might have an easier time focusing on preferred stimuli or tasks. It may be easier for them to stay relaxed and calm, for example, when falling asleep at night or concentrating on desk work at school.

- *Problem if:* Conversely, **hypersensitivity to hearing speech or noise** can be a problem if it causes distractibility. Such children might have trouble filtering out background chatter or noise. Attention can be pulled away from more important stimuli, activities, or tasks. Some children may find that ordinary background noise can be quite irritating. **Low sensitivity to hearing speech** can be a problem when children are expected to register and respond to the spoken word. This difficulty is compounded if information is presented exclusively to the ears without accompanying visuals. **Low sensitivity to hearing noise** can have safety repercussions if auditory warning signals go unnoticed. These children are more likely to miss some nonverbal cues, such as tone of voice, inflection, or throat-clearing. They may also miss other important auditory-social signals, like bells, gongs, or whistles that mark the end of recess. Children with low auditory sensitivity might speak too loudly or make loud noises, unaware of how this is perceived by others.
- *Parent-child fit:* Parents with high sensitivity to hearing may be good "noticers." On the other hand, they may feel annoyed by the normal sounds of children. Parents with low sensitivity to hearing may be poor "noticers" but more able to let potentially irritating chatter or noise float on by. When parents and children have very different thresholds for registering auditory stimuli, any conflicting tendencies to overreact or underreact might be mutually confusing, frustrating, or irritating.

Accommodations:

- Strategies to accommodate **high auditory sensitivity** include directing preferred input toward your child's ears while keeping distracting input away. Especially if other sensory pathways are weak, parents can use a child's relatively strong speech registration channel to help their child compensate. For example, reading aloud or "talking books" can help registration of the printed word. Vocal repetition, paraphrasing, and discussion can improve comprehension. Words can be set to music. The workspace should be designed with attention to the auditory environment. If auditory hypersensitivity is a source of distraction, then background noise should be kept to a minimum. Silence or at least soften other sounds that could be disturbing. Turn off or turn down the volume of other stimuli. Create a quiet space. Consider earplugs, headphones, white-noise machines, or fans. Background music can be a source of distraction for some but an effective filter for others. See what works for your child. Adults can provide auditory forecasts: "It will probably be pretty noisy in there." Before entering loud environments, the child can linger outside and take time to gradually acclimate. Adults should understand that some of these children speak softly or avoid making noise because they are irritated by the very sounds they produce, not necessarily because they are shy.

- Strategies to accommodate **low auditory sensitivity** begin with understanding and accepting that your child is not deliberately tuning you out. Remember, hearing happens in the ears, but listening and understanding happen in the brain. Working ears need receptive brains, just like a movie projector needs a movie screen and a dark room. Many of these children are falsely accused of "selective" hearing. They may be chastised for not listening. But low sensitivity to hearing is not a matter of willful ignoring, disobedience, or low intelligence.
    - Even when children with low sensitivity to auditory input are not deaf, we should think about interacting with them as if they are (Marschark, Lang, & Albertini, 2002). Do not call to these children from another room or across a noisy

space. First, come over and be sure to get your child's full visual and/or touch attention. Then keep it short and simple. Don't talk too fast. Although increasing your voice volume a bit might help, avoid shouting. Distractions should be kept to a minimum. In a classroom, these children should sit up front, close to the teacher and away from the hallway door. If a child has a one-sided or asymmetric hearing deficit, speakers should take care to position the "good ear" closer.

- Use a multimedia approach to communication rather than relying exclusively on the weak auditory channel. Don't just explain, demonstrate. If a child is known to have other "input routes" that work well, use these to get and keep attention. Use touch and movement. Some children hear spoken language better when it is put to music. Above all, think about visual communication. Exaggerate your facial expressions, gestures, and body language. Use visual aids, such as pictures, charts, and clocks. Visual aids should change along with the content of speech. For example, when the topic changes, those visual aids should be put away and new pertinent ones brought to the forefront. Sign language is now commonly used outside of the deaf community, not as the sole means of communication, but as a liberating supplement.
- Some children with low sensitivity to hearing require extra supervision and facilitation. For example, a relative lack of auditory awareness could create a serious street safety problem. To compensate for poor processing of auditory social cues, rely on visual strategies or touch. In advance, before the auditory environment becomes difficult to navigate, preview and rehearse social expectations.

Side notes: Mixed auditory sensitivity profiles are common and complicated. Some children are not just over- *or* undersensitive to speech. They can be over- *and* undersensitive to different *types* of voices; for example, low versus high-pitched. The same complexity pertains to different types of noises. The same child can be oversensitive to the sound of birds quietly chirping but impervious to the loud rumble of an old air conditioner. An infinite variety of mixed auditory sensitivities exists because different types of sounds are processed by different parts of the brain, and different children grow up under diverse environmental conditions. All that being said, the most common problem with mixed auditory sensitivity seems to be the combination of high sensitivity to noise and low sensitivity to speech. This is especially challenging when environmental noise and speech registration demands are both high; for example, a noisy classroom. The obvious solution, as discussed previously, is to turn down the background noise, turn up the foreground speech, and use nonauditory supplementary aides. All this customization depends on anticipating the situation and understanding your child's sensory profile.

Vision

What it means: Every child should have regular vision screening for vision deficits. Whether vision is normal or not, some children just seem especially alert to their visual environment. Other children seem relatively oblivious to visual signals.

Vision is the most complex of the human senses. There are many different types of visual input. We have different nerves, brain regions, and networks for night vision and day vision; for central vision and peripheral vision; for shape, object, motion, depth, number, and color; for facial identification and expression; and more. In this sensory section of the Gander, we will consider sensitivity to visual stimuli in general. In the skills section of the Gander that follows, we will discuss more specific visual channels and networks pertaining to reading, spatial relations, and social skills. As emphasized in the discussion of hearing—and true for all facets of the sensory system—awareness of a sensory signal is different from, interpretation and understanding. Here, we mean simple registration (eyes to brain), not complicated processing (across many different brain regions).

GOODNESS OF FIT:

- *Good for:* **High visual sensitivity** is good for situations where visual registration is required. Visual responsiveness is often an advantage regarding learning, recreation, and safety. These children may have enhanced appreciation of nature or art. **Low visual sensitivity** is good for filtering out visual distractions; for example, if the teacher is talking when there's a lot going on out the window.
- *Problem if:* **High visual sensitivity** can be a problem if the child is distracted from important tasks or signals. Some children have trouble listening because they are just so busy looking around. They look at one thing, then another, then another. Some children are so sensitive that they are irritated—even distressed—by ordinary light, patterns, or movement. **Low visual sensitivity** is a problem if these children miss information that is important for safety, learning, social interaction, or pleasure; for example, red traffic lights, blackboard instruction, and facial expressions. Sports that are intensely visual (such as baseball and soccer) may be more difficult than others that are less visually taxing (such as swimming and running).
- *Parent-child fit:* When parent and child have similar patterns of visual sensitivity, they might both underreact or overreact, but at least they tend to react in sync. Parents may assume that their children see the world in much the same way, but this is not always the case. For visually mismatched adults and children, what's visually obvious, irritating, or important to one might be missed, difficult, or inconsequential to the other. These kinds of

sensory system mismatches can lead to confusion or frustration, leading some parents or teachers to think or say: "What's your problem? It's right in front of your face!"

ACCOMMODATIONS:

- Strategies to accommodate **high sensitivity to visual stimuli** include elimination or minimization of visual distractions. The child can be seated with his or her back toward visual fields that are *too* interesting, such as the window. Of course, TVs, computers, and other electronic screens might have to be turned off or put out of sight. Some rooms are too full of bright, colorful, or moving objects. Visual aids can help capture and sustain the child's attention, but they must be directly relevant to the subject at hand. Maps, graphs, pictures, diagrams, colors, and demonstrations can all help, but off-topic "visuals" should be put away so that they do not distract. If there is a tendency toward light sensitivity, use window shades, low lighting, or sunglasses. Some children need to take visual breaks from prolonged reading or electronics to avoid eye strain.
- Strategies to accommodate **low sensitivity to visual stimuli** avoid exclusive reliance on visual input. Before communicating with these children, parents should ensure engagement by using sound, touch, or movement. In school, maps, graphs, and pictures—designed to make information processing easier for others—may make things harder for these children. They may actually require more verbal explanation and less visual communication. Color-coding can be confusing if color insensitivity or true color blindness goes undiagnosed. Across the life span, if safety requires visual vigilance, extra supervision may be required. This is true for the young child stepping in front of a moving swing or the teenager learning to drive a car. Like

looking into the sun, excessive TV or computer screen time can cause eye damage if a child is not "bothered enough" by extended staring into bright lights.

Side notes: Of course, visual acuity changes over time. That's why all children should have yearly vision screenings. More complicated and more interesting, the interplay between visual and other sensory systems also changes over the course of the life span. To demonstrate the point, consider Stevie Wonder, Blind Lemon Jefferson, Jose Feliciano, the Blind Boys of Alabama, Ray Charles, Doc Watson, and George Shearing. All great musicians; all blind, either from birth or very early in life. Their extraordinary ears for music probably developed—at least in part—as compensation for their visual deficits. Many musicians with normal vision close their eyes while playing or listening to enhance their musical experience. Conversely, deaf people learn to use sign language and lipreading for communication, plus floor vibrations for music. This capacity for the human brain to "grow" compensatory sensory systems also occurs in degrees with lesser sensory impairment.

With shifting environmental demands, the need for accommodation of sensory difference can change over time. One of the brightest students in my medical school class failed his first histology (microscopic anatomy) exam. He knew his stuff, but before medical school, his inability to distinguish between subtle shades of red and blue had never been so specifically tested. Given the incidence of color blindness in the general population, our professor was accustomed to discovering one or two color-blind med students each year. For the next exams, my classmate was provided with written descriptions of cell color. He aced the rest of his histology exams and went on to a stellar career in primary care pediatrics. It was no coincidence that he stayed away from medical specialties that require excellent ability to distinguish shades of red and blue; either under a microscope or on an operating room table; such as, pathology or surgery.

Taste and smell

What it means: On the tongue, there are four main types of taste receptors: sweet, sour, salty, and bitter. From the nose to the brain, there are many specialized cells and nerve tracts for different odors. Some children have **high sensitivity to taste and smell**. Others have **low sensitivity to taste and smell**. Children have a wide range of differences regarding how easily they notice these many types of sensory stimuli. Sensitivity to taste and smell often travel together.

Goodness of fit:

- *Good for:* **High sensitivity to taste and smell** can be good for noticing potential hazards. These children may be the first to report spoiled food, smoke, or other hazards. They may be able to appreciate and enjoy certain foods and odors on a more discriminating "aesthetic" level (Ackerman, 1991). There are even professional tasters and sniffers who must be so endowed. Children and adults with these hypersensitivities might be less likely to experiment with drugs of abuse, either inhaled (marijuana, cigarettes) or ingested (alcohol). On the other hand, **low sensitivity to taste and smell** can be can be good for olfactory and gustatory flexibility. These children may not be bothered by foods or smells that would turn others away. They may be more open to trying new and different foods. They might fit more comfortably into social situations that revolve around eating different foods. They have less difficulty with pungent environments—or pungent people.
- *Problem if:* **High sensitivity to taste and smell** can be a problem if the child will not accept a healthy diet or lacks the flexibility expected for social eating. Extreme sensitivity to certain smells can make ordinary environmental exposures excessively irritating, unsettling, or even anxiety-provoking. Some children

cannot stand even a whiff of perfume, autumn leaves, or kitchen or body odors. These children might feel uncomfortable when their air is even a bit "impure." **Low sensitivity to taste and smell** can be a problem if children do not notice certain hazards. They may not avoid harmful or unhealthy foods and may be oblivious to warning odors. Some of these children may seek or even crave unhealthy foods, "nonfoods," or dangerous chemicals. They might be more likely to mouth, eat, or inhale in an unhealthy and socially inappropriate manner. They may need to substitute safe alternatives to satisfy undesirable cravings.

- *Parent-child fit:* There are pluses and minuses here as everywhere. Parents with high sensitivity to taste and smell might be more attuned to warning signals, or they might overreact and influence their children inappropriately. Parents with low sensitivity to taste and smell might either miss these sensory cues or better communicate tolerance of sensations to their children. These low-sensitivity parents might also have a hard time understanding their high-sensitivity child's limited tolerance for different foods. Either way, if parent and child have significantly different sensory thresholds, this may lead to mutual misunderstanding, tension, and frustration.

Accommodations:

- Strategies to accommodate **high sensitivity to taste and smell** boil down (pun intended) to avoiding unnecessary exposure. Remember, your child's sensory experience may be very different from your own. Force-feeding is never a good idea. Very gradual exposure may be necessary. Unpleasant foods can be masked by hiding one food in another, but for many of these children, that simply doesn't work. To a degree, parents may have to accept a poorly balanced diet and view improved nutrition as a very long-term project. Odors that are noxious to these children can be countered by improving ventilation, spraying deodorizers, or burning candles. If such exposures cannot be avoided, older children can be warned and taught socially acceptable ways of reacting.

- Strategies to accommodate **low sensitivity to taste and smell** involve increasing supervision and controlling the environment. Parents of these underreactive children have to be more deliberate and regular in teaching rules of health, safety, and society. This includes explicit and wide-ranging instruction; for example, in nutrition, substance abuse, and manners. High-salt and high-sugar diets should be discouraged. Parents should control the availability of such foods. Also, parents should be knowledgeable about inhaled or snorted drugs; not just cigarettes, marijuana, and cocaine, but also glue, household products, liquid paper, and automobile fluids. (Drug Enforcement Administration & US Department of Education, 2012). All early adolescents should be warned that infectious diseases can be transmitted by oral sex.

Side notes: About that last sex comment. For some readers, the connection just made between taste, smell, and sexuality might have been unexpected and uncomfortable. But the connection is real, and some more general points are worth further discussion.

In addition to taste and smell, almost all sensory systems are involved in sex. Sex is affected by over- or undersensivity to light touch, deep touch, hearing, vision, spatial position, and internal physical signals. Sexual development also depends on individual differences in behavioral style, including motor activity level, impulsivity, attention, initial reaction, adaptability, intensity of reaction, mood, and regularity. Furthermore, there are complicated connections between sexuality and the whole range of skill strengths and weaknesses, including fine motor, gross motor, expressive and receptive language, spatial relations, visual arts, music, math, time awareness, planning, organization, implementation, and social skills. And last but not least, sexuality is profoundly affected by environmental, physical, and life stresses.

I have elaborated on this connection between taste, smell, and sex to make some more general points. First, there is not a single aspect of individual difference that might not be relevant to human development throughout the life span. Some of these connections are just more hidden or surprising than others. Second, no one aspect of developmental difference ever wholly explains variations in individual or interpersonal function. Rather, it's the complex combination of developmental differences that underlies all human behavior. Third, goodness of fit should be considered, not just by parents of children with challenging behavior or just by adolescent and adult couples regarding the potential interplay of their sensory-sexual differences, but across all human relationships and activities. These individual differences are sometimes hidden, but they are always intertwined and fascinating. Understanding how all these factors affect you and your child can be empowering and liberating.

Light touch and deep touch

What it means: From the hair on your head to the nails on your toes, there are many different types of touch receptors that send different electrical signals along different nerve pathways to different regions in the brain. We have specialized networks for a range of touch stimuli: vibration, indentation, and movement; velocity and duration; heat, cold, and rate of temperature change. There are different kinds of nerve systems for different kinds of pain and for different kinds of movement in joints, muscles, and tendons. To simplify discussion and focus on sensory differences that are most relevant to understanding challenging behavior, the Gander is artificially limited to just light touch and deep touch.

As for other facets of the Gander, most children have a "mixed pattern" of sensory preferences. They can be oversensitive to some types of touch and undersensitive to others. It is not unusual to be undersensitive to deep touch while being oversensitive to light touch. Children with this pattern of tactile incongruity love big hugs, cuddling, and intense physical contact, but they hate caresses, tickles, and certain types of clothing. It is also common to have just the opposite sensory mix; that is, high sensitivity to deep pressure ("Don't hug me!") coexisting with low sensitivity to light touch ("Tickle me! Tickle me!").

GOODNESS OF FIT:
Different sensitivities to touch can have a significant impact on behavior, mood, socialization and learning.

- *Good for:* **Low sensitivity to light touch** is good for tolerating minor skin discomfort and different textures. These children have an easy time with clothing, shirt collars, tags, shoes and socks; bathing, haircuts, and hairbrushing; Band-Aids, and lotions. If these children are accidentally brushed up against, it's not a big deal. **Low sensitivity to deep touch** is good for fun, comfort, and interpersonal physicality. These children love big hugs and prolonged cuddling. They do not mind hard knocks on the athletic field, on the playground, or in the playroom. If the desire for deep touch is shared and safe, some roughhousing can be fun and socially connecting. (What's good for children with low sensitivity to light touch and deep touch is a problem for children with ***high sensitivities*** to the same stimuli.)
- *Problem if:* **Low sensitivity to light touch** can be a problem if the child is slow to notice danger. The relative absence of certain withdrawal reflexes can result in failure to protect against burn, frostbite, or some types of unwanted or inappropriate physical contact. Having **low sensitivity to deep touch** can

result in unhealthy or socially problematic cravings. For example, some children can be too physical, too aggressive, or too interested in seeking out socially unacceptable touching. (What's a problem for children with low sensitivity to light touch and deep touch is good for children with ***high sensitivities*** to the same stimuli.)

- *Parent-child fit:* Individual sensitivities to touch may or may not fit well with social expectations, daily routines, or other sensory preferences. Parents with high sensitivity to certain types of touch may not be comfortable with children who have the opposite craving. Parents with low sensitivity to touch may be frustrated, confused, or upset when their children seem bothered by certain types of physical contact. If the desire for certain types of touch is not shared, this can contribute to interpersonal problems across peer and sibling relations as well. Again, it can be uncomfortable but important for parents to consider the sexual implications of these variations.

ACCOMMODATIONS:

- Strategies to accommodate **low sensitivity to light touch and deep touch** may require extra preview, more explicit rules, and tighter supervision. These children need careful instruction about how to recognize and avoid various dangers. They need well-defined and clearly communicated social norms. For example, using dolls or drawings, parents can show how rules for touching change depending on social context. Green zones (OK to touch), red zones (not OK to touch), and yellow zones (maybe OK to touch) change according to setting (public vs. private, classroom vs. playground), context (dancing, greeting, sports), and person (parent, sibling, close friend, acquaintance, teacher, sexual partner).

- As with all other hypersensitivities, strategies to accommodate **high sensitivity to light and deep touch** begin with understanding and acceptance. If easy and inconsequential, parents can eliminate or at least minimize exposure to irritating tactile stimuli. For example, parents can respect their child's preferences in clothing texture. They can minimize baths and modify hugs. After all, we adults make these kinds of choices for ourselves all the time.

Side notes: At this point, a disclaimer seems warranted. As stated earlier, we have limited our discussion so far to accommodations, not interventions. Readers might be growing impatient. Isn't there a limit to how much we should cater to our children's developmental differences? How are they going to learn navigating the real world? Doesn't avoidance reinforce hypersensitivities? Every time we accommodate our challenging children, don't we deny them an opportunity to develop flexibility, learn new skills, and work things out on their own? Is the approach advocated here tantamount to permissive parenting? When do we stop spoiling, coddling, and enabling? How about setting some limits? How about letting them learn that the world doesn't revolve around their personal preferences? In the context of this section on sensory differences, what about the child who refuses to get dressed and has a tantrum every morning because, "This shirt is too scratchy!" The harder these parents try to find "the right shirt," the more this child insists, "There aren't any shirts that feel right! I can't go to school!"

Your Gander Instruction Manual emphasizes accommodation. The preceding ten-mile *Journey* is mostly about intervention; including desensitization, limit setting and natural consequences; plus, a host of other behavioral interventions that promote self-care, flexibility, and independence. In the end, parents are encouraged to put it all together and determine the right balance of accommodation *and* intervention; acceptance *and* change.

Movement/body position in space

What it means: The inner ear sends signals to the brain about balance, position, movement, and acceleration. Children with **high sensitivity to movement and positional change** experience distress or, more often, avoid such activities altogether. Other children with **low sensitivity to movement and positional change** are not bothered by even sudden or extreme positional changes. They may seek out spatial disorientation adventure.

Goodness of fit

- *Good for:* **High sensitivity to movement** can be good for avoiding potentially dangerous activities. Such children are more likely to opt out of truly risky jumps, slides, and high-speed misadventures. They might naturally resist ill-advised dares from peers. They are more likely to exercise caution on skates, bikes, hikes, and playgrounds. **Low sensitivity to movement** is good for having certain kinds of fun or tolerating unavoidable acceleration or turbulence. Many childhood activities involve hurtling through space. A wide variety of sports and recreational activities require a high tolerance of positional change; for example, gymnastics, boating, skiing, skating, and amusement-park rides. Many good times and friendships are launched and shared on swing sets, slides, rides, hills, and diving boards. Traveling by car, bus, train, or plane can be a true pleasure for these children and their parents.
- *Problem if:* A **high sensitivity to movement** and positional change can be a problem for many desirable or necessary activities. These children are not born for space travel. They can have significant discomfort with very ordinary car rides, slides, and swings. Even walking down stairs and hills can feel like torture. Anxiety and nausea are no fun. Adults who don't understand this

source of secondary behavioral disturbances might feel frustrated. **Low sensitivity to movement** can be a problem if children engage in daredevil behaviors and put themselves at risk of serious injury.

- *Parent-child fit:* Parents with high sensitivity to movement might find themselves mismatched with a movement-craving child. Parents with low sensitivity to movement might have difficulty understanding their child's reluctance to travel or participate in certain activities.

ACCOMMODATIONS:

- Strategies to accommodate **high sensitivity to movement** involve avoiding or at least minimizing unwanted changes in position and velocity. These children should not be forced into distressing activities just because it's somebody else's idea of fun. For unavoidable travel, parents and children should experiment with different strategies, such as distraction with music or conversation; relaxation with breathing awareness, muscle exercises, or positive mental imagery; or preferential seating (if safe) in the front seat. Car drivers should take it easy, avoiding sudden braking, accelerating, and turning. If necessary, consider using Dramamine or Scopolamine.
- Strategies to accommodate **low sensitivity to movement** require extra supervision in high-risk environments. As they grow up, these movement-seeking children need to be carefully watched and taught, beginning with stairs and followed by playgrounds, streets, and "extreme" recreational activities. These children should not be allowed to shun appropriate safety gear and equipment. Rules should be reviewed and enforced. Dance, skating, gymnastics, and other relatively safe outlets should be provided for immediate pleasure and long-term health.

Side notes: What's the difference between high sensory reactivity and anxiety? These two aspects of a child's profile often "travel" together. In the context of this discussion, it may be difficult to know which came first: a child's fear of flying and driving or a sensitivity to movement through space. In chicken-egg relationships, things change over time. A child with sensory reactivity might get more and more tense about airplanes and cars. Although this aversion may have started with motion sickness, the secondary anxiety can "take on a life of its own." Even as the child gradually "outgrows" his or her sensitivity to motion, the anxiety may continue. Just as possible, a child with a primary anxiety problem could easily develop secondary sensitivity to changes in spatial position. In theory, treatment might depend on which came first: the sensory reactivity or the anxiety. Accordingly, interventions would target either the "sensory brain" or the "emotional brain." If a child is impaired by coexisting motion sensitivity and anxiety, should parents call an occupational therapist who specializes in sensory strategies or a psychotherapist who specializes in therapy for anxiety?

I recommend steering clear of such artificial "either/or" approaches. Clearly, in this and most cases like it, there are sensory components to the anxiety *and* anxiety components to the sensory experience. Anxious children tend to have heightened sensory reactivity, and hypersensitive children tend to experience more anxiety. As Levine would say, "There is dysfunction at the junction of the functions." So should this child see a psychotherapist *and* an occupational therapist? Perhaps. But it's better to see one professional who *integrates* research and wisdom across disciplines: a therapist who truly sees the whole child, not one who treats coexisting facets as if they were isolated and unrelated. In this case, that means finding a psychologist who knows a lot about sensory differences *or* an occupational therapist who knows a lot about cognitive-behavioral therapy. Unfortunately, the paucity of cross-disciplinary training makes integrationists scarce and hard to find.

Beyond the chicken-egg question, should this child's interrelated motion sickness and anxiety be accommodated or fixed? Quite simply, both. The complicated part is determining the right balance of accommodation versus intervention. Such management decisions cannot be found in consensus statements written by isolated therapeutic camps. Rather, the right blend of accommodation *and* intervention—in this example, sensory therapy *and* cognitive-behavioral therapy—is determined on a case-by-case basis and then modified according to the child's progress over time. How to do this? A comprehensive, integrated, multidimensional program. Not simple, but I hope that this *Parent Child Journey* proves to be a useful start.

Internal body awareness/physical symptoms

What it means: Some children have **high sensitivity to internal body sensations.** They are remarkably aware of physical symptoms. Infantile colic may be the earliest manifestation of hypersensitivity to intestinal discomfort. Over the years, children with this kind of body awareness are quicker to notice fatigue, fever, headaches, stomachaches, and other bowel and bladder signals. The list of potential sources of physical discomfort encompasses the whole field of pediatric medicine (Schmitt, 2005). Children with **low sensitivity to internal body sensations** do not readily notice these internal stimuli. They are relatively oblivious to body signals.

Goodness of fit:

- *Good for:* **High sensitivity to internal body sensations** is good for getting sympathy and necessary medical attention. It helps with toilet training and self-care. **Low sensitivity to internal body sensations** is good for tolerating minor discomforts and carrying on despite illness.

- *Problem if:* **High sensitivity to internal body sensations** is a problem if it interferes with normal functioning. Some children run to the bathroom more than they need to. Others can be "bellyachers" or "somaticizers"; true hypochondriacs. They overreact to normal physiologic changes or experience any degree of emotional distress as physical symptoms. In addition to the child's amplified misery, his or her distorted reporting can cause diagnostic confusion and frustration for others. **Low sensitivity to internal body sensations** is a problem if significant medical problems go unnoticed and underreported. Some of these children might rupture an eardrum or an appendix before anybody knows they've been sick. Sometimes relative insensitivity to bowel and bladder signals can interfere with toilet training or timely toilet use. For safety and optimal care, some chronic medical conditions—such as asthma and diabetes—require a certain level of body signal awareness.
- *Parent-child fit:* Parents who have a high sensitivity to body discomforts may project this heightened awareness onto their children. This can cause parents to overreact to their child's symptoms, model poor coping, or make the child unnecessarily anxious. Parents who are distracted by—or obsessed with—their own physical discomforts might be less emotionally available to their children. On the other hand, parents who have a low sensitivity to body discomforts may find it difficult to empathize with a child who seems to be a "bellyacher" or "always crying wolf."

Accommodations:

- Strategies to accommodate **high sensitivity to internal body sensations** involve minimizing physical distress whenever possible. For example, if a child is more sensitive to pain or fever, parents may be somewhat more liberal with medications. As these hypersensitive children get older, it may be appropriate to allow brief and infrequent breaks from certain activities—"until you feel better"—as long as they do return and a tendency to withdraw does not spiral out of control. With children who are unreliable overreporters, parents and doctors may need to rely more heavily on objective data from physical exams, laboratory tests, or radiologic imaging. Adults can avoid overreacting or underreacting to the child's "drama" by carefully monitoring trends and then distinguishing between symptoms that are mild and transient versus serious and persistent. When in doubt, parents should contact their pediatrician.

- Strategies to accommodate **low sensitivity to internal body sensations** require parents and other caregivers to have a "high index of suspicion." These underreporting children can put themselves at increased risk. Parents should learn their child's subtle cues. For some young children, vague and minor changes in behavior or sleep pattern might be reliable indicators of ear infection. The increased risk of undetected illness should condition these parents to err on the safe side and go to the doctor for relatively mild symptoms. For children with chronic or recurrent medical conditions, parents might have to rely more often on objective physiologic measures, such as peak flow meters if asthmatic and thermometers if immunocompromised.

Side notes: In describing your child's sensitivity to body sensations—or any other facet of their sensory profile—remember that these are just generalizations about predispositions and tendencies, not 100 percent reliable indicators or predictors. Parents and doctors who know a child too well should not let history bias their judgment too much. For underreporters, there might be a tendency to overcompensate with excessive assessment and unnecessary treatment. On the other hand, each time a chronic bellyacher's symptoms are too quickly dismissed—"there he goes again"—it could be the one time that he or she has a serious medical or surgical problem. Even if the physical symptoms are "all in their head," emotional distress is no less deserving of attention, evaluation, and support—albeit of a different kind. After all, the distinction between "mind" and "body" is never so clear and clean. We all experience physical symptoms in different ways. Our perceptions depend not just on our temperament and physiology, but also on our culture, experience, and conditioned behavior. These sensitivities change over time.

This concludes our discussion of behavioral style including temperament and sensory profile. We now turn to a discussion of various skills.

Discussion of Skills Profile

In this section of the Gander, you will rate your child's relative strengths and weaknesses in the following developmental domains:

- Fine motor
- Handwriting
- Gross motor
- Speaking
- Listening
- Writing
- Reading
- Understanding spatial relations
- Visual arts
- Music
- Math
- Time awareness
- Planning, organization, and implementation
- Social skills

We all have strengths and weaknesses. Your child's "skills profile" represents a combination of affinity, opportunity, instruction, and practice.

Understanding your child's skills profile will further help explain the source of your child's challenging behavior. This description of skills will guide individualized and effective management strategies. Also, the skills profile represents a road map to success and fulfillment.

These skill categories are artificial. Each facet of your child's skills profile exists in dynamic interplay with every other facet. Language and math affect each other, fine motor and time management affect each other, gross motor and social skills affect each other, and so on. All developmental domains are intertwined.

These important interconnections are sometimes obvious; other times they are hidden. Many skills that are considered prerequisites for academic success are at least as important for social-emotional functioning. For example, strengths or weaknesses in expressive language are important both in the classroom and on the playground. Conversely, social skills are necessary both for making friends and for group academic learning. All other facets of your child's profile—including behavioral style, sensory profile, and life stresses—affect each facet of the skills profile, and vice versa. Mild weaknesses in different areas may be of no consequence when viewed in isolation. However, in combination, minor differences can cause surprisingly significant impairment. Take the child who has just a little trouble with attention, a little trouble with receptive language, a little trouble with time management, and a little trouble with writing efficiency. It might not be immediately obvious why he or she never knows what to do for homework. Each weakness by itself is no big deal. However, if parents and teachers take a step back and view the overlap of these subtle differences, there is no mystery at all. In fact, this broader perspective makes the source of difficulty painfully clear. Skill by skill, we will be considering many of these important interconnections.

As with all facets of the Gander, your child's skills profile will change over time. Some children overcome or "outgrow" disabilities. Other children experience progressively increasing impairment. For all children, we should do our best to accommodate and remediate skill deficits. In addition—and perhaps more importantly—we should make every effort to identify and nurture each child's natural strengths and interests. A strengths-based approach to skills development lays the foundation for social connection, positive self-image, and success.

This does not mean that every child has some hidden talent or genius. We have all heard incredible stories about amputees climbing Mount Everest or autistic savants quickly mastering complicated foreign languages. Although such tales are inspiring, as discussed in the Tenth Mile, some people in the disability rights movement sardonically call them "super crips" because their heroism can also be demoralizing. After all, such compensatory abilities are truly extraordinary. Not every blind person can be Stevie Wonder. Not every child with language disability can be Albert Einstein. And not every child with a mood disorder can be Abraham Lincoln. For most people, there is a limit to how much can be achieved. To suggest that anyone can overcome his or her disability if he or she just tries hard enough is unrealistic and insulting. Still, as emphasized by Gardner (2006) in his writings on multiple intelligences, there are "different kinds of smart." To a certain degree, areas of relative ability can be tapped to facilitate progress in areas of relative weakness. And these strengths can be strengthened for their own sake. Just because a child has difficulty in some areas of development does not mean that he or she must be denied any measure of success.

As you complete your child's skills profile, describe his or her current level of functioning. Do not dwell on the past or speculate about the future. Let's not place any artificial ceiling on his or her developmental potential or assume a certain life path. Do not define your child's destiny by just one narrow facet of his or her profile. Rather, the current skills profile should simply take the mystery out of everyday struggles and guide effective solutions. If we take care of today, who knows what tomorrow will bring?

Similar to the explanation of behavioral style and sensory profile, for each facet of your child's Gander skills profile, I will offer comments regarding:

- "What it means" including developmental norms
- "Goodness of fit"
  - "Good for/"Problem if"
  - "Parent-child fit"
- Accommodations
- Strengthening strengths
- Side notes

Let's start with motor skills.

Fine motor, handwriting, and gross motor

What it means: For some children, motor performance comes easily. Others have difficulty with motor control due to lack of practice, lack of natural ability, or both. For the first few years of life, we have very well-established norms for motor development (Frankenburg, Dodds, Archer, Shapiro, & Bresnick, 1992). Average ages for achieving early motor milestones can be found in any standard textbook (Illingworth, 2013; Kliegman, Stanton, St. Geme, & Schor, 2015).

Gross motor milestones

- prone	
- head up	1 month
- chest up	2 months
- up on elbows	3 months
- up on hands	4 months
- roll front to back	3 to 4 months
- roll back to front	4 to 5 months

sit with support	5 months
sit without support	6 to 7 months
come to sit	8 months
crawl (quadruped)	8 months
pull to stand	8 to 9 months
crawl	9 to 10 months
walk (two hands held)	10 months
walk (one hand held)	11 months
walk alone (ten steps)	12 months
stoop and recover	14 months
run (stiff leg)	15 months
walk upstairs (with rail)	21 months
jump in place	24 months
pedal a tricycle	30 months
downstairs (alternating feet)	3 years
balance (five secs each foot)	4 years

Fine motor milestones

retain ring (rattle)	1 month
hands unfisted (< 50%)	3 months
reach	3 to 4 months
hands to midline	3 to 4 months
transfer hand to hand	5 months
take one-inch cube	5 to 6 months
take pellet	6 to 7 months
immature pincer	7 to 8 months
mature pincer	10 months
voluntary release	12 months
tower of four cubes	18 months
tower of eight cubes	2.5 years

GRAPHOMOTOR MILESTONES

• scribble	13 months
• copy vertical line	2.5 years
• copy circle	3.5 years
• copy + sign	4.5 years
• copy square	5.5 years

CURRENT MOTOR SKILLS

Once your child has these basic motor skills down, assessment of higher-level motor function becomes more qualitative and subjective. With increasing age, judgments about relative motor strengths and weaknesses are more about "how well" rather than "can or can't." Across the range of motor skills, how coordinated, fluid, and efficient is your child? Clumsy or graceful? Accident-prone or "cat-like"? What about your child's muscle tone, posture, and strength? Stamina and endurance? Ability to learn new movements and work toward mastery of more complicated and specialized motor skills? Without clear-cut norms for higher-level motor skills, we are left making rough comparisons with age-matched peers and speculating whether even subtle differences in motor ability might interfere with skill acquisition. Think about the quality of your child's motor skills with regard to the following:

- Gross motor skills: walking, running, bike-riding, skating, sports
- Fine motor skills: grasping or manipulating small objects, taking, transferring and releasing, using fingers or utensils to eat, tying shoes, brushing teeth, dressing, buttoning clothes, zipping, drawing, keyboarding, playing musical instruments, using tools
- Graphomotor skills: printing, cursive

Goodness of fit:

- *Good for/Problem if:* Good motor skills are crucial for many types of tasks, including self-care, academics, and play. Sometimes motor weaknesses are obviously disabling. Other times their impact can be subtler but still significant. Ultimately, motor difficulties don't just complicate the performance of specific tasks. Motor struggles can also have a negative impact on self-image, motivation, and socialization.
    - Gross motor skills are important for sports, playground activities, peer interaction, exercise, health, and ordinary transitions from place to place. At school, motor competence is most obvious in physical education class, but it may be just as important for simply moving around the classroom, up and down stairs, and through the halls. At home and play, children with motor weaknesses might have a hard time keeping up.
    - Fine motor skills are important across a wide range of life skills: for self-care, such as dressing, tying shoes, and eating; for play, such as building and playing games; for crafts, such as cutting, sewing, and folding; and for academics, such as keyboarding and managing a notebook.
    - Graphomotor skills are important for written expression, school performance, time management, and organization.
- *Parent-child fit:* When parents and children have mismatched motor skills, they may find it difficult to help one another with certain tasks or enjoy the same activities. What's easy for one can be difficult for the other. This can lead to misunderstanding, frustration, and anger. On the other hand, when parent and child have the same pattern of motor strengths and weaknesses, it may be easier to sympathize, share, and enjoy. Goodness of fit can be an issue across all kinds of motor activities at home, at school, and with friends.

Accommodations:
Simply recognizing weak motor skills allows parents and teachers to respond empathetically and lessen the child's frustration. Parents and other adults should not push a child to "just try harder." They should not admonish: "You can do better than that!" Instead, empathize: "That sure is hard, isn't it?" An understanding response is deeply appreciated by children, whether their frustration is with motor performance in sports, crafts, writing, or self-care.

If motor difficulties impair learning, socialization, self-help, or health, then it may be necessary to provide special instruction, accommodations, and support. Parents should consider allowing their child to opt out only if a difficult motor activity is frustrating and unimportant. Children should not be forced to do things just because they are *supposed* to be fun. Many adults have preconceptions about what makes for a happy and meaningful childhood. Some parents, and our culture at large, attach undue value to success in competitive athletics. Certain activities that are fun for many children can be pure torture for a child with motor impairments. If the activity is supposed to be pleasurable but it only brings pain, then parents should reexamine their motivation.

In public settings, bypass strategies can be employed to lessen handicaps and avoid humiliation. Bypass strategies usually require modification of the task itself. Adults should ask: What is the educational or developmental bottom line? Why does this task need to be done? Why is total avoidance inappropriate? What does the child really need to do? The answers to these questions will guide management. Usually, there are different roads that can lead to the same destination. Why jump over a hurdle when you can remove it or just run around it? Ideally, task modification is done in such a way that the child can successfully participate and enjoy without calling undue attention to his or her weakness. Universal accommodations, such as ramps for wheelchairs, can destigmatize disability and make the climb easier for all. Whenever possible, modifications should be normalizing, not humiliating; empowering, not demoralizing.

Here are some examples of accommodation strategies for a variety of motor tasks.

For fine motor problems:

- Loafers, Velcro, or self-tying shoes can substitute for standard tie shoes. Here, the goal is independence in getting shoes on and off, not shoe tying per se.
- Electric toothbrushes and short haircuts can make personal hygiene less physically demanding.
- Finger paints, touch screens, or drawing software can facilitate artistic creation without requiring "a fine hand." Instead of freehand drawing, children can use rulers, stencils, tracing paper, lined paper, and graph paper when it might otherwise be too difficult to connect points or reproduce images. Digital cameras can come in handy too.
- Simplified guitar or ukulele chords (on just two strings) or electronic pianos (that create full band sounds by just touching one key) can help children enjoy music without having to master finger technique. Some instruments, such as sax, clarinet, and violin, are less forgiving of poor motor coordination than others, such as piano, trumpet, autoharp, drums, and harmonica. The pace of instruction and complexity of material should be slowed and simplified to match the child's rate of skill acquisition.
- For lack of a better place to comment on (nonspeech) oral-motor control problems: Children (or adults) who cannot swallow whole pills or capsules can take crushed, sprinkled, or liquid medicines. Some medicines come in dissolvable tablets that melt in the mouth or patches that get absorbed through the skin.

For writing mechanics problems:

- Children with problems writing should not be forced to write on the blackboard in front of others. They should not be pushed to write faster than they really can.
- When poor handwriting interferes with self-expression, demonstration of knowledge, or recording important information, consider the following bypass strategies:
  - keyboarding
  - dictation to a scribe or voice recognition software
  - note-takers, recording devices, teacher notes, and teacher websites
  - word prediction software
  - reduced written workload
  - oral, dramatic, or other modes of presentation
  - PowerPoint
  - grading on content, not penmanship
  - extended time
  - write-in test booklets instead of on separate "fill in the bubble" sheets
- Teachers can use a team approach for writing assignments and assign jobs such that each child's strengths compensate for another child's weaknesses. For example, one child is the reader, another is the idea kid, another takes care of supplies, another is the illustrator, another the scribe, and another is the project manager.

For gross motor problems:

- Toilet step stools
- Sports accommodations:
  - For baseball, extra-fat baseball bats, hitting-Ts, Velcro gloves and balls
  - For basketball, low hoops and small, lightweight balls

    - For soccer, playing goalie, assistant goalie, or defense instead of midfield or forward
- Noncompetitive exercise: dance, water play, swimming, gardening, hiking, kayaking, martial arts, playground, camping skills, climbing, wrestling, yoga.
- Stationary bike (in front of TV or movie if necessary, or while reading, looking at magazines, or listening to music or audiobooks if possible).
- If your child likes sports but has gross motor difficulties, consider alternative modes of participation such as team trainer, manager, scorekeeper, statistician, or photographer.
- If the goal is getting from here to there rather than physical fitness, then provide ramps, rides, and lifts.

Strengthen strengths: For children with an affinity for motor activities, parents should provide plenty of opportunity for fun, health, social connection, positive self-image, and possible mastery. For fine motor and gross motor, the range of possibilities is wide and deep: sports and fitness, dance, arts and crafts, outdoor recreation and yard work, to name just a few.

Side notes: Even minor lags in gross motor, fine motor, or writing skills can have a major impact. Early in life, subtle differences may not be obvious. The child might appear to be well within normal limits for acquisition of early milestones, but only because it is impossible to assess later-developing skills until they are due to come online. For example, there is no way to know about a two-month-old's walking skills, a one-year-old's ability to tie shoelaces, or a two-year-old's cursive writing. Time must pass. Over the years, as motor demands increase, inconsequential weaknesses might become significant sources of impairment and frustration. Only when expectations regarding workload and quality go up are difficulties with efficiency and endurance exposed. Standardized measures and competition amplify the importance of seemingly minor skill deficits. Even as your child makes progress, other children make progress too. The performance gap can widen when your child's rate of development is help up against his or her peers.

On the other hand, some very obvious and worrisome early motor delays might turn out to be surprisingly inconsequential. Some children do just fine despite their awkward way of running, fingering the guitar fret board, or holding a pencil. On standardized assessments they might score low, but in life, they do plenty well enough. They might learn to compensate for a motor disability by leaning on other offsetting strengths. They might be extremely late bloomers. Through special support, expert instruction, perseverance, and the passage of time, they might overcome physical handicaps.

Accurate developmental assessment must take place over time. One point on a graph of motor abilities may fall well below average. But we must draw lines between many points to see meaningful trends. Relative to most other children, is your child's motor skills gap widening, closing, or staying the same? Also consider: do these data points reflect real-world functioning or just isolated skills? Long-term, natural-environment assessment is crucial, not just in understanding motor development, but in all other facets of your child's skills profile as well.

Language: speaking, listening, writing, and reading

What it means: Here, we will focus mostly on verbal language; that is, the development and use of words. Nonverbal language—including facial expression, tone of voice, gesture, and so on—will be covered below in the section on social skills. For the sake of simplicity, verbal language skills can be categorized as expressive or receptive, spoken or written: speaking, listening, writing, and reading. As with other skills, your child's language development can be compared to the majority of typically developing children. Has your child achieved the following language milestones at these average ages? Earlier or later? As you work through this section, remember that different facets of language are controlled by different brain networks. So, just because you are good at speaking does not necessarily mean that you are good at listening.

For speech:

imitates speech sounds	5 months
combines syllables	6 months
first words	10 months
combines words, 2 to 3-word phrases	18 months
names one picture	18 months
50 percent understood by strangers	18 months
entirely understood by strangers	3 years

What about your child's quality, fluency, and comfort with higher-level speech skills, such as putting increasingly complicated thoughts into words, organizing language on demand, and enjoying conversation?

For writing, how does your child do putting his or her thoughts onto paper? Organizing thoughts into good sentences and paragraphs? Does your child enjoy writing?

For listening, when did your child achieve his or her milestones relative to these average ages?

Points to six different body parts when asked, "Where's your____?"	18 months
Points to four pictures, when asked "Where's the _____?"	20 months
Understands four prepositions, four verbs, and three adjectives	3 years
Defines seven words and gives two opposites	4.5 years

For higher-level listening skills, how does your child do:

- Understanding spoken communication?
- Learning the alphabet, days of the week, months of the year, phone number, address, and birthday?
- Following a spoken story or lesson?
- Understanding directions without needing repetition?

For reading, how does your child do with:

- Letter recognition?
- Word recognition?
- Speed and fluency naming (letters, number, and words)?
- Following a line of print without losing place?
- Reading for a long time?
- Understanding written instructions?
- Overall reading comprehension?
- Overall pleasure reading?

For now, these guidelines are designed to keep things simple. But it may be hard to know what's normal. Try comparing your child to other children his or her age. If you're not sure, ask an experienced teacher or consider consulting a speech-language pathologist. In the side notes that follow, I will discuss some complexities of language assessment.

GOODNESS OF FIT:

- *Good for/Problem if:* Language skills are important for school success. Children are tested and graded on their ability to read, write, and participate in classroom discussions. These academic performance skills may also be crucial for many future jobs. Although language strengths and weaknesses are systematically measured and reported against academic benchmarks, the very same expressive and receptive language skills can also have relatively hidden but profound impact outside of the classroom.

Across all settings, language disorders often interfere with learning, problem-solving, social communication, behavior, and even mood regulation. Virtually every aspect of human functioning depends on language. For many children, even subtle weaknesses in language comprehension can present as "oppositional" behavior or "selective hearing." These children may have relative difficulty understanding exactly what parents or teachers are saying. They may have problems asking for clarification. They may struggle to put their frustrations into words. Especially when stressed or anxious, they may freeze, act out, or explode. If a child cannot easily describe his or her own emotions, it's awfully hard to problem-solve. Instead of recognizing and accommodating these underlying language deficits, adults may assume that such secondary "noncompliant" behaviors represent willful "disobedience," "laziness," or "stupidity." Moreover, your child might not understand the connection between his or her own language weaknesses and his or her trouble meeting expectations.

Beyond academic and behavioral issues, children with weak expressive and receptive language skills usually struggle in peer interaction. So much of social success depends on fluent speaking and listening skills. Imagine trying to make friends and keep friends if you were suddenly dropped off in a foreign country (Duke et al., 1996). For children with language weaknesses, navigating complicated and fast-paced verbal back-and-forth can be that daunting.

- *Parent-child fit:* When parents and children share strong verbal language abilities, it can be easier to communicate expectations. When conflicts arise, language-able dyads have an easier time problem-solving together. If a parent or child has weak expressive or receptive language, it's harder for them to understand and help each other. This can lead to misunderstanding and anger. Parent and/or child might unwittingly communicate frustration rather than repair what was "lost in translation."

Accommodations:

Strategies to accommodate language skills deficits require adults to remain attuned to possible academic, behavioral, and social repercussions. Parents and teachers need to understand the child's language level and adjust their verbal communication accordingly. The child's developmental age for language might not match their chronological age. Expectations must match abilities. Parents and teachers need to remember that these children talk, understand, read, and write at "younger" levels. At the same time, it is important not to confuse language abilities with intelligence. Even children with severe language disability can learn. Adults just need to stay calm, patient, and sensitive to the frustration these children experience. Parents and teachers should take care not to embarrass or humiliate. They should be sure not to mistake language disability for defiance, anxiety, or global delays. They should not mistake paucity of expression for disinterest, rudeness, or inability to learn.

In general:

- Find the mode of language processing and production that is easiest for your child, and let him or her rely on that input and output channel, such as listening versus reading, speaking versus writing.
- Supplement verbal communication with nonverbal modes; for example, demonstration, not just pure explanation.
- If language inefficiency interferes with the child's ability to show what he or she knows, consider reduced workload and

extra time for tests and assignments. Warning: extra time is often very helpful—but not always. If a child just doesn't know what he or she is reading or how to begin formulating a response, all the time in the world will not vanquish a true learning disability. In fact, extra time might even lead to extra frustration. The longer a child just sits and stares at a blank piece of paper or struggles to speak, the more anxious he or she may become. Extra time may be necessary, but not sufficient.

- In school, foreign language requirements can be modified or even waived if a child is bound to have difficulty with just his or her native language.

For speech problems:

- Make sure that more verbal children do not always jump in and take away speaking opportunities from a less fluent child.
- If a verbal response is necessary, extra processing and production time can help. Let the child know the question in advance. Give assistance preparing an answer. Do not call on these children in class or in certain social settings if the result would only be embarrassment.
- Sign language, picture exchange, and symbol selection can empower speech-delayed children to communicate (Bondy & Frost, 2011; Heller, 2004). A plethora of new technologies "speak for the child" when he or she touches various pictures on customized electronic app screens (Green, 2013). These alternate modes of expression do not delay language acquisition; rather, they give speech a developmental lift.
- Multiple-choice or true-false formats can help, both in casual conversation and class discussion.
- "Comic strip conversations" can help children slow down and express emotionally complicated thoughts (Gray, 1994). Using

sequential panels, just like a cartoon strip, you can draw simple figures and then have your child suggest how to fill in thought or feeling bubbles. "What is he thinking now?"

For written expression problems:

- Again, extra time, adjusted workload, *and* extra help can be crucial.
- Avoid total reliance on weak writing skills. These children should be allowed and encouraged to share their thoughts and feelings by other means: drawing, acting, demonstrating, singing, speaking, dictating—whatever alternate mode of presentation takes advantage of the child's strengths to bypass his or her written output weakness.
- Use multiple-choice or true-false formats in testing. Avoid essay exams.
- Sometimes it is appropriate to de-emphasize the importance of spelling or grammar if the primary educational goal is self-expression or demonstration of understanding. Spelling and grammar can be taught separately.
- For organization of language, prewriting exercises can make a huge difference (Graham & Harris, 2005). Consider graphic organizers, PowerPoint, and specialized computer software.

For problems understanding spoken language:

- Speak slowly and clearly. Keep it short and simple. Many children just need more time, smaller chunks, or simpler paraphrasing. Repeat instructions. No shouting.
- Get visual engagement before speaking, then work hard to keep your child's eyes on you throughout the communication.
- Supplement speech with nonverbal communication aids: gesture, animation, pictures, charts, graphs, drama, music, demonstration, and hands-on activities (Tufte, 1997).

- If a child has a special passion—sports, video games, TV shows—relate new and difficult concepts to those familiar interests.

For problems understanding written language:

- Minimize the reading content in nonverbal tasks. For example, language-rich "everyday math" is great for some children, but language-impaired children would do better with a more traditional, pure math approach or a multi-sensory approach like Math-U-See.
- Use the auditory channel. Some children do much better with books on tape, electronic readers, reading aloud, group reading, and taped instructions.
- Help your child make up a rhyme or use a mnemonic or acronym when he or she is trying to learn and remember written material.
- Act it out. Have fun with role-playing written narratives.
- Demonstrate. Some children understand best when adults model and help them walk through a set of instructions. Especially for multistep tasks, first do it together. Your child has a better chance of understanding and remembering what he or she is supposed to do if you show versus command.
- To overcome problems with inconsistent eye-tracking, your child can be taught to use a finger, marker, index card, or reading window.
- Associate reading materials with previously acquired knowledge or special interests.
- Preview new material. Read comprehension questions before reading the text. Use notes, outlines, or study guides. Preteach concepts and vocabulary. Prehighlight main ideas.
- Provide an easier text on the same content.
- Use an alternative to reading to present the same material, such as movies, exhibits, or field trips.
- Again, when appropriate, consider extended time and/or reduced reading load.

Strengthen strengths: Children with strong language skills can take full advantage of their natural gifts. Reading and writing should not just be considered academic necessities, but inherently valuable and fulfilling activities. Children should be encouraged to read for pleasure and growth, write creatively and persuasively, and journal for emotional release and self-discovery. Our culture attaches status to skillful speaking, but family, friends, classmates, and coworkers value skillful listening at least as much.

Side notes: No domain of child development is more crucial or complex than language. Although expressive and receptive language disorders are the most common source of impairment in childhood, the many different types of language difficulty often go unrecognized and are misunderstood. Due to the complexity of language and communication, careful assessment must move beyond simplistic distinctions between expressive or receptive, spoken or written. Though some children have discrete language problems, many have a combination of different language disorders.

Comprehensive discussion, complete developmental norms, and myriad diagnostic instruments are available (Paul & Norbury, 2011). A complete review of language assessment is beyond the scope of this book—and the expertise of this author. However, to understand how speech-language pathologists dissect language problems, it is important to have some familiarity with the range of differences in language development.

As outlined previously, **receptive verbal language** problems relate to incoming words: what a person "hears or reads" and what was actually "said or written." **Expressive verbal language** problems relate to outgoing words: what a person actually "says or writes" and what he or she would have liked to communicate. Children can also have **receptive and expressive nonverbal language disorders**. These social-pragmatic language problems will be discussed in detail in the section on social skills. Here, we will focus on the subtypes of **verbal language** problems.

Phonemes or speech sounds are the most elementary building blocks of language. Phonemes are like the atoms of language. To say the word "bat," three distinct speech sounds are pronounced: /b/, /a/, and /t/. These three phonemes blend together to form the word as it is said and heard. These three phonemes are also coded into alphabetical representations to form words as written or read. Much has been made of how the English language does not have one-to-one correspondence between phonemes as they are said and written. True enough. But English is not as haphazard as many people think. Patterns of phoneme-alphabet coding-decoding can be taught (McGuinness, 1999; McGuinness & McGuinness, 1999). Some children have a hard time recognizing or vocalizing these distinct sounds. They have problems with phonological processing or production. These children can have associated problems with decoding (reading), encoding (spelling), listening (registration), and/or speaking (articulation).

Semantics refers to word meaning and word retrieval; that is, understanding and using vocabulary. We create words by combining phonemes. If phonemes are like atoms, then words are like molecules. Many words must simply be learned through repeated exposure or memorization, but knowledge of word roots helps with vocabulary building. (This is especially true for medical students, such as, oto = ear, larynx = upper airway, "-ology" = study of the ear, nose, and throat.) Similarly, suffixes ("-ful" and "-ness") and prefixes ("ex-" and "pro-") can further facilitate understanding of semantic language. But many words have meaning only if understood in context. These semantic-pragmatic language difficulties are most obvious when children miss the inference or metaphor and take the meaning of idioms too literally, such as "it's raining cats and dogs" or "let's shoot for the moon." Some children have difficulty understanding that the same word can have different meanings. For example, the word "bank" can refer to rivers or money. Despite good phonological processing and production, some children can still struggle with expressive and/or receptive language at the semantic level. Some readers decode phonemes fluently but have a hard time understanding the meaning of single words. Some speakers have perfect articulation but have difficulty finding the right word.

Syntax refers to the structure of language, especially as it pertains to sentence meaning. Syntax is like the chemical bonds and architecture of language. For example, the same three words can carry very different messages when their order is changed; for example, "dog bites man" means something very different from "man bites dog." A failure to understand and use rules of grammar can turn past into future (walked vs. walk), many into one (feet vs. foot), and nouns into verbs (runner vs. run). Many children have difficulty using and understanding pronouns. Children who have difficulty with syntax and grammar can misunderstand or miscommunicate in subtle but significant ways.

Discourse refers to how sentences are put together. Depending on how many data points or ideas are being connected, discourse is like the organs or organisms of language. Some children have increasing difficulty as chunks of language become progressively longer, more complex, or more abstract. Metalinguistics, or language about language, can be especially difficult for many children and adults. For example, it might be hard to understand discussions about foreshadowing in a novel or passive voice in an essay. Some children do very well with early and simple language milestones but have significant impairment when they are expected to use language at these higher levels of complexity and sophistication. These children often have difficulty with concept formation, inferential reasoning, and memory.

Fluency refers to how quickly and efficiently language is processed (receptive) or produced (expressive). There can be dysfluency at the phonological level. For example, kindergarten screening should include *naming speed* for letters, numbers, and words. Some children might be able to "decode" phonemes just fine on standardized tests or when the pace is leisurely but struggle mightily when required to read quickly or under high-volume demands (Wolf & Bowers, 1999). Similarly, children can perform within the normal range for basic spelling and writing skills but fall apart with increased demands on efficiency, pace, and complexity. This can present as a dysfluency in writing or speech. *Speech dysfluencies*, such as stuttering and stammering, are the traditional domain of the speech therapist. But many children, especially when stressed or emotionally flooded, have subtler problems with auditory processing speed and organization of language for expression on demand.

This discussion only begins to unpeel the complexities of language development. Fortunately, parents can usually make very educated guesses about the source of a language problem without getting their own PhD or obtaining formal assessment by a speech-language pathologist. Referring to the previous explanation of different language domains: Does your child have difficulties with receptive, expressive, written, and/or oral language? At what level(s): phonological, semantic, syntactical, discourse, and/or fluency? Are there significant language problems in more than one of these domains? For sure, designing an effective language intervention program might require the expertise of reading, language, speech, and/or hearing specialists. However, parents can understand their child's language profile well enough to accommodate language differences, understand how these differences explain behavior, customize behavioral strategies, and know when it's necessary to seek expert help.

Although the Gander is designed to keep assessment simple and practical, I hope that this dive into the deep end of language assessment was interesting and served fair warning: there's often more to child development than meets the eye. In fact, for every facet of the Gander, there are many more layers of analysis than I could try to cover. Beyond the Gander, expert assessment might be necessary to sufficiently understand certain aspects of your child's profile. This is especially true regarding language. Despite these limitations, I hope the Gander proves to be a sufficiently useful springboard for understanding and helping your challenging child.

Understanding visual-spatial relations and visual arts

What it means: All children should have regular screening for vision deficits. But even with normal vision, children vary in their aptitude for visual-spatial relations and visual art. Compared to other children of the same age, how does your child do with the following types of visual processing and production skills?

- Identifying different types of lines, such as long and short, thick and thin, straight and curved
- Recognizing geometric shapes: circle, square, triangle, hexagon, and so on
- Recognizing the difference between geometric shapes (clear edges as made by tools) versus organic shapes (flowing, curving, and irregular as found in nature)
- Picking out hidden or different forms and objects
- Understanding pattern, line, shape, color, value (shading), space, and texture
- Understanding balance, symmetry, asymmetry, and proportion
- Understanding the difference between 2D and 3D; foreground, middleground, background; and other positional relationships
- Understanding depth, such as relationships between near-large and far-small

- Identifying and telling colors apart, knowing the difference between secondary and intermediate colors
- Understanding graphs, diagrams, and maps

Good for/problem if: Understanding visual-spatial relations and acquiring visual-art skills are obviously important for drawing, painting, crafts, sculpture, photography, building, and puzzles. These visual-art activities may be emphasized in some schools, but sadly not in others. A sense of visual-spatial relations is also important in math (geometry, graphing), science (astronomy, anatomy, computers, and chemistry), geography (maps), and architecture (drafting). Also, the ability to visualize can be important for comprehension in listening and reading. Children and adults with poor visual-spatial skills can get lost navigating standardized test answer sheets, pictures, graphs, and other modes of visual communication. Some children have legitimate trouble finding their way about school or around town. Eventually, they grow up to have difficulty hiking, driving, or boating. Depth perception has a significant impact on sports performance; for example, catching or hitting a ball, or finding the right position on the court or field. From an early age, children vary in their appreciation of visual art and their enjoyment of the creative process. Countless visual activities can provide fun and challenging activities for social connection, personal development, and pleasure.

Accommodations: Strategies to accommodate visual-spatial weaknesses include the following:

- Preview and coach the child when visuals are too complicated for his or her level of understanding or skill.
- Demonstrate and teach the child how to break down complicated visual wholes into simple isolated parts.
- Translate visuals into written or spoken directions. For example, maps can be converted to step-by-step instructions.

- Some children get lost even within the classroom—more so navigating larger buildings and neighborhoods. Color codes can be used to mark paths. Landmarks can be clearly identified. Peer travel partners can serve as escorts. Adult shadows can prompt as needed. GPS has been a lifesaver for the directionally challenged.

Strategies to accommodate visual arts weaknesses include the following:

- Scaffold output by providing stencils, outlines, and paint-/draw-by-number.
- Reduce art workload by finding alternate means of expression.
- Break down assignments or tasks into smaller chunks.
- For children who might feel hesitant or even embarrassed about their artistic skills, adults can provide extra encouragement and privacy.

Strengthen strengths: Children with visual-spatial strengths should be given plenty of opportunity to see great art, design, graphics, and architecture. This includes geography, navigation, and astronomy. They should have regular opportunities for informal practice and formal instruction.

Side notes: Here, a personal note. My friends and family know all too well: I should never be trusted to leave the house without GPS. Ever since I was a very young child, my life has been marked by a long series of navigation misadventures. My mother tells a story from when I was boy. I was playing in the neighborhood and got home late—as usual. Worried, she asked, "Where have you been?" With feigned nonchalance, I answered, "Guys don't like saying where they go." The truth is, I never had a clue where I was! In my defense, then and now, I am always on time. I'm just never in the right place. My wife, on the other hand, struggles with "on-time arrival," but she has a great sense of direction. I imagine that she must have an extraordinarily well-developed "mapping region" in her brain, just like the London taxicab drivers described in a famous MRI study. Lucky for me, I married the right person—a very good fit—and not just for her stellar directional abilities. Plus GPS came along, granting me some independence.

One snowy winter, when I was a fourth-year medical student and GPS apps had not yet been invented, I went to Madison, Wisconsin, for an extraordinary child neurology rotation with the revered Dr. Ray Chun (b. 1926–d. 2014). The first Monday morning, allowing plenty of extra time to walk through the snow from my apartment to the pediatric medical center, I got lost—as usual. Very late and flustered, I finally arrived in the middle of neurology rounds. Dr. Chun was addressing a group of medical trainees. Covered with snow and obviously embarrassed, I paused in the back of the room.

With a warm smile, Dr. Chun interrupted his lecture and said, "You must be Dan Shapiro."

Sheepishly, I said. "Yes."

Then he said a few words that changed my life: "Well, we were just talking about Krabbe Disease, but let's change up and talk about your brain instead. You traveled all the way from DC to spend the month in Wisconsin. My guess is that you were very motivated to get here on time. You probably wanted to make a good first impression? Something must have made that hard."

Apologetic but feeling a strange sense of relief, I explained, "As always, I got very lost."

He smiled and said, "Then let's talk about your right parietal lobe."

This was my introduction to the idea of brain-based developmental differences. In that moment, Dr. Chun became for me (as he had for so many others) a model of nonjudgmental, empathic, and compassionate care. From that day on, I have remained intrigued about the whole range of developmental differences.

Although I was happily dependent on my wife and cell phone for navigation, I had never been satisfied with my drawing skills, and nobody could hold the pencil for me. Michelangelo was one of my childhood heroes, but my own drawing development plateaued out at the stick figure/prekindergarten level. For years, I remained jealous of people who could sketch so naturally. But then, midcareer, I needed a series of cervical spine operations. This meant some time out of work and some long prednisone-fueled nights awake. Just when I was starting to go stir-crazy, a friend brought me a care package, including a sketch pad, pencils, and an instruction book (Edwards, 2012). For lack of anything better to do, I went through the exercises. I learned how to forget about drawing things and focus instead on lines, angles, and spaces. Much to my amazement, I learned to draw.

What would have happened to my visual-spatial development without my wife and GPS? Would I have learned to draw if not for neck surgery and a thoughtful friend? Similarly, in ways unforeseen, your child's disabilities might not matter as much in the future. Or skill deficits might prove more modifiable than you'd ever imagined.

Music

What it means: Some children have difficulty acquiring musical skills. Just like verbal language, musical language has its expressive and receptive aspects (Levitin, 2007). Various components of making and hearing music are well defined—melody, rhythm, harmony, tone, composition, and performance. The brain basis of musical ability and disability can be understood at various levels of complexity. Developmental norms for musical ability are fuzzy. At what ages should children be able to recognize or sing a melody, imitate songs, keep rhythm and tempo, read music, understand meter, hear and make harmony, understand the emotional character of music, sing or play in an ensemble, improvise, and compose? When should a child be able to learn different musical instruments, and at what level of proficiency? To a large degree, music development depends on exposure, opportunity, and positive instruction. Assessment of musical development depends on subjective comparisons of ability, ease, and pleasure.

Goodness of Fit:

- *Good for/Problem if:* In musical settings and activities, children have different levels of comfort, joy, distress, or aversion. Children who are relatively tone-deaf and rhythm-deaf can have a hard time fitting in with musical activities. Ironically, children with perfect pitch might feel irritated by the imperfect pitch of others. But the extraordinary range of benefits should make music exposure and music education an essential part of growing up (Sacks, 2008). Music can help children learn and thrive in every other area of development. Many studies demonstrate that music helps with language, reading, math, problem-solving, reasoning, imagination, and flexibility. Music can promote listening skills and memorization. Music training can help with the development of eye-hand coordination, spatial abilities, and timing. Music can fuel people to maximize physical exercise. Music training can help children learn perseverance, discipline, and hard work—plus how to tolerate mistakes and overcome anxiety. Music can reduce stress, help with relaxation, and improve overall emotional health. Musical ability correlates with better scores on standardized tests of achievement and intelligence. Music can motivate children to go to school. Music can be a wonderful source of connection with other people and a foundation for meaningful friendships. Learning to make music together means learning cooperation and teamwork. Music can be a means of self-expression, achievement, and positive self-image.

- *Parent-child fit:* Parents who have poorly developed music skills may have difficulty enjoying or helping with their child's musical activities. On the other hand, musically inclined parents might feel sadness, frustration, or disappointment if they have a child for whom music does not seem as easy or important. Because music can be central to self-image, parents and children with differences in musical taste can experience secondary tension or even conflict. Parents may feel threatened when their child's musical preferences pull him or her away, especially if these other musical influences seem powerful, undesirable, or even dangerous.

Accommodations: Strategies to accommodate are based on understanding and acceptance that children can have very significant differences in musical ability and affinity. Some children just don't seem to enjoy music. They might even seem irritated, covering their ears or withdrawing to music-free zones. Children with poorly developed musical ability should not be put on the spot or embarrassed. In very loud musical environments, volume can be reduced, or the child can use earplugs or headphones. Such children can be allowed to hang at the periphery and enter these music zones gradually.

Efforts should be made to discover pleasurable modes of musical exposure and expression. The child with fine motor coordination problems should probably not be started on saxophone or harp; rather, voice, trumpet, or autoharp. The child with easy fatigability should not be started on trombone or French horn; rather, electronic piano. The visual child should play the piano, guitar, or other instruments that allow him or her to see melodic lines and chord structures on the key or fingerboard. Conversely, the auditory child might do well on harmonica; the tactile child, strings; the kinesthetic child, percussion; and the child with good oral-motor control, brass or woodwinds. For many, the computer has become an extraordinarily flexible and welcoming musical instrument.

For instruction, children with weak language processing might do best with Suzuki Method, which is based simply on hearing, imitating, and repeating. Standard musical notation can be converted to fingering charts or tab notation. Demonstration and imitation can replace note-reading altogether. Motivation might depend heavily on respecting your child's song and style preferences. This might mean abandoning traditional method books and simply asking the child, "What's your favorite song?"

Strengthen strengths: Every school, from kindergarten through college, should have a strong musical arts program. From an early age, all children should be encouraged to sing or learn an instrument; hopefully more than one. Those with special abilities and affinities should receive extra instruction to maximize their musical potential and pleasure. Adults should help create opportunities for children to make music together; ranging from school bands and choirs to garage bands and electronic music.

Side notes: As with every other aspect of your child's profile, musical ability does not develop in a vacuum. As discussed previously, differences in behavioral style and skills affect music development. Conversely, musical abilities can have a profound impact on other facets of development. Nowhere is this dialectic more remarkable than in the interplay between musical and social development.

Social and environmental factors can have a profound impact on the development of musical ability. Think about your child's level of music exposure across settings: home, school, and other activities. Is your child's environment music-rich or music-poor? Does your child listen to, sing, or play music with family, schoolmates, and friends? Is music a vehicle for sharing emotional experiences, interpersonal connection, fun, and creativity? Has your child's music education been dry or moving, perfunctory or inspirational, programmatic or beautiful? Your child's success in developing musical ability may depend in large part on whether the music teacher was "really nice" or "way cool." Your child's motivation in music and all other pursuits depends on his or her interpersonal relationships.

On the other hand, musical ability can have a profound impact on social development. Many children with ADHD, learning disabilities, autism, and mood disorders have difficulty with interpersonal relationships. When so many other parts of their lives can be filled with frustration and disappointment, relative strengths in music can represent both a launching point and safe harbor. Looking back on their lives, how many children will most value those people with whom they sang and played music? How many children will be lucky enough to have had a musical instrument as an ever-present best friend?

Math

What it means: Some children are naturally drawn to math. They enjoy number problems and take pencil to paper with confidence. Other children feel the "wrath of math." They might become anxious and avoid all kinds of mathematical tasks (Levine, 1992). Difficulty with basic number concepts can appear early in life. The average age for first counting one block is 3.5 years; for first counting five blocks, 4.5 years. Other children struggle only when confronted with higher-level mathematics. Moving into the early school years, your child might have difficulty with simple calculations, such as addition, subtraction, multiplication, and division. Other children struggle with math concepts, such as fractions, decimals, variables, and irrational numbers.

Often difficulties in nonmath areas sabotage success in math:

- Visual perception problems may cause fractions such as 41/5 to be seen as 1/45 or 4 (and) 1/5. "Figure-background deficits" can cause difficulty locating the decimal point. Numbers can blur and run together.
- Abstract reasoning problems can be very difficult. For example, although "2/5" and "two out of five" are represented in different ways, they mean the same thing. Some curricula are heavy on "everyday math" applications. Such emphasis on solving word problems can be especially burdensome for children with language difficulties. Some children are confused by the way "third, fourth, and fifth" changes the meaning of the numbers "3, 4, and 5" to mean fractions instead of whole numbers. Instructions to "shade in $^3/_4$" will leave some children baffled if they do not know what it means to shade.
- Some words in common use can be confusing when applied to math; for example, *improper* fractions, *mixed* numbers, and *lowest* terms. One-quarter means 25 cents in everyday language but can mean one-fourth (¼) in math.
- Auditory discrimination problems can create confusion hearing the difference between tenths/tens, hundredths/hundreds, and so on.
- Difficulties with attention, memory, strategic thinking, and anxiety can have a profound impact, especially with increasing mathematical complexity. It is not unusual for some children to easily master math concepts but have surprising difficulty generalizing application to different types of routine problems.

Goodness of Fit:

- *Good for/Problem if:* Of course, math ability is important for academic success—but not just in math class. Mathematical and statistical concepts are also relevant in language processing and production, science, social studies, economics, psychology, arts and crafts, music, study skills, and more. Outside of school, math concepts underlie sports, social interaction, time and money management, cooking and play, and many more household and self-care tasks. The range of everyday math-based activities may be surprising, including card and board games, pizza cutting, batting averages, phone numbers, computer use, and medication management.
- *Parent-child fit:* As with all other skills, when parent and child share a strong interest and ability, there is less likely to be a frustrating discrepancy between expectations. However, parents with poor math skills may have difficulty doing math activities with their children. And woe to parent and child when neither one knows how to do the math homework.

Accommodations: In math, as elsewhere, strategies to accommodate are based on understanding and accepting the child's difficulties. Again, care should be taken to spare the child embarrassment and unnecessary frustration. Math anxiety is common, especially because of math's relentlessly cumulative nature (Tobias, 1995). Unlike many other subjects, performance at each level of math depends on mastery of skills at lower levels. Fail to learn your addition or multiplication facts and you are a goner with long division. Parents and teachers should be especially careful not to fuel a child's frustration by expressing their own exasperation. These children should not be called to the blackboard unless the teacher knows that they will "get it right." Sometimes the child can be given a problem the day before to rehearse the answer before called on to perform in front of others. Although basic skill gaps must be remediated, temporary deficits or dysfluencies can be bypassed by allowing calculators or extra time on some tests and assignments. Such accommodations can help math-challenged students keep pace with new concepts. Math anxiety should be reduced by presenting new information in small chunks, breaking down multistep tasks, and cutting the volume of some homework assignments.

In school and out, some more specific techniques for bypassing math-learning problems include the following:

- Use visual cuing. Highlight important details with boxes, circles, and lines (such as the operational sign). Use specific color cues, such as write the whole number in red and the fraction in blue, or change the decimal point to a different color than the numbers.
- Try big-boxed graph paper to help keep numbers lined up for proper calculations. If not available, lined paper can be turned sideways. Make sure to provide extra workspace on the page to avoid visual clutter; perhaps even a separate page for each problem.
- Use manipulatives as crucial comprehension and calculation aides. For example, use coins, unit strips, fraction boards, blocks, pies, and other foods.
- Assign fewer problems and give more time.
- Alter, adjust, or reinforce the text. For example, in word problems, highlight key words and number multiple steps.
- Test for understanding, not rote memorization or speed. Allow calculators, open-book tests, multiplication and formula charts.

Strengthen strengths: Geeks rule! In today's world, the mathematically inclined enjoy some huge advantages. STEM (science, technology, engineering, and math) as well as accounting and business career paths are wide open to those so gifted. Statistics now underlie an extraordinary range of vocations (Greenhouse, 2013). The opportunities for math development are now innumerable! It has become cool to do Sudoku puzzles, participate in math bowls, and program computers just for fun.

Side notes: By now, I hope that you have come to see the interplay between developmental domains as a central theme of this book. Here's another example of developmental cross-pollination: using math to help children understand and modulate their own activity level, initial reaction, intensity of reaction, and adaptability. Math for self-regulation and social-emotional development!

As discussed elsewhere, children who have difficulty with emotional flexibility and modulation operate on a binary system, as if the only numbers are zero and one. The only possible states are on or off. The only possible choices are black or white. If it's not heaven, it's hell. If it can't be perfect, it can't be anything at all. For these children, it's as if the numbers two through nine do not exist, not to mention two through ninety-nine! Parents and professionals can use numbers to teach a broader range of behaviors, emotional states, coping strategies, and solutions. By teaching a larger set of representational numbers, children can learn better self-awareness. This can be the first step toward improved self-regulation. For example:

- How is your motor running (Kuypers, 2011)? 0 = off, 1 = idling, 2 = slow, 3 = medium, 4 = fast, 5 = superfast. How fast should it be running: At home? On the playground? In the classroom? At the store?
- Fear thermometer (Zucker, 2017). 0 = no big deal, 3 = I'm a little uneasy, 5 = maybe I can handle it but I'm not sure, 7 = I don't think so, 9 = really hard, 10 = no way.
    - How much fear or anxiety *do* you experience when exposed to specific stimuli or situations?
    - How much fear or anxiety *should* you experience?

  - How much of a gap is there between *do* and *should*?
  - Let's try some strategies and see what happens to those numbers in one week.
  - How long do you think it will take for you to close the gap?
- Rate possible solutions (Kendall, 2007). Given a specific problem (home, school, or with friends), let's rate possible solutions: 0 = stinks, 1 = bad, 2 = OK, 3 = good, 4 = very good, 5 = excellent.
- Assess progress. If zero is where you started and one hundred is your goal, what percentage improvement do you think there's been so far?
- Behavior modification (Cooper et al., 2007). Parents and children can quantify degrees of success by using money, tokens, points, puzzle pieces, marks, marbles, and so on.
- Turn-taking can be tied to number concepts such as fixed ratios ("I do one, and you do two.") or games of chance ("Guess a number between zero and ten.").

In these ways and more, math concepts are key to much of modern (measurable outcomes-based) psychotherapy.

Time awareness, planning, organization, and implementation

What it means: Children have very significant differences in their ability to initiate, sustain, inhibit, and shift. Some children have trouble keeping track of time or things. These so-called executive functions, based in the prefrontal cortex of the brain, also include time awareness, planning, organization, and implementation (Fuster, 2015). It is difficult to assess these skills in very young children, but typically developing preschoolers should be starting to develop some rudimentary executive skills. How does your child do knowing the difference between morning, afternoon, and night? Being aware of the hour, day, date, month, and season? Learning to tell time? Being aware of time passing? Estimating how long activities will take and minding their pace? Is your child successful at planning, strategizing, sequencing, and preparing? Is your child able to self-assess and self-monitor? How does your child do organizing his or her materials and spaces? Knowing where to put or find clothing and supplies for school or play? How about bringing school or play materials? Keeping the school desk, cubby, or locker organized? Maintaining a neat bedroom?

Goodness of fit:

- *Good for/Problem if:* Organization skills are essential for academic success, especially as homework and study demands increase. With each passing school year, task complexity and performance expectations both rise. How is your child about knowing what to do and how to do it? Handing homework in on time? Tracking assignments and work at an appropriate pace? Employing strategies for test-taking? Proficiency with these types of executive skills is essential for academic success and positive self-image. Difficulty with this type of planning and implementation can lead to underperformance, stress, and loss of motivation (Cooper-Kahn & Dietzel, 2008). Time awareness, planning, organization, and implementation skills are also crucial for success outside of school. Knowing when, where, and how is also important for family functioning, social interaction, and adaptive life skills. Think about the crucial role of executive functions in morning routines, evening routines, self-care, chores, getting together with friends, and participating in extracurricular activities. From taking care of the family dog to finding a baseball mitt, these managerial skills are essential.
- *Parent-child fit:* The complex and demanding job of raising children requires parents to have adequate time awareness, planning, organization, and implementation skills. If parent and child share excellent organization skills, many of life's stresses can be

anticipated and minimized. However, parents with good executive function skills may have difficulty understanding how hard it is for their child with poor executive function skills. Parents with weak executive skills may feel overwhelmed, anxious, or depressed. Especially if parents and children share a problem with staying organized, chaos can reign. The parent-child relationship can be stressed and strained. Such households can put children at a disadvantage.

Accommodations: Strategies to accommodate children with executive dysfunction amount to "outsourcing your child's prefrontal cortex" to an executive secretary (Dawson & Guare, 2010). Usually, this means a high degree of parent involvement, but the planning and organization team might also include other family members, teachers, and tutors (Gordon, 2007). Children with executive dysfunction should not be admonished to just try harder (Levine, 2004). However, they do need to accept help and use compensatory organization systems. If parent and child acknowledge these skills deficits, then supports can be put in place and stress lowered.

Starting at an early age, morning and evening routines should be well established. Day-to-day variation should be kept to a minimum. In general, these children do well with regularity, routine, and ritual. The schedule must be structured but flexible. Your child will need help with contingency planning. More strategic thinking means less stress.

Parents and teachers should work together to schedule up the typical day. From waking in the morning until falling asleep at night, the schedule should be comprehensive and detailed.

You might need to divide the day into routines, subroutines, and ministeps. There should be regular planning periods; for example, every

Sunday for the week ahead, every Friday for the weekend, and every afternoon for the time left until bedtime. In broad outline:

- The *morning routine* involves waking up at a certain time, getting dressed, eating breakfast, brushing teeth, grabbing the backpack (prepared the night before as part of evening routine), and getting out the door.
- *School routines* should be clear. If necessary, the schedule should be posted and reviewed at the beginning of each day. The child should know the progression of events: where to go, when to go, and what to have ready each step of the way.
- *Homework routines:* At the end of the school day, teachers can check the backpack and assignment book. Parent-teacher communication should be regular and sufficiently detailed. Teachers can provide homework accommodations, such as comprehension checks, advance notice, assignment breakdown, and grading on understanding, not work efficiency. At home, work and activities for the afternoon and evening should be broken down into doable chunks and assigned to the schedule. As needed, parents should help with jump-starting, supervision, pacing, and positive reinforcement.
- *Evening routines* include dinner, homework, play, family time, electronics, reading, next-day preparations, cleanup, wind-down time, bathroom, bedtime, and lights out.
- *Family-social planning:* Family, social, and free time should also receive scheduling priority, including family activities, extracurricular activities, playdates, hanging out with friends, appointments, travel, vacations, and eating out. Common stress points can all receive advance discussion and problem-solving; for example, TV, video, computer, homework, and time with friends.
- *Clarity:* Across environments, try to keep the routine front and center. Use electronic calendars, cell phone apps, pictures,

posters, to-do lists, checklists, timers, clocks, hourglasses, alarms, and sticky notes—whatever external props, cues, and prompts are necessary, age-appropriate, and effective.

Children with executive skill deficits need help organizing their materials and environment. From a very early age, children should learn proper places for everything—coat, backpack, lunch bag, and so on. Whether preparing for work or play, parents and teachers should preview and supervise proper use of drawers, cubbies, folders, boxes, lockers, notebooks, and desks. Life-skills prep should take place across all settings: home, school, and social. Once these skills are mastered, adults can gradually withdraw their support.

Strengthen strengths: While looking out for children with executive dysfunction, we should not fail to appreciate others who seem to be natural-born organizers and problem-solvers. Managers are essential to every ball game, band practice, home video production, and trip. Such directors and coordinators might enjoy minding the details that others avoid. Parents and teachers can look for these positive planning and leadership opportunities.

Side notes: But what about the long term for those who struggle with executive dysfunction? To some parents, accommodation for these kinds of difficulties may sound like coddling, enabling, and spoiling. "When," you might ask, "will my child learn to accept responsibility and take care of him- or herself?" Throughout the *Parent Child Journey*, we discuss behavioral interventions to promote self-care and independence. Whether we are talking about executive dysfunctions or any other set of skills deficits, accommodation is never enough. If you only accommodate without correcting skills deficits, your child will become more dependent and poorly equipped to make his or her way in the world (Levine, 2006).

So why, throughout Your Gander Instruction Manual, is there such an emphasis on accommodation? Quite simply, accommodation is quick. Skill building takes time. Until your child's abilities improve sufficiently, accommodation will be necessary. While your child gradually works toward greater degrees of independence, a certain amount of accommodation will be necessary to avoid frustration, loss of motivation, and avoidant behaviors. Over the years, your child will grow, and the landscape will change. But for now, you and your child need to make adjustments and find the right balance of both accommodation and intervention.

How long will this level of support be necessary? Every child is different. In general, serial MRIs of the brain's executive centers show ongoing maturation even beyond thirty years of age (Giedd et al., 1999). Remember: your child will not be a fully formed adult on the day of graduation from high school. Think for a moment about the maturational difference between most twenty- and thirty-year-olds. There's no need to despair if your child needs ongoing support. Brain maturation and cumulative life experience will continue to make a positive difference into adult life.

Social skills

What it means: A complex network of brain modules and networks underlies the development of social skills (Goleman, 2007). Some children have primary deficits in social development, such as autism. Other children have social delays secondary to differences in behavioral style, such as attention deficits, impulsivity, inflexibility, high intensity of reaction, and sensory hyperreactivity. Still others have social difficulties because of other skills deficits, such as disorders of expressive or receptive language, fine or gross motor coordination, and executive function. Finally, many children have social struggles because of environmental factors, such as deprivation, abuse, or other life stress. Often there is a combination of factors.

Social development continues lifelong. Here are some average ages for early social milestones:

- Smile responsively at one month
- First wave bye-bye, play pat-a-cake and indicate wants at eight months
- First imitate another person and play ball back and forth at ten months
- Point to share interest at twelve months
- First "help" in the house at fourteen months
- Feed a doll at seventeen months
- Engage in simple symbolic and imaginary play by twenty months
- Share and take turns by twenty-four months
- Play board or card games by thirty-six months
- Complicated dramatic play with plots and emotional themes by thirty-six months

Over the ensuing years, children with strong social skills are natural "mind readers" and "situation readers." Intuitively, they understand what other people are thinking or feeling. They "get" the social context and modify their behavior accordingly. These children are very attuned to other people. They reliably read nonverbal cues, such as body language, tone of voice, and facial expression. They show affection and compassion. They are motivated to initiate, respond, and reciprocate in social interaction. They enjoy playing and talking with other children their age. They are pleasant and appropriate with peers. They fit in easily and make good friends. They are skillful at solving interpersonal conflicts. They show sympathy and come to the aid of social outliers. They feel good about their social life.

Children with weak social skills are relatively "mind blind" or "context blind" (Baron-Cohen, Cosmides, & Tooby, 1997; Vermeulen, 2012). Other people's actions, thoughts, or feelings may be mysterious, confusing, or negligible. These children struggle with cultural norms and act in unexpected ways. They have difficulty recognizing and processing important nonverbal cues. They may not interact much with peers. They tend to do better with adults and older or younger children. They feel anxious in social situations. They have trouble fitting in. They may have poor play skills. They are not consistently successful making and keeping friends. They have difficulty with social problem-solving and relationship repair. Naïve and gullible, they easily fall victim to bullying or teasing. They wish they had more friends or better friends. They might lose social motivation and say they don't care about friendships at all (Lavoie, Reiner, Reiner, & Levine, 2006).

Goodness of fit:

- *Good for/Problem if:* Social skills are crucial across a broad range of activities. When we think about social skills, we usually think about success in peer interactions. Whether or not your child develops friendships and positive peer relations is the most obvious and important measure of social development.
  Social skills are also crucial for success in school; not just on the playground but in the lunchroom, the hallway, and the classroom. Academic skills are learned, in large part, through interaction with classmates. If school is largely about preparation for life, then education should move beyond independent worksheets and standardized test performance to group discussion, collaborative learning, and joint problem-solving. Study after study demonstrates that school success—and future success in

the workplace—depends on social-emotional intelligence, not just IQ, SAT, or ACT scores. The ability to work with others is central to academic achievement. A successful childhood should not be measured by admission to prestigious colleges, but rather by the development of ethics, morality, self-control, grit, and compassion.

Social skills are also essential to the development of life skills and healthy family functioning. Mealtime behavior, sharing, taking turns, participation in family and community activities, doing chores, morning and evening routines, resolving conflicts, and sibling relations all depend on social awareness, social skills, and self-regulation.

- *Parent-child fit:* Parents who have problems with social awareness, self-awareness, and social skills may have difficulty modeling for—or even relating to—their own children. These parents might also struggle working with other adults who are involved in their children's lives, such as their spouse or coparent, other family members, health professionals, teachers, or other parents. Parents with strong social skills are usually more comfortable setting an example for their children at home and advocating for them across settings. However, such parents might take it personally or feel frustrated if their socially unskillful child does inappropriate things. It may be hard to remember that their child's social skills deficits do not indicate a personality disorder.

Accommodations:

There are many ways to help your child develop social skills. However, on the playground and in the playroom, most children with social skills deficits depend on parents and teachers for different levels of real-time support. Here, we will only consider strategies to accommodate social skills deficits.

These accommodations are based on understanding and accepting your child's current level of social development. For some children, their "social development age" might lag quite a bit behind their chronological age. We should not give sixth-grade reading material to a dyslexic child who can only read at the second-grade level. Likewise, we need to choreograph and modify the interpersonal experience of socially delayed children to match their developmental readiness (Winner, 2016). These children should not be put into social situations that cause confusion, embarrassment, frustration, or loss of motivation. Parents and teachers should customize and choreograph social interaction. This adult facilitation usually requires their sustained attention, supervision, and role-modeling. Once the child is successful at one level of socialization, he or she can advance to the next and extra support can be gradually withdrawn.

Social choreography should address the following factors:

- *Structure:* Quite simply, children with social skills deficits need more social support. Unstructured time should be structured up. Social activities should be tightly scripted. Direct social coaching and facilitation may be necessary. Adult supervision can be faded over time, but not too quickly.
- *Familiarity:* Children with social skills delays will do better with activities that are well within their comfort zone. Social success can be derailed if a child is forced to simultaneously interact with peers and experience new things. This social multitasking can lead to sensory or emotional overload and increasing social anxiety. These children have an easier time interacting with other children if activities and settings are old and familiar. Novelty should be limited or introduced gradually and incrementally. The unfamiliar can be rendered more familiar through preview and rehearsal. Use visual schedules, social calendars, social stories, comic-book conversations, social scripts, rule reviews, guided practice, and role-plays (Gray, 2015; Gray, 2016). All

these techniques can help socially awkward children anticipate interpersonal expectations and complexities.

- *Competence and interest:* For children with social skill deficits, social success is more likely if they are operating in areas of relative strength and interest. Follow your child's bliss. Instead of thinking about *who* your child might connect with, consider *what* your child enjoys doing. Then find another kid who shares the same interest. After all, adults have different friends for different types of activities. Children can learn to match friends to interests as well. Teachers and parents can spotlight special talents and interests, raising such "outliers'" social status and self-image (Gladwell, 2008).
- *Play skills:* Children need plenty of play opportunities that are well matched to their play skills (Lifter, Suzler-Azaroff, Anderson, & Cowdery, 1993). Some children use toys indiscriminately, not according to their specific functions. Others use toys according to their properties, but in a very limited way. Over the years, children learn to use play objects in a greater variety of ways and combinations. With progressively more imagination and creativity, they learn to use objects to symbolize different things. Plots and emotional themes become more elaborate, thematic, and dramatic. It is important to match play partners who are at roughly the same level of play skill.
- *Partners:* Ironically, peer play is hardest. It is much easier to play with parents, other adults, or children who are much older or much younger. For children with social delays, such age-mismatched play partners are often better suited for social success. Older or younger play partners are usually more accommodating, tolerant, or accepting. Sometimes boys do better with girls, and girls do better with boys. And that's ok.
- *Group size:* The larger the group size, the greater the social complexity. Social stress can increase with a larger number of play partners. Children with limited social skills should have limited

social demands. If two's company, three might be a crowd. Before children can be successful one on two, they should be consistently successfully one on one.

- *Time:* Playtimes or other social activities should not go on too long. Parents should know how long their child usually lasts before things fall apart and plan to end the social activities fifteen minutes earlier. Then play can end on a positive note, leaving both children wanting more. This is better than having things end on a sour note of misunderstanding, conflict, or boredom. As my father-in-law would say, "Thanks for coming. Thanks for going."
- *Warm-up time:* Children who are slow to warm up should be given extra warm-up time. This is like putting one toe in the pool at a time. Some children need just a few extra minutes hanging at the periphery to gradually acclimate. Others need extra hours, days, weeks, or even months. As discussed in the section on negative initial reaction, beware the child who is tortured by prolonged transitions. He or she will do better just "jumping into the deep end" and then adjusting quickly.
- *Sharing, flexibility, and social skills:* Children need to learn sharing attention and sharing toys. Finally, they need to learn sharing thoughts and feelings. There can be delays along the way. Again, parent expectations should match the child's developmental level. Some children might need explicit teaching and prompting to form a triangle of joint attention between an object and another child, and similarly between their thoughts and feelings. Over the years, they need to be coached out of a self-absorbed mindset toward other-awareness and true interpersonal reciprocity (Winner, 2007). There is a developmental progression from "my way" to "your way" to "our way." Emotional intelligence evolves from primitive, black-and-white thinking to intermediate awareness of primary feelings (happy, sad, angry, scared) to advanced understanding of emotional complexity and nuance (embarrassed,

jealous, disappointed) (Attwood, 2008). Children need to learn about these emotions both in themselves and in others. In the meantime, again, expectations should match abilities.

Strengthen strengths: If your child is naturally a "social animal," nourish his or her interpersonal life. Do not feel threatened if he or she looks beyond your nuclear family to a second family of friends. Especially for children who struggle in other areas, be thankful for a vibrant and grounding network of companions.

Side notes: What if your child remains socially different? It is important to remember that many people value their work over their relationships. Some children and adults are content not to socialize. This may run contrary to your idea of the "meaningful life." It is contrary to some science that emphasizes the importance of relationships for a happy and healthy existence. However, many of history's most admired and important individuals were not at all socially successful (Silberman & Sacks, 2015). Thanks largely to the growing importance of physics, science, computers, and the Internet, a relatively isolated existence is no longer synonymous with failure (Prizant & Fields-Meyer, 2016). To quote Temple Grandin (D. Shapiro, personal communication, 2002), the most famous autistic person in the world: "You so-called normal people and your relationships! Don't give me an interview. Just look at my work portfolio. I don't need a marriage or even your idea of a friend. Just let me have my special interests and a good job." The autism pride and neurodiversity movements are based on the idea that our society needs to expand its narrow idea of success and meaning (Donvan & Zucker, 2016). This is not to say that we should neglect to intervene where correction of skills deficits can improve quality of life. But sometimes accommodation is more realistic—and more respectful too.

People can be quick and harsh. Ironically, this insensitive rush to judgment can be more pernicious and problematic when the social impairment—or any disability—is relatively mild and hidden. It is not easy needing a white cane, a wheelchair, or a helmet. However, such specialized equipment is obvious and more likely than not to illicit a sympathetic reaction. What about children who "look normal" but act differently? They too are at risk for success deprivation, mental illness, and unemployment. Yet these children with subtle but significant social disabilities—*and their parents*—might be less likely to get a helping hand and more likely to incur blame, shame, reprimand, or punishment. Their relatively unexpected and misunderstood behaviors do not usually inspire respect and compassion. All too often children with subtle social disabilities are dealt exasperated reproaches, such as, "What's your *problem*!" Note the exclamation mark instead of a question mark. After all, these are prejudiced verdicts, not compassionate appeals for understanding. People with disabilities do not want pity, but they do need accommodation, no matter how mild or severe the impairment may seem (Shapiro, 1994). If the last chapter to be written in the civil rights movement is about disability rights, then perhaps the last pages will be about hidden impairments.

Physical health, family, environmental, and other life stresses

What it means: Many children have very significant problems with physical health or environmental stresses. These stresses may seem minor when considered in isolation. Although frequently discounted, such stresses can have a major impact, especially when considered in combination. The Gander Life Stresses checklist includes a wide range of such challenges. Health problems include hospitalizations, surgeries, physical or mental illnesses, disabilities, injuries, and allergies; in the child, family members, or significant others. Many parents, struggling with the stress of raising a challenging child, experience anxiety and depression. Family stresses can be secondary to death, mental illness, strained or fractured relationships, family restructuring, abuse, violence, financial hardship, work pressures, social and cultural challenges, and school problems. Ranging from overscheduling and playground conflicts to poverty and tragedy, a child's behavior problems can be amplified or caused by a broad range of real-world hardships (Elkind, 2006; Greenspan & Salmon, 1994; Kotlowitz, 1992). Parents should never underestimate the impact of these life stresses on their children—and themselves.

GOODNESS OF FIT:

- *Good for/Problem if:* Although children are born with different temperaments and predispositions, they do not grow up in a vacuum. Brain-based differences are modified by the environment. Your child's development is all about nature *and* nurture. Down at the level of your child's DNA, epigenetics is a fascinating new field that looks at how environmental factors actually turn on and off different genes (Ridley, 2003). On a more mundane and familiar level, your child's behavior and mood are clearly modified by a multitude of life circumstances. Study after study shows that family, social, and economic factors have a profound impact on learning, resilience, and development.
- *Parent-child fit:* Some families are extraordinarily lucky. When environmental stresses are at a minimum, it is easier for your child to cope and overcome his or her developmental challenges. But many families are not so fortunate. Life can be complicated. Every family has limited time, money, and energy, but some families are much more constrained than others. For many parents, essential resources may prove insufficient. A necessary minimum of environmental stability might be lacking. Beyond these environmental pressures, just raising a challenging child will stretch and strain any parent. When a child has special needs, mothers, fathers, siblings, and other family members often feel confused, angry, guilty, or overwhelmed. Parents might

have physical or emotional stresses of their own. Due to the genetics of developmental difference, children and parents often share difficult temperaments, ADHD, learning disabilities, mood disorders, autism spectrum disorders, and other developmental differences. The apple may not have fallen far from the tree. Although parent disability on top of child disability can pose special challenges, shared experience can allow parents to be more sensitive and supportive of their children—and other children with developmental differences too. For all these reasons, for every child with special needs, there's a family with special needs too.

ACCOMMODATIONS:
Throughout *Parent Child Journey*, especially the Second and Ninth Miles, I emphasize the importance of parent self-care and stress reduction. Here, suffice it to say, parents who do not take care of themselves will have a much harder time taking care of their children. Parents do not have to face these life challenges alone. To reduce child and family stresses, parents should turn to their pediatrician or family doctor; schoolteachers, counselors, and administrators; mental health providers, religious organizations, social services, and government agencies; support groups and online communities; and family and friends. People care. They want to help. They need to know what you are dealing with behind the scenes. If they know, then they can give you and your child a little extra sensitivity and support. There is no shame in seeking help for your child. There is no shame in seeking help for yourself.

Side notes: For decades, there has been a movement to reduce child development and human behavior down to genes and neurons (Development, 2000). The study of the brain has yielded groundbreaking and paradigm-shifting insights into the basis of developmental variation. Parents should no longer feel blamed or guilty for causing their children's difficulties. We have fascinating new tests and promising new treatments for the neurophysiologic abnormalities that underlie real-life impairment. This biological perspective is crucial to further advances in our ability to help children. However, such an increasingly narrow focus on biology is insufficient to explain the complexity of human variation and so falls short of providing the kind of help people really need (Khoury, Evans, & Burke, 2010; Mukherjee, 2016).

As stated repeatedly throughout this book, children's brains do not develop in some kind of isolation vat. Neurodevelopment is the product of inborn differences *and* life experience. Developmental and behavioral pediatrics does include genetics and neurology—but also, and no less importantly, we should be informed by research and concepts from the worlds of social work, anthropology, economics, education, epidemiology, public health, toxicology, political science, law, history, art, philosophy, and more. Let's consider the profound impact of just one such extraneurologic perspective: family systems theory (Papero, 1990).

No matter what kind of brain your child has, family relationships matter (Nichols, 2013). Family connections are usually lifelong, interactive, dynamic, and deep. These intimate interpersonal forces exert a powerful impact on personality development and life trajectory. Family relationships can be nurturing and intensely positive. Family members represent our primary source of play, social learning, support, and love. Of course, families can also be a source of tension (Napier & Whitaker, 1988). For some families, conflicts can be deep and frequent. There can be rivalry for attention, love, and approval. This can take the form of teasing, insulting, competition, and aggression. Family turmoil can cause serious physical and emotional harm. Whether positive or negative, the impact of family relations on development and behavior is undeniable.

Child development and behavior are affected by a large number of complicated family variables: family size; birth order and spacing of siblings;

multiple births (i.e., twins, triplets); temperament of parents and siblings; step-, adoptive-, and foster-family structures; homosexual, heterosexual, single, or separated parents; family members with chronic illness or special needs; death of a family member; plus an extraordinary network of different family relationships.

As discussed, "goodness of fit" between family members is highly variable across relationships, situations, and phases of development. Parents have different levels of insight and skill. Going back to families of origin, those relationships and role models have a profound effect on how parents treat their own children and each other. Each family member has different types of relationships with every other family member: "indifferent," "distant," "estranged," "conflicted," "harmonious," "close," "friendly," "loving," "hostile," "violent," "abusive," "manipulative," "controlling," "admiring," and so on (McGoldrick, Gerson, & Shellenberger, 1999). Usually, relationships cannot be summed up using just one such label. Relationships between siblings and parents are more accurately described by an ever-changing combination of such characteristics.

The complexity of these interlocking family relationship triangles and their downstream effects can be as dizzying as any nerve network in the brain. One classic example: In a marriage, an overly responsive and controlling parent can cause his or her spouse to feel dependent, helpless, and depressed. The child with the least emotional separation from the controlling parent might be especially vulnerable to tension in the parents' relationship. The child's anxiety might appear as physical symptoms (e.g., stomachaches) or behaviors (e.g., acting out). This can cause parents to shift attention away from their conflict with each other and turn together toward their child's symptoms. In this way, the developmental or behavioral problem might be caused—or at least influenced by—an unhealthy family dynamic. Clearly, such a child's symptoms are not entirely biological in the making. And these family dynamics can be passed down from one generation to another. What kind of brain scan, blood test, or prescription can address all of this? Only the family systems perspective brings these important factors to light.

Life stresses and *Parent Child Journey*

For parents seeking developmental-behavioral services, the crisis of limited availability and affordability might be one of your most significant life stresses. The Gander cannot take the place of comprehensive neuropsychological and multidisciplinary assessment. However, when asked the right questions, I have found that most parents can give a very accurate description of their child's profile. The Gander profile might even be more comprehensive and nuanced than some narrow and expensive subspecialty evaluations. A book and parent training group is no substitute for individualized evaluation and treatment, but I hope that the *Parent Child Journey* represents a useful and accessible starting point.

YOUR GANDER INSTRUCTION MANUAL: PARTS B, C, AND D

• • •

AND NOW FOR SOMETHING COMPLETELY different. So far, I have presented the Gander in a conventional way. You've circled some numbers and read some text. These next sections are still very much in development and not for everybody. But for those of you who are artistically, musically, or graphically inclined, I hope you have some fun playing with these multimodal treatments of the Gander. I've offered some suggestions, but please use your own creativity and imagination. And thanks for contacting me directly to share what you've done and offer any suggestions for further development.

Your Gander Instruction Manual Part B: Know Your Boat

You and your child might choose to draw your own Gander picture. As you complete the Gander, feel free to have some fun creating a metaphorical picture. Start with a rough outline of Raph's (your child's) boat. Outline Raph's (your child's) body and head in the boat. Then, according to the suggestions that follow, add different parts to the boat and Raph. Better yet, exercise your own creativity and make up your own boat and parts. Do not draw every feature listed. Rather, choose to picture only those aspects of the Gander that are most important; meaning the key features of your child's profile. Here are some ideas:

- ***Motor activity:*** Children with high motor activity act as if they have a big motor driving their boat. Children with low motor activity act as if they have a little motor (or just a little paddle) driving their boat.
- ***Impulsivity:*** Children with high impulsivity act as if the anchor for their boat is too little—or there's no anchor at the end of the rope at all! Children with low impulsivity act as if the anchor for their boat is too big.
- ***Attention span:*** Children with short attention spans act as if they have a constantly rotating, 360-degree scanning radar for their boat. It notices everything, but only for a moment. Children with long attention span act as if they have a fixed telescope for their boat. It stays focused on one thing for a long time.
- ***Initial reaction:*** Children with negative initial reaction act as if their boat is very securely docked, tied up tight. The rope goes around and around a post or tree. There's a big knot. Children with positive initial reaction act as if their boat is unmoored. The rope is untied, and the boat is easily swept away down the river.
- ***Adaptability:*** Children with high adaptability act as if their boat can turn and easily avoid obstacles in the river. They have both

hands on the wheel. Children with low adaptability plow right ahead. They just go over obstacles without considering a change of direction. Their hands are off the wheel, so they can't turn the boat.

- ***Intensity of reaction:*** Children with high intensity of reaction act as if their motor runs very loud. Children with low intensity of reaction act as if their motor runs very quiet.
- ***Mood:*** Children with generally positive mood usually have a smile. Children with negative mood often carry a frown.
- ***Regularity/predictability:*** Children with high regularity and predictability act as if they have a big centerboard and rudder. Their boat tracks steady and handles true. Other children act is if their centerboard and rudder are broken. Their boats too easily veer and change course with the current.
- ***Hearing sensitivity:*** Children with high sensitivity to hearing speech act as if they have a walkie-talkie on one ear. Children with high sensitivity to noise act as if they have one ear that's especially huge. Children with low sensitivity to hearing speech act as if they have an ear plug. Children with low sensitivity to hearing noise act as if they have "tiny little ears." Children with "mixed profiles" have two different types of ears.
- ***Visual sensitivity:*** Children with high visual sensitivity act as if they have big eyes. Children with low visual sensitivity act as if they have little eyes.
- ***Taste and smell sensitivity:*** Children with high sensitivity to taste act as if they have a big tongue. Children with high sensitivity to smell act as if they have a big nose. Children with low sensitivity to taste act as if they have a little tongue. Children with low sensitivity to smell act as if they have a little nose.
- ***Touch sensitivity:*** Children with high sensitivity to deep touch act as if everything that touches them is a stingray or bumblebee stinger. Children with high sensitivity to light touch act as if they have extra fingers. Children with low sensitivity to deep

touch act as if everything that touches them should be an eight-armed hugging octopus. Children with low sensitivity to light touch act as if they have mittens on their hands.

- ***Movement sensitivity:*** Children with high sensitivity to movement always stay seated in the boat. Children with low sensitivity love to stand up—even dance—in the boat.
- ***Internal body awareness/physical symptoms sensitivity:*** Children with high sensitivity to internal body sensations act as if they often have a high thermometer reading. Children with low sensitivity to internal body sensations act as if they have a normal thermometer reading.
- ***Fine motor skills:*** Children with above-average fine motor skills act as if they could easily thread a small hook on a thin fishing line. Children with below-average fine motor skills act as if they could only catch a fish with a net.
- ***Writing mechanics:*** Children with above-average writing mechanics act as if they could do professional calligraphy on the side of their boat. Children with below-average writing mechanics could only make a sloppy "X."
- ***Gross-motor skills:*** Children with above-average gross motor skills act as if they could easily get out of a boat climbing a ladder. Children with below-average gross motor skills act as if they would need a slide to get out of a boat.
- ***Oral expression skills:*** Children with above-average oral expression act as if they speak with exclamation marks. Children with below-average oral expression act as if they speak with question marks.
- ***Written expression skills:*** Children with above-average written expression act as if they could send a long note in a bottle. Children with below-average written expression act as if they would rather send the pencil in the bottle.
- ***Listening skills:*** Children with above-average listening skills act as if their brain registers an exclamation mark. Children with

below-average understanding of oral language act as if their brain registers a question mark.

- ***Reading skills:*** Children with above-average reading skills act as if they always want to carry a book. Children with below-average understanding of written language act as if they would rather throw a book in the river.
- ***Visual-spatial/art skills:*** Children with above-average visual-spatial and visual art skills act as if they always have a camera ready. Children with below-average visual-spatial and visual art skills act as if they are wearing dark sunglasses.
- ***Music skills:*** Children with above-average music development act as if they have music notes dancing in their heads. Children with below-average music development act as if a musical note is lying down asleep in their heads.
- ***Math skills:*** Children with above-average math skills act as if the brain understands "infinity." Children with below-average math skills act as if the brain understands "zero."
- ***Time awareness, planning, organization, and implementation skills:*** Children with above-average time awareness act as if time stands still. Children with below-average time awareness act as if time flies. Children with above-average planning and organization skills act as if signs along their way reliably point them in the right direction. Children with below-average planning and organization skills act as if signs along their way point in multiple directions at once.
- ***Social skills:*** Children with above-average social skill act as if they have a life ring ready to throw to others. Children with below-average social skill act as if they have a rope to throw to others, but it is not attached, either to the side of the boat or to a life preserver.
- ***Physical/environmental health:*** For children with above-average physical and environmental health, it seems as if the sun is always shining. For children with below-average physical and environmental health, it's like the sky is full of dark clouds.

Your Gander Instruction Manual Part C: Know Your Song

"Raph's Song" (child) and "Hawk's Song" (parent): One day Your Gander Instruction Manual might go online. Then, a song could be written and played for you as you complete the Gander. But for now, those of you who are musically inclined can give it a try. Pick your own melody—perhaps, "Row, Row, Row Your Boat." Make up your own words.

Music: My version of Raph's and Hawk's songs represent variations on a simple melody I wrote as a teenager. Hawk's soaring melody starts a perfect fifth above the earthbound Raph's. Then, for each developmental domain, the melody in each of my songs moves up or down, depending on Gander individual differences. Also, Hawk's song moves to the long and graceful 4/4 beat of his wings. Raph's song moves in shorter beats and more incremental 6/8 time. In this way, both songs are melodically and rhythmically intertwined. Although Hawk's and Raph's songs may be different, they can still be sung together in beautiful harmony. This actually works! For a musical sample, go to Your Gander Instruction Manual at ParentChildJourney.com.

Words: Don't write a verse for every facet of the Gander, just the most important ones. First write lyrics to sum up your child's profile in song. Then do your own. Riffing on the *Tale of Raph and Hawk* in *Parent Child Journey*, here's what I came up with.

> ***Chorus (together):***
> *Raph and Hawk travelin' Miles and Miles*
> *Up the river together*
> *Logs and lightning and rocks on their way*
> *Tambalacoque forever*
>
> > ***High motor activity:*** Fast I go
> > ***Low motor activity:*** Slow I go

High impulsivity: I can't stop
Low impulsivity: I can't go

Short attention span: Hey, what's that?
Long attention span: Locked right in

Negative initial reaction: Don't wanna go
Positive initial reaction: Hey let's go

Low adaptability: Stay the course
High adaptability: Let's change course

High intensity of reaction: Crash so loud
Low intensity of reaction: Slip so soft

Negative mood: Feel so blue
Positive mood: Feel so good

Low regularity and predictability: Centerboard broke
High regularity and predictability: Straight and true

Chorus (together):
Raph and Hawk travelin' Miles and Miles
Up the river together
Logs and lightning and rocks on their way
Tambalacoque forever

High sensitivity to hearing speech: What's that talk?
Low sensitivity to hearing speech: Huh, what talk?

High sensitivity to hearing noise: What's that sound?
Low sensitivity to hearing noise: Huh, what sound?

High sensitivity to vision: What's that? See?
Low sensitivity to vision: Huh, see what?

High sensitivity to taste: What's that taste?
Low sensitivity to taste: Huh, what taste?

High sensitivity to smell: What's that smell?
Low sensitivity to smell: Huh, what smell?

High sensitivity to light touch: Feel that breeze?
Low sensitivity to light touch: Huh, what breeze?

High sensitivity deep touch: Vest too tight
Low sensitivity to deep touch: Vest too loose

High sensitivity to internal body/physical sensations: It all hurts
Low sensitivity to internal body/physical sensations: Nothing hurts

Chorus (together):
Raph and Hawk travelin' Miles and Miles
Up the river together
Logs and lightning and rocks on their way
Tambalacoque forever

Above-average fine motor skills: Tie my line
Below-average fine motor skills: Drop my line

Above-average writing mechanics: Need my pen
Below-average writing mechanics: Eraser please

Above-average gross motor skills: Jump on shore
Below-average gross motor skills: Ladder please

Above-average oral expression: Talk it out
Below-average oral expression: Don't talk out

Above-average written expression: Write it out
Below-average written expression: Don't write out

Above-average listening skills: Got you say
Below-average understanding of oral language: What you say?

Above-average reading skills: Read that right
Below-average understanding of written language: Can't read that

Above-average visual-spatial skills: Know my way
Below-average visual-spatial skills: Lost again

Above-average visual-art skills: Draw my boat
Below-average visual-art skills: Can't draw that

Above-average music skills: Sing my song
Below-average music skills: Can't sing that

Above-average math skills: Know my miles
Below-average math skills: How many miles?

Above-average time awareness: Time stands still
Below-average time awareness: Time flies by

Above-average planning and organization skills: All shipshape
Below-average planning and organization skills: What forecast?

Above-average social skills: Welcome aboard
Below-average social skills: Lone traveler

Above-average physical and environmental health: Smooth sailing
Below-average physical and environmental health: Rough water

Chorus (together):
Raph and Hawk travelin' miles and miles
Up the river together
Logs and lightning and rocks on their way
Tambalacoque forever

Your Gander Instruction Manual Part D: Know Your Map

It might be easier for some of you to sum up your child's Gander profile on a graph. And it's kind of cool to see how a Gander graph maps out over a river—for both your child and for you. *For ease of use, I repeat the following presentation of the river map in both the First Mile of the Journey and as part D of* Your Gander Instruction Manual.

Behavioral Style and Sensory Profile

Near shore, midriver, or far shore

For behavioral style and sensory profile, go ahead and plot points on the river map that correspond to each facet of your child's Gander profile. Then connect the dots and see your child's natural path through the water. Does your child tend to travel along the near shore, up the middle of the river, or along the far shore? Maybe your child's profile is all over the river?

With great hesitation, let me make some very imperfect generalizations about temperament and this river map. In the context of our cultural expectations, the "near shore" tends to be easier; the "far shore" more difficult; the "middle of the river" not a big deal either way. This is consistent with the work of Chess and Thomas (1989), who made generalizations about certain temperament constellations or groupings being relatively "easy" and others more "difficult." Although often helpful, labeling these personality types or river paths in such a way will not be accurate for all children in all situations. As emphasized throughout part A of the Your Gander Instruction Manual, there is no such thing as a "good" or "bad" temperament, just "goodness or badness of fit," depending on the task or situation at hand. Sometimes the "near shore" is harder and the "far shore" is easier. Even so, I offer these labels and generalizations because they tend to apply more often than not. Whatever your child's differences in temperament, it's up to you to decide when that behavioral style represents an advantage (near shore) or a disadvantage (far shore).

Staying mindful of this warning against generalizations, go ahead. See how your child's Gander behavioral style and sensory profile maps onto the river. Then, if you like, use a different color to map your own natural path onto the same graph. This makes it easier to see when you and your child tend to travel together or apart.

MAPPING BEHAVIORAL STYLE AND SENSORY PROFILE

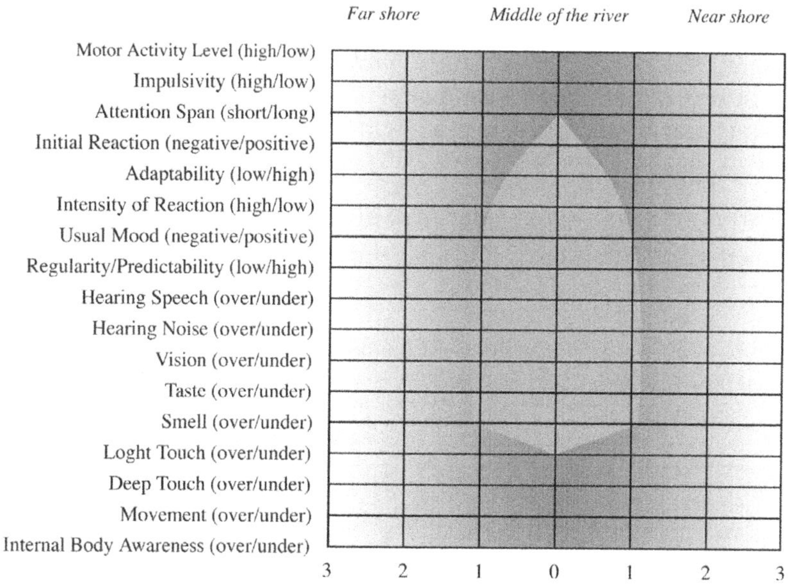

Skills (Strengths and Weaknesses)

Fly above water level (sails) or sink below (holes)

Now do the same thing for your child's skills profile. Plot your child's Gander strengths and weaknesses, then connect those dots. For which developmental domains does your child's boat tend to "fly" above the water, travel along at water level, or "sink" below? (See the Tenth Mile for more detailed discussion of strengths and weaknesses.) Most children have uneven profiles, with some skills in the average range, others above, and others below. Most children will have some weaknesses—"holes in their boats"—that require bailing (accommodations) or patching (interventions), but also some strengths—"sails"—for catching favorable winds (enrichment). As before, using a different color, plot your own skills profile on the same graph with your child's. Which of your strengths and weaknesses map along with your child's? Which of your skills are different from each other?

MAPPING SKILLS PROFILE

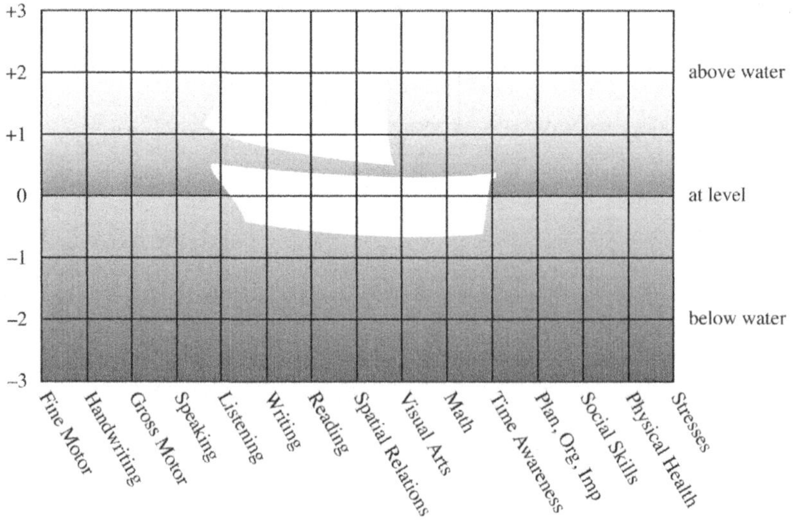

TALON NOTES AND EGG-STRA READING

• • •

THIS IS A BOOK FOR parents. As such, these "talon notes" are provided to guide additional reading. This is not a scholarly work, but it is built on the work of many others. By providing these references, I hope to give credit and thanks where due.

Ackerman, D. (1991). *A natural history of the senses.* New York, NY: Vintage Books.

Allen, R. (n.d.) Behavioral Services and Products, Inc. Retrieved from http://www.robinallen.com/

American Academy of Pediatrics. (2011). ADHD: Clinical practice guideline for the diagnosis, evaluation, and treatment of attention-deficit/hyperactivity disorder in children and adolescents. *Pediatrics, 128* (5).

American Academy of Pediatrics. (2012). Sensory integration therapies for children with developmental and behavioral disorders. *Pediatrics, 129* (6).

American Psychiatric Association. (2013). *Diagnostic and statistical manual of mental disorders* (5th ed.). Arlington, VA: American Psychiatric Association.

Angelou, M. (2009). *I know why the caged bird sings.* New York, NY: Ballantine Books.

Attwood, T. (2008). *The complete guide to Asperger's syndrome.* London, UK: Jessica Kingsley Publishers.

Azrin, N., & Foxx, R. M. (1989). *Toilet training in less than a day.* New York, NY: Pocket Books.

Barkley, R. A. (2005). *ADHD and the nature of self-control.* New York, NY: The Guilford Press.

Barkley, R. A. (2013a). *Defiant children: A clinician's manual for assessment and parent training* (3rd ed.). New York, NY: The Guilford Press.

Barkley, R. A. (2013b). *Taking charge of ADHD: The complete, authoritative guide for parents* (3rd ed.). New York, NY: The Guilford Press.

Barkley, R. A. (2014). *Attention-deficit hyperactivity disorder: A handbook for diagnosis and treatment* (4th ed.). New York, NY: The Guilford Press.

Barkley, R. A., & Benton, C. M. (2013). *Your defiant child: Eight steps to better behavior* (2nd ed.). New York, NY: The Guilford Press.

Baron-Cohen, S., Cosmides, L., & Tooby J. (1997). *Mindblindness: An essay on autism and theory of mind.* Cambridge, MA: A Bradford Book.

Baumrind, D. (1966). Effects of authoritative parental control on child behavior. *Child Development, 37* (4), 897–907.

Beck, J. S., & Beck, A. T. (1995). *Cognitive therapy: Basics and beyond.* New York, NY: The Guilford Press.

Bondy, A., & Frost, L. (2011). *A picture's worth: PECS and other visual communication strategies in autism* (2nd ed.). Bethesda, MD: Woodbine House.

Brazelton, T. B., & Nugent, J. K. (2011). *Neonatal behavioral assessment scale* (4th ed.). London, UK: Mac Keith Press.

Brooks, R., & Goldstein, S. (2002). *Raising resilient children : Fostering strength, hope, and optimism in your child.* Lincolnwood, IL: McGraw-Hill Education.

Buber, M. (2010). *I and thou.* Mansfield Center, CT: Martino Publishing.

Burns, D. D. (1999). *The feeling good handbook.* New York, NY: Plume.

Cain, S. (2013). *Quiet: The power of introverts in a world that can't stop talking.* New York, NY: Broadway Books.

Carey, W. B. (2004). *Understanding your child's temperament.* New York, NY: Xlibris.

Carroll, L. (1898). *Alice's adventures in wonderland.* New York, NY: McMillan Company.

Chess, S. (1995). *Temperament in clinical practice.* New York, NY: The Guilford Press.

Chess, S., & Thomas, A. (1989). *Know your child: An authoritative guide for today's parents.* New York, NY: Basic Books.

Christophersen, E. R. (1998). *Little people: Guidelines for common sense child rearing* (4th ed.). Shawnee Mission, KS: Overland Press Inc.

Coles, R. (1998). *The moral intelligence of children: How to raise a moral child.* New York, NY: Plume.

Committee on Integrating the Science of Early Childhood Development. *From neurons to neighborhoods : The science of early childhood development.* J. P. Shonkoff & D. A. Phillips (Eds.). Washington, DC: National Academies Press.

Cooper, J. O., Heron, T. E., & Heward, W. L. (2007). *Applied behavior analysis* (2nd ed.). Upper Saddle River, NJ: Pearson.

Cooper-Kahn, J., & Dietzel, L. (2008). *Late, lost, and unprepared: A parents' guide to helping children with executive functioning.* Bethesda, MD: Woodbine House.

Cousins, N. (2005). *Anatomy of an illness: As perceived by the patient.* New York, NY: W. W. Norton & Company.

Cuthbert, B. N., & Insel, T.R. (2013). Toward the future of psychiatric diagnosis: The seven pillars of research domain criteria. *BMC Medicine, 11*, 126.

Darwin, C., & Huxley, J. (2003). *The origin of species: 150th Anniversary Edition.* New York, NY: Signet.

David, L., Uhrenholdt, K., Baker, M., Foer, J. S., & Karp, D. H. (2010). *The family dinner: Great ways to connect with your kids, one meal at a time.* New York, NY: Grand Central Life & Style.

Dawkins, R. (1996). *River out of Eden: A Darwinian view of life.* New York, NY: Basic Books.

Dawkins, R. (2006). *The selfish gene: 30th anniversary edition.* Oxford, UK: Oxford University Press.

Dawson, P., & Guare, R. (2010). *Executive skills in children and adolescents: A practical guide to assessment and intervention* (2nd ed.). New York, NY: The Guilford Press.

Dennison, P. E., & Dennison, G. E. (1992). *Brain gym: Simple activities for whole brain learning.* Glendale, CA: Edu Kinesthetics.

Donvan, J., & Zucker, C. (2016). *In a different key: The story of autism.* New York, NY: Crown.

Drug Enforcement Administration and US Department of Education. (2012). *Growing up drug free: A parent's guide to prevention.* Washington, DC

Duke, M., Martin, E. A., & Nowicki, S. (1996). *Teaching your child the language of social success.* Atlanta, GA: Peachtree Publishers.

Dweck, C. (2007). *Mindset: The new psychology of success.* New York, NY: Ballantine Books.

Edwards, B. (2012). *Drawing on the right side of the brain: The definitive* (4th ed.). New York, NY: TarcherPerigee.

Eichenstein, R. (2015). *Not what I expected: Help and hope for parents of atypical children.* New York, NY: TarcherPerigee.

Elkind, D. (2006). *The hurried child: 25th anniversary edition.* Cambridge, MA: Da Capo Press.

Featherstone, H. (1981). *A difference in the family: Living with a disabled child.* New York, NY: Penguin Books.

Feuerstein, R., & Rand, Y. (1998). *Don't accept me as I am: Helping retarded performers excel.* Arlington Heights, IL: Skylight Professional Development.

Frankenburg, W. K., Dodds, J., Archer, P., Shapiro, H., & Bresnick, B. (1992). The Denver II: A major revision and restandardization of the Denver developmental screening test. *Pediatrics, 89* (1), 91–97.

Frost, R. (1969). *The Poetry of Robert Frost.* E. C. Lathem (Ed.). New York, NY: Holt Rinehart & Winston.

Furlong, M., McGilloway, S., Bywater, T., Hutchings, J., Smith, S. M., & Donnelly, M. Behavioural and cognitive-behavioural group-based parenting programs for early-onset conduct problems in children aged 3 to 12 years. *Cochrane Database of Systematic Reviews, 2012* (2), CD008225.

Fuster, J. (2015). *The prefrontal cortex* (5th ed.). Boston, MA: Academic Press.

Garber, S. W. (1997). *Beyond Ritalin: Facts about medication and other strategies for helping children, adolescents, and adults with attention deficit disorders.* New York, NY: William Morrow Paperbacks.

Gardner, H. E. (2006). *Multiple intelligences: New horizons in theory and practice.* New York, NY: Basic Books.

Gardner, H. E. (2011). *Frames of mind: The theory of multiple intelligences* (3rd ed.). New York, NY: Basic Books.

Gardner, H. E., & Laskin, E. (2011). *Leading minds: An anatomy of leadership*. New York, NY: Basic Books.

Giedd, J. N., Blumenthal, J., Jeffries, N. O., Castellanos, F. X., Liu, H., Zijdenbos, A.,...Rapoport, J. L. (1999). Brain development during childhood and adolescence: A longitudinal MRI study. *Nature Neuroscience, 2* (10), 861–863.

Ginott, D. H. G. (2003). *Between parent and child: The bestselling classic that revolutionized parent-child communication*. A. Ginott & H. W. Goddard (Eds.). New York, NY: Harmony.

Gladwell, M. (2008). *Outliers: The story of success*. New York, NY; Boston, MA: Little, Brown and Company.

Glasser, H., & Easley, J. (1999). *Transforming the difficult child: The nurtured heart approach*. Tucson, AZ: Nurtured Heart Publications.

Goleman, D. (2005). *Emotional intelligence: Why it can matter more than IQ: 10th anniversary edition*. New York, NY: Bantam Books.

Goleman, D. (2007). *Social intelligence: The new science of human relationships*. New York, NY: Bantam Dell.

Gordon, R. M. (2007). *Thinking organized for parents and children: Helping kids get organized for home, school & play*. Silver Spring, MD: Thinking Organized Press.

Gottman, J., & DeClaire, J. (1997). *The heart of parenting: Raising an emotionally intelligent child*. New York, NY: Simon & Schuster.

Graham, S., & Harris, K. (2005). *Writing better: Effective strategies for teaching students with learning difficulties*. Baltimore, MD: Brookes Publishing.

Gray, C. (1994). *Comic strip conversations.* Arlington, TX: Future Horizons.

Gray, C. (2015). *The new social story book: Over 150 social stories that teach everyday social skills to children and adults with autism and their peers* (15th ed.). Arlington, TX: Future Horizons.

Gray, C. (n.d.). *Home.* Retrieved from http://carolgraysocialstories.com/

Green, J. (2013). *Assistive technology in special education: Resources for education, intervention, and rehabilitation* (2nd ed.). Waco, TX: Prufrock Press.

Green, M., & Solnit, A. J. (1964). Reactions to the threatened loss of a child: A vulnerable child syndrome. *Pediatrics, 34* (1), 58–66.

Greene, R. W. (2014a). *The explosive child: A new approach for understanding and parenting easily frustrated, chronically inflexible children* (5th ed.). New York, NY: HarperCollins.

Greene, R. W. (2014b). *Lost at school why our kids with behavioral challenges are falling through the cracks and how we can help them.* New York, NY: Scribner

Greenhouse, J. B. (2013). *Statistical thinking: The bedrock of data science.* Retrieved from http://www.huffingtonpost.com/american-statistical-association/statistical-thinking-the-bedrock-of-data-science_b_3651121.html

Greenspan, S. I., Salmon, J. (1994). *Playground politics: Understanding the emotional life of your school-age child.* Reading, MA: Perseus Books.

Greenspan, S. I., and J. Salmon. (1996). *The challenging child: Understanding, raising, and enjoying the five "difficult" types of children.* Cambridge, MA: Perseus Books.

Greenspan, S. I., Wieder, S., & Simons, R. (1998). *The child with special needs: Encouraging intellectual and emotional growth.* Reading, MA: Perseus Books.

Grinker, R. R. (2008). *Unstrange minds: Remapping the world of autism.* New York, NY: Basic Books.

Hallowell, E. M., & Ratey, J. J. (1995). *Driven to distraction: Recognizing and coping with attention deficit disorder from childhood through adulthood.* New York, NY: Touchstone.

Hanh, T. N. (2002). *Anger: Wisdom for cooling the flames.* New York, NY: Riverhead Books.

Harvey, P., & Penzo, J. A. (2009). *Parenting a child who has intense emotions: Dialectical behavior therapy skills to help your child regulate emotional outbursts and aggressive behaviors.* Oakland, CA: New Harbinger Publications.

Heller, L. (2004). *Sign language for kids: A fun & easy guide to American sign language.* New York, NY: Sterling.

Heraclitus. (2001). *Fragments: The collected wisdom of Heraclitus.* (B. Haxton, Trans.). New York, NY: Penguin.

Howard, D. (2000). *Einstein: The formative years, 1879–1909.* Boston, MA: Birkhauser.

Hyman, S. L., Stewart, P. A., Foley, J., Cain, U., Peck, R., Morris, D. D.,...Smith, T. 2016. The gluten-free/casein-free diet: A double-blind challenge trial in children with autism. *Journal of Autism and Developmental Disorders, 46* (1), 205–220.

Illingworth, R. S. (2013). *The development of the infant and the young child: Normal and abnormal.* M. K. C. Nair & P. D. Russell (Eds.). (10th ed.). New Delhi, India: Elsevier.

Jamison, K. R. (1996). *An unquiet mind: A memoir of moods and madness.* New York, NY: Vintage Books.

Kalat, J. W. (2013). *Introduction to psychology* (10th ed.). Belmont, CA: Cengage Learning.

Kaufmann, W. A. (2013). *Nietzsche: Philosopher, psychologist, antichrist* (4th ed.). Princeton, NJ: Princeton University Press.

Kendall, P. C. (2007). *Cognitive-behavioral therapy for impulsive children: Therapist manual* (3rd ed.). Ardmore, PA: Workbook Publishing.

Kendall, P. C., & Hedtke, K. A. (2006). *Coping cat workbook* (2nd ed.). Ardmore, PA: Workbook Publishing.

Kerr, M. E., & Bowen, M. (1988). *Family evaluation.* New York, NY: W. W. Norton & Company.

Khoury, M. J., Evans, J., & Burke, W. (2010). A reality check for personalized medicine. *Nature 464* (7289), 680.

Kliegman, R. M., Stanton, B., St. Geme, J., & Schor, N. F. (2015). *Nelson textbook of pediatrics* (Vols. 1–2) (20th ed.). Philadelphia, PA: Elsevier.

Kohn, A. (1999). *Punished by rewards: The trouble with gold stars, incentive plans, A's, praise, and other bribes* (2nd ed.). Boston, MA: Mariner Books.

Kohn, A. (2006). *Unconditional parenting: Moving from rewards and punishments to love and reason.* New York, NY: Atria Books.

Kohn, A. 2007. *The homework myth: Why our kids get too much of a bad thing.* Cambridge; London: Da Capo Press.

Koplewicz, H. S. (2003). *More than moody: Recognizing and treating adolescent depression.* New York, NY: Perigee Trade.

Kotlowitz, A. (1992). *There are no children here: The story of two boys growing up in the other America.* New York, NY: Doubleday.

Kranowitz, C., & Miller, L. J. (2006). *The out-of-sync child.* New York, NY: TarcherPerigee.

Kübler-Ross, E., & Kessler, D. (2014). *On grief and grieving: Finding the meaning of grief through the five stages of loss.* New York, NY: Scribner.

Kurcinka, M. S. (2015). *Raising your spirited child: A guide for parents whose child is more intense, sensitive, perceptive, persistent, and energetic* (3rd ed.). New York, NY: William Morrow Paperbacks.

Kuypers, L. (2011). *Zones of regulation.* San Jose, CA: Think Social Publishing.

Lancy, D. F. (2015). The *anthropology of childhood: Cherubs, chattel, changelings* (2nd ed.). Cambridge, UK: Cambridge University Press.

Lavoie, R., Reiner, M., Reiner, R., & Levine, M. (2006). *It's so much work to be your friend: Helping the child with learning disabilities find social success.* New York, NY: Touchstone.

Leibenluft, E. (2011). Severe mood dysregulation, irritability, and the diagnostic boundaries of bipolar disorder in youths. *American Journal of Psychiatry, 168* (2).

Levine, M. (1992). *All kinds of minds: A young student's book about learning abilities and learning disorders.* Cambridge, MA: Educators Publishing Service, Incorporated.

Levine, M. (2003). *A mind at a time: America's top learning expert shows how every child can succeed.* New York, NY: Simon & Schuster.

Levine, M. (2004). *The myth of laziness.* New York, NY: Simon & Schuster.

Levine, M. (2006). *Ready or not, here life comes.* New York, NY: Simon & Schuster.

Levitin, D. J. (2007). *This is your brain on music: The science of a human obsession.* New York, NY: Plume/Penguin.

Lifter, K., Sulzer-Azaroff, B., Anderson, S. R., & Cowdery, G. E. (1993). Teaching play activities to preschool children with disabilities: The importance of developmental considerations. *Journal of Early Intervention, 17* (2), 139–159.

Lovaas, O. I. (1987). Behavioral treatment and normal educational and intellectual functioning in young Autistic children. *Journal of Consulting and Clinical Psychology, 55* (1).

Mandela, N. (1995). *Long walk to freedom: The autobiography of Nelson Mandela.* Princeton, NJ: Back Bay Books.

Marschark, M., Lang, H. G., & Albertini, J. A. (2002). *Educating deaf students: From research to practice.* Oxford, UK: Oxford University Press.

Maurice, C., & O'Hanlon, M. E. (2000). *Autism's battle within*. Retrieved from https://www.brookings.edu/opinions/autisms-battle-within/

May, R. (1994). *The courage to create*. New York, NY: W. W. Norton & Company.

McClannahan, L. E., & Krantz, P. (2010). *Activity schedules for children with autism: Teaching Independent Behavior* (2nd ed.). Bethesda, MD: Woodbine House.

McClellan, J., Kowatch, R., Findling, R. L., & Rand Work Group on Quality Issues. (2007). Practice parameter for the assessment and treatment of children and adolescents with bipolar disorder. *Journal of the American Academy of Child and Adolescent Psychiatry, 46* (1), 107–125.

McGoldrick, M., & Gerson, R. (1986). *Genograms in family assessment*. New York, NY: W. W. Norton & Co Inc.

McGoldrick, M., Gerson, R., & Shellenberger, S. (1999). *Genograms: Assessment and intervention* (2nd ed.). New York, NY: W. W. Norton & Co Inc.

McGuinness, D. (1999). *Why our children can't read and what we can do about it: A scientific revolution in reading*. New York, NY: Free Press.

McGuinness, C., & McGuinness, G. (1999). *Reading reflex: The foolproof phono-graphix method for teaching your child to read*. New York, NY: Free Press.

McMahon, R. J., & Forehand, R. (2005). *Helping the noncompliant child: Family-based treatment for oppositional behavior* (2nd ed.). New York, NY: The Guilford Press.

McNeil, C. B., Hembree-Kigin, T. L., & Anhalt, K. (2010). *Parent-child interaction therapy* (2nd ed.). New York, NY: Springer.

Miller, W. R., & Rollnick, S. (2012). *Motivational interviewing: Helping people change* (3rd ed.). New York, NY: The Guilford Press.

Mogel, W. (2008). *The blessing of a skinned knee: Using Jewish teachings to raise self-reliant children*. New York: Scribner.

Mogel, W. (2011). *The blessing of a B minus: Using Jewish teachings to raise resilient teenagers*. New York, NY: Scribner.

The MTA Cooperative Group. (1999). A 14-month randomized clinical trial of treatment strategies for attention-deficit/hyperactivity disorder. *Archives of General Psychiatry*, *56* (12), 1073–1086.

Mukherjee, S. (2016). *The gene: An intimate history*. New York, NY: Scribner.

Myles, B. S., & Southwick, J. 2005. *Asperger syndrome and difficult moments: Practical solutions for tantrums, rage and meltdowns*. Shawnee Mission, KS: Autism Asperger Publishing Company.

Napier, A. Y., & Whitaker, C. (1988). *The family crucible: The intense experience of family therapy*. New York, NY: Harper and Row.

National Education Association. (2016). *Research spotlight on homework*. Retrieved from http://www.nea.org//tools/16938.htm

Nichols, M. P. (2013). *The essentials of family therapy* (6th ed.). Boston, MA: Pearson.

Papero, D. V. (1990). *Bowen family systems theory*. Boston, MA: Pearson.

Papolos, D. (2007). *The bipolar child: The definitive and reassuring guide to childhood's most misunderstood disorder* (3rd ed.). New York, NY: Broadway.

Patterson, G. R. (1977). *Living with children: New methods for parents and teachers.* Champaign, IL: Research Press.

Paul, R., & Norbury, C. (2011). *Language disorders from infancy through adolescence: Listening, speaking, reading, writing, and communicating* (4th ed.). St. Louis, MO: Mosby.

Pfaff, D. W. (2015). *The altruistic brain: How we are naturally good.* Oxford, UK: Oxford University Press.

Phelan, T. W. (2010). *1-2-3 magic: Effective discipline for children 2–12* (4th ed.). Glen Ellyn, IL: Parentmagic, Inc.

Prizant, B. M., & Fields-Meyer, T. (2016). *Uniquely human: A different way of seeing autism.* New York, NY: Simon & Schuster.

Rapee, R., Wignall, A. D., Spence, S., Cobham, V., & Lyneham, H. (2008). *Helping your anxious child: A step-by-step guide for parents* (2nd ed.). Oakland, CA: New Harbinger Publications.

Reischer, E. (2016, February 22). Against the sticker chart: Priming kids to expect rewards for good behavior can harm their social skills in the long term. *The Atlantic.* Retrieved from http://www.theatlantic.com/health/archive/2016/02/perils-of-sticker-charts/470160/

Ridley, M. (2003). *Nature via nurture: Genes, experience, and what makes us human.* New York, NY: HarperCollins.

Sacks, O. (1996). *An anthropologist on mars: Seven paradoxical tales.* New York, NY: Vintage Books.

Sacks, O. (2008). *Musicophilia: Tales of music and the brain.* New York, NY: Vintage Books.

Satter, E. (1987). *How to get your kid to eat: But not too much.* Palo Alto, CA: Bull Publishing Company.

Schlitz, D. (1978). The gambler [Recorded by Kenny Rogers>. New York, NY: Sony/ATV Music Publishing LLC

Schmitt, B. D. (2005). *Your child's health: The parents' one-stop reference guide to symptoms, emergencies, common illnesses, behavior problems, and healthy development.* New York, NY: Bantam.

Seligman, M. E. P. (2004). *Authentic happiness: Using the new positive psychology to realize your potential for lasting fulfillment.* New York, NY: Atria Books.

Seligman, M. E. P. (2006). *Learned optimism: How to change your mind and your life.* New York, NY: Vintage Books.

Seligman, M. E. P. (2007). *The optimistic child: A proven program to safeguard children against depression and build lifelong resilience.* Boston, MA: Mariner Books.

Shapiro, J. P. (1994). *No pity: People with disabilities forging a new civil rights movement.* New York, NY: Broadway Books.

Shapiro, D. (2016, August). SCADS of children with coexisting ADHD, autism and anxiety: Understanding and treating complicated problems with self-control and attention dysregulation. *Attention*. Retrieved from http://www.chadd.org/

Silberman, S., & Sacks, O. (2015). *NeuroTribes: The legacy of autism and the future of neurodiversity*. New York, NY: Avery.

Silverman, S. M., Iseman, J. S., & Jeweler, S. (2009). *School success for kids with ADHD*. Waco, TX: Prufrock Press, Inc.

Skinner, B. F. (1976). *About behaviorism*. New York, NY: Vintage Books.

Skinner, B. F. (1991). *Verbal behavior*. Acton, MA: Copley Publishing Group.

Skinner, B. F. (2005). *Walden two*. Indianapolis, IN: Hackett Publishing Company, Inc.

Smith, S. (2004). *Live it, learn it: The academic club approach for students with learning disabilities and ADHD*. Baltimore, MD: Brookes Publishing.

Sundberg, M. L., & Partington, J. W. (2010). *Teaching language to children with autism or other developmental disabilities*. Concord, CA: AVB Press.

Time Timer. (n.d.). Visual timers, classroom timers, time timers. Retrieved from http://www.timetimer.com/

Tobias, S. (1995). *Overcoming math anxiety*. New York, NY: W. W. Norton & Company.

Tufte, E. R. (1997). *Visual explanations: Images and quantities, evidence and narrative*. Cheshire, CT: Graphics Press.

United States Department of Agriculture. (2015). *MyPlate.* Retrieved from http://www.choosemyplate.gov/MyPlate

Vermeulen, P. (2012). *Autism as context blindness.* Shawnee Mission, KS: AAPC Publishing.

Ward, S. (n.d.). *Cognitive connections.* Retrieved from http://efpractice.com/

Walton, M., & Deming, W. E. (1988). *The Deming management method.* New York, NY: Perigee Books.

Weil, S. (1952). *Gravity and grace.* New York, NY: Putnam.

Weinfeld, R., & Davis, M. (2008). *Special needs advocacy resource book: What you can do now to advocate for your exceptional child's education.* Waco, TX: Prufrock Press.

Weinfeld, R., Jeweler, S., Barnes-Robinson, L., & Shevitz, B. R. (2013). *Smart kids with learning difficulties: Overcoming obstacles and realizing potential* (2nd ed.). Waco, TX: Prufrock Press.

Whitman, W. (1959). *Leaves of grass.* New York, NY: Viking Penguin.

Whyte, W. H. (1950). Is anybody listening? *Fortune Magazine.*

Wilens, T. E., & Hammerness, P. G. (2016). *Straight talk about psychiatric medications for kids* (4th ed.). New York, NY: The Guilford Press.

Winner, M. G. (2007). *Thinking about you, thinking about me* (2nd ed.). San Jose, CA: Think Social Publishing.

Winner, M. G. (n.d.). *Socialthinking—Home.* Retrieved from https://www.socialthinking.com/

Wolf, M., & Bowers, P. G. (1999). The double-deficit hypothesis for the developmental dyslexias. *Journal of Educational Psychology, 91* (3), 415–438.

Wozniak, J., Biederman, J., Kiely, K., Ablon, J. S., Faraone, S. V., Mundy, E., & Mennin, D. (1995). Mania-like symptoms suggestive of childhood-onset bipolar disorder in clinically referred children. *Journal of the American Academy of Child and Adolescent Psychiatry, 34* (7), 867–876.

Wyatt Kaminski, J., Valle, L. A., Filene, J. H., & Boyle, C. L. (2008). A meta-analytic review of components associated with parent training program effectiveness. *Journal of Abnormal Child Psychology, 36* (4): 567–589.

Zucker, B. (2017). *Anxiety-free kids: An interactive guide for parents and children* (2nd ed.). Waco, TX: Prufrock Press.

ABOUT THE AUTHOR

• • •

The Author

Dr. Shapiro is a native of East Lansing, Michigan. He moved to Washington, DC, to attend the George Washington University School of Medicine and stayed for pediatric residency training at Children's National Medical Center. Dr. Shapiro practiced primary-care pediatric and adolescent medicine in Silver Spring, Maryland, before shifting his focus to developmental and behavioral pediatrics. Currently, in addition to his office practice, Dr. Shapiro observes children and collaborates with educators at dozens of area schools. He developed the Parent Child Journey Program and offers behavior-management training groups throughout Greater Washington. He is a fellow of the American Academy of Pediatrics and a member of the Society for Developmental and Behavioral Pediatrics. He is married with four children and two grandchildren, all wonderfully different. Dr. Shapiro's hobbies include playing music, reading, unicycling, and floating down the Potomac in a kayak.

For more information, go to ParentChildJourney.com.

ABOUT THE ILLUSTRATOR

• • •

JOHN WATKINS-CHOW WAS BORN IN New Jersey and somehow ended up with three degrees from MIT, which he has failed to parlay into anything noteworthy. John has been drawing all of his life, though this book is likely the first place nongeek (and geek-adjacent) folk might see his art. He has been fortunate to work in animation, comics, and sketch card art on properties such as *Star Wars*, *Lord of the Rings*, and Marvel Comics—and very occasionally, his own comic, *Talismen*. During the day, John teaches math in a private school in suburban Maryland. When not producing sketchy art or stumbling in the classroom, John can reliably be found in the doghouse, a source of frustration for his lovely wife and embarrassment for his two talented daughters.

Made in the USA
Las Vegas, NV
19 March 2021

19817613R00266